Lands and Peoples

THE WORLD IN COLOR

Volume 3

EASTERN EUROPE   SOVIET UNION
MIDDLE EAST

Grolier

INCORPORATED

New York

DISTRIBUTED IN THE UNITED STATES BY
THE GROLIER SOCIETY INC.

DISTRIBUTED IN CANADA BY
THE GROLIER SOCIETY OF CANADA LIMITED

Volume 3

TABLE OF CONTENTS

THE CRAGS of Mount Olympus loom over the great gorge of Tempe. For the gods the mountain was the court of Zeus and for men it defended Thessaly from Macedonia. The cloud-wreathed summit is almost 10.000 feet high.

BOISSONNAS

Greece ... *the twentieth-century nation*

SAY "Greece" and what usually leaps to mind is classic Greece and the giant figures of ancient myth and history. The modern nation comes as an afterthought, even with some faint astonishment that there *is* a present-day Greece. Yet the twentieth-century nation is one of the most vital forces in the Mediterranean world. Its people, for all their pride in their glorious past, impress the observer as being more youthful and vigorous than many other Europeans with a less weighty history.

Ravaged by World War II and scourged by civil war, Greece in 1949 was unstable, poor and depopulated. But lavish foreign aid, including almost $1,500,000,000 from the United States, saved it from disaster. The loss of labor by emigration was offset. Public health was improved by the con-

4

quest of malaria. Newly irrigated and scientifically fertilized farms blossomed. The national income rose steadily some 6 per cent a year. By the late 1950's Greece could play a full part in the European economy and reap technical assistance from West Germany, benefits from the Common Market and new riches from the tourist trade.

Today Greece has moved ahead of its prewar position. Agriculture is thriving and the country is more than self-sufficient in wheat and rice. Orchards, vineyards and truck farms are flourishing on the northern plain, yielding enough vegetables and fruit, especially apples, for sale abroad. The outstanding crop, however, is tobacco, which has taken the place of currants as the country's most important export. Offsetting this rosy picture is the fact that Germany, the best customer for tobacco, is turning to the Virginia leaf grown in the United States.

Progress and Perils

Starting practically from scratch, industry is striding ahead. Greece has begun developing its many valuable minerals: bauxite (aluminum ore), high-grade iron ore, uranium and free Europe's sole nickel supply. Most promising is the vast electrification program. As new plants—both water power and steam generation—go into operation the goal draws nearer of bringing electricity to every village. This will not only raise living standards but provide the necessary power for industrial expansion.

Much of the above has come about because, for the first time in years, Greece has a relatively stable government. The runaway inflation of the postwar years has been halted and the Greek currency strengthened. It has also made foreign investment—needed capital—in Greece more inviting.

There are dangers nonetheless. In 1959, for instance, troubles in the tobacco trade caused a depression in the Salonika area and foreign agricultural tariffs imperiled the stability of the whole economy of the country.

The Communists remain a serious threat. Though the Communist Party is outlawed and its numbers have dwindled, there is a die-hard, tightly disciplined core. Moreover, it is strongly supported by the communist regimes to the north. Greek communist leaders are heard frequently on the Bucharest radio.

The end of the Cyprus trouble in 1959 meant the end of Turkish hostility, Greece's most serious problem, and an end also to the strain on NATO, to which they both belong.

Greece still has a long way to go before it overcomes the poverty of most of the people. The poverty is shown strikingly in such fields as publishing, radio and motion pictures. Less than 2,000 books are issued a year. In a population of more than 8,000,000 there are only about 545,000 radio sets. Few films are produced though those few are excellent. This does not mean that the creative arts are dying in Greece. It is simply that most Greeks have no money left to support their artists. Culturally there have always been strong links between Greece and France. Greek painters and sculptors are likely to go to Paris. Naturally they are influenced by the French school but their basic inspiration stems from their native land. Writers find it hard to choose between modern Greek and classic Greek. Contemporary writers also remain rather obscure to the world at large as few of their works are translated. An outstanding exception to this was Nikos Kazantzakis. The English translations of his novels *Zorba the Greek* and *The Greek Passion* and his superb verse sequel to Homer's *Odyssey* won international acclaim.

Rocks Tossed at Random

Let us see what this storied land looks like. According to an old story, when God finished making the earth, some rocks were left over and He tossed them away at random. This is how Greece was created, with 500 or so islands on the east and 116 islands on the west. Each island is as individual as the Greeks themselves.

Wherever you go in Greece you can see

the glitter of the sea somewhere in the distance. No part of the country is more than sixty miles from the sea. To the west is the Ionian Sea and to the east the Aegean. For its size, Greece has one of the longest coast lines in the world. The southern portion of the mainland, the Peloponnesus, is somewhat the shape of a maple leaf, dangling by a mere stalk of land, the Isthmus of Corinth. This is cut by a canal, which shortens the sea route between eastern and western Greece.

About 60 per cent of Greece is mountainous. Even the Aegean islands are really mountaintops of a land that in prehistoric times collapsed into the ocean. The highest peak, Mount Olympus, rises nearly 10,000 feet above sea level. This is where the old Greek gods were supposed to have their home. The summit is bald but the sides are covered with spruce and beech trees. Stands of emerald-green pines and sometimes merely gray-mauve sagebrush clothe the lower mountain slopes. Almost everywhere the ground is strewed with rocks.

Villages nestle on mountainsides or spread out in valleys among silver-gray olive trees, sunny vineyards or patches of wheat. Depending on the season, the tilled land is green or gold, or the brown of fallow.

There are no mighty rivers in Greece, only a few creeks and streams. Perhaps this is why the Greeks never had river boats as people do on the Nile, the St. Lawrence, the Mississippi.

Mariners from Ancient Times

Seafaring ships? Oh, yes. Long before Columbus crossed the Atlantic Ocean, the Greeks were sailing all over the Mediterranean. Their vessels hugged the coasts all the way to Gibraltar—the Pillars of Hercules to the ancient mariners. Some sailors even ventured out into the Atlantic. Others sailed south from Crete to Egypt, or northeast through the Dardanelles and the Bosporus into the Black Sea and to the land of the Scythians, Russia.

Now Onassis, Niarchos and other shipping magnates follow the course of Ulysses and Jason, but under foreign flags. Greece, seeking their return, is building new argosies and gaining a higher place among the world's traders.

You may have a twentieth-century Hellene for neighbor. He is Nick the Greek or Mr. Poulos, who runs the food shop or owns the flower store. Possibly he came from Ulysses' home, Ithaca, the beautiful island off the west coast of Greece, which earthquakes shook severely in the 1950's. Your acquaintance is friendly and curious to learn. He likes to talk, especially about politics. He may know more about the prime minister or the president than you or I. Or perhaps a twentieth-century Ulysses is selling peanuts at the corner. This man is from Sparta, once renowned for its warriors, though today it is only a little town, drowsing among orange groves and cypress trees, close to a sorry mass of stones. They are all that is left of the city of ancient glory.

Rocky Soil Is Made to Yield

Almost 60 per cent of the Greeks earn their living by cultivating the rocky land. Wherever there is a patch of soil, however thin, it is tilled. In some parts of the country, particularly in Thessaly and other northern sections, wheat and other cereals are grown for bread. Also in northern Greece—Macedonia and Thrace —tobacco is cultivated, small in leaf but fine in quality.

Olive trees flourish. On the islands of Mytilene (Lesbos), Corfu (Kerkyra) and Crete, the livelihood of the villagers depends on the olive crops. The fruit is picked, usually between October and December, by beating the laden branches with sticks and then scooping up the fallen olives. They may be preserved in brine or in vinegar, or pressed to extract the oil. Some of the best olive oil in the world comes from Greece. The Greeks themselves use it in cooking, instead of butter or lard. When a Greek has olives and bread, he is not afraid of hunger.

In the fertile countryside around Corinth and along the northern coast of the

Peloponnesus, currants thrive. (Did you know that the word "currant" comes from the name Corinth?) They are really small seedless grapes. The delicious bits in cinnamon buns are the dried fruit. The Greeks cultivate their currants carefully. Small ditches are dug around each vine to collect rain water; and for protection against pests, the leaves are sprayed with copper sulfate. After the grapes have been picked, they are put out to dry in the sun. The same regions produce luscious tomatoes and other vegetables. Around Argos, melons are grown that are prized throughout the country for their sweetness. Hardly less noted are the oranges of Crete, the apples and pears of Macedonia, and the figs of Attica—greenish violet outside, purple within.

In grape-growing sections, August and September mean fun for the youngsters.

To press the grapes, barefoot lads romp on the masses of freshly picked clusters. These are piled on huge shallow receptacles made of wood and with an opening out of which the juice drains. It goes into barrels to ferment into wine.

Since the lean years following World War II, there has been a great increase in the production of rice, especially in the region around Thermopylae. The Greeks used to import much of it from abroad. Today they grow all the rice they need and have some left for export.

The Greeks cherish their fields and vineyards, olive groves and orchards, even though a single plot may be smaller than a North American backyard. The small size of holdings makes life hard for the farmers, especially those of the mountain villages. Let us see how an average farmer, Niko, must spend his working day. Niko gets up at five o'clock in the

GREECE

morning. Then he either walks or rides a burro for two hours, to reach one little strip of land. There he plows, sows, weeds or reaps for a while. He cannot stay all day, however, for he has another strip to tend, two or three hours away in the other direction. So Niko must waste a good bit of his time simply in traveling between his little fields.

A Village Boy's Life

Though the situation might be better, it might be worse. Suppose you were a Greek village boy. It would be your job to lead sheep and goats up the mountain late in spring. Down in the valley only dried thistles and sun-parched sagebrush remain. So you must take the animals to the greener pastures on the slope. There you stay all summer, in cool, sweet-smelling air, looking after your flock. For meals, you have brown whole-wheat bread, olives, some goat cheese occasionally, a little milk and some greens picked on the mountainside. You boil the greens and then sprinkle them with olive oil. When the grass in the valley, under the first autumn rain, sprouts green again, down you go with your goats and sheep, their bells tinkling, to the village.

The village has been called the backbone of Greek life. About half of the total population lives in more than 5,000 villages, with an average of about 1,000 persons each. The rest of the Greeks live in 365 larger villages, with about 3,500 persons each; in 46 small towns, with 22,000 each; and in 3 cities. Athens, the capital, including its port, Piraeus, is first in size. Salonika (Thessalonica), in northern Greece, is next; and Patras, on the west coast of the Peloponnesus, is a poor third.

Gardens and Pink Tiles

Village houses, mostly one or two stories high, are built of stone. Wood is scarce in Greece. In the Aegean islands the roofs usually are flat and the walls whitewashed. Against the sea they make a color pattern like that of the Greek flag with its stripes of white and blue. In the mainland villages, roofs are gabled and covered with slate or tiles. The latter are in various tones of pink, depending on the earth from which they have been made and how much they have been battered by the weather. Some houses stand flush with the street and have small gardens at the side. An almond, a peach or a pomegranate tree peeps over the garden wall. Other dwellings are built around open courts. Again there is a tree or two, and sometimes geraniums and gardenias growing in whitewashed gasoline cans. Balconies are adorned with potted plants—flaming amaryllis, green balls of sweet basil.

Heat and Water for Homes

Greece can get bitterly cold in winter, particularly in the mountains and in the north. Village houses have no central heating, however. Warmth is provided by fireplaces, wood-burning stoves or open charcoal braziers. Wells or mountain springs supply water. The women carry it home in large red earthenware pitchers, balanced on their heads. The custom gives the women a proud erect carriage. Some island villages, however, have neither wells nor springs. So rain water is collected. As it falls on the flat roofs, it is held by gutters, from which it flows through pipes to underground cisterns.

Modern Penelopes

Greek women usually stay at home. They take pride in keeping their houses spotless and are excellent cooks. They are also skilled at crafts, such as weaving blankets and many-colored rugs on hand looms, from wool that they have spun themselves.

Every village has a square and sometimes several. Around the sides are shops and at least one coffee house, its tables out in the open air. The church and the school are usually close by. Greek men, after the day's work is done, gather in the coffee house. They smoke cigarettes and sometimes hookahs—pipes in which the smoke is drawn through water, to cool it. The favorite beverage is "turkish" coffee, very thick and served in small

© E. N. A.

ATHENS, since ancient times the most famous of Hellenic cities, is situated in Attica on and around a group of hills. It is about three miles from the coast and five miles from its port, the Piræus. As we stand upon the northern ramparts of the Acropolis, or citadel, we look west-wards across the city towards the Theseum to the distant hazy Poikilon Hills. Athens was made the capital of Greece in 1833 after the War of Independence, and has since grown rapidly in size and importance, but its chief attraction is in its historic ruins.

9

THREE LIONS

DRYING WOOL. Farm women usually dry wool, for their homespun clothing, in the open. Drying must be gentle if the yarn is to be strong.

Part of the charm of the coffee house is talk. The men discuss the merits of this or that politician in Parliament (in Greek, *Boule*) or a recent visit of the king and queen to the rural community center. One man may read aloud to the others from the latest newspaper received from the *politeia,* the city.

An Ancient Tongue Lives On

Soon the village priest joins the group, sitting down and settling his black robes about him. He keeps his high brimless hat on his head and, as he talks, he strokes his long beard. Into the debate, in all likelihood, he injects a quotation from the Old or New Testament, perhaps from the Gospel of St. Luke in its original language. For this gospel was written in Greek. His audience understands. Greeks may not look like the ancient marble statues of gods and goddesses but they still speak basically the same language as Praxiteles or Aristotle or Aristophanes did.

Belief in the old deities has, of course, vanished. Most Greeks are Christians, members of the Greek Orthodox Church. A Greek ignores his own birthday and celebrates the name day of his patron saint. If your name is John, you celebrate on St. John's Day.

Although special religious services are held on Christmas, it is less important than in many other countries. New Year's Day, dedicated to St. Basil, is the day of gifts, joyously festive. In the streets, children carry red or blue paper ships in memory of the ship that brought St. Basil from Cappadocia (in Asia Minor) to Greece. From house to house they go, singing carols in the saint's honor. For New Year's Day, Greek housewives bake a rich cake in which a coin, preferably of gold, is hidden. Whoever finds the coin in his slice is sure to have a very lucky year.

January 6 is another holiday. By tradition it was on a January 6 that Christ was baptized in the River Jordan. In the country, to mark the occasion, the fields are sprinkled with holy water. At towns along the coast, crowds gather for another

cups. It is washed down with water. A spoonful of morello-cherry jam or mastic (resin from the mastic tree) preserve may accompany the coffee. Another sweet is a candied baby bitter orange, as green as jade. Again the sweetness is chased with a glass of water. The men smack their bearded lips in delight because, they say, "This water is good; it comes from the spring near St. George's."

ceremony. The priest tosses a cross into the sea, and then the village boys dive for it. The lad who recovers the cross is considered specially blessed.

There are gay carnivals before Lent begins. City dwellers don all kinds of fancy costumes and dance in the streets. Through the crowds prance absurd "camels," shouting jokes.

Of all the religious celebrations, Easter is the most impressive. The Day of Resurrection is also the day of renewed life in nature. Then spring bursts forth in all its glory. At midnight on Easter Eve, the churches are full. Just at the stroke of twelve, the priest, in his finest vestments, announces, "Christ hath risen." In one voice the people sing the Easter hymn, and light white candles. Outside, fireworks explode and light up the sky. After the service the faithful carry their candles home, trying to keep the flame from going out. Now the strict Lenten fast that preceded Easter is broken. The Easter Day feast is lamb, roasted on a spit, accompanied by dyed red eggs, and kokoretsi—crackly roasted lamb entrails.

On May 1, in a survival of a pagan custom, the Greeks hang wreathes of flowers on the front doors of their homes. St. John's Eve—midsummer eve—marks another festival. Small bonfires are lit and then the boys and men take turns at jumping over the fires. On August 15 comes the Dormition (known elsewhere as the Assumption into Heaven) of the Virgin Mary. Thousands throng to her shrine on the island of Tenos, in the Aegean, where the holy icon is credited with miraculous cures.

The Greeks have a natural talent for communal gaiety. Such occasions are

PIX

ELECTRIC-RAILWAY STATION in Piraeus. From here you can take a train for Athens, only five miles away. Piraeus has been the port for modern Athens since 1834—as Piraeus was in ancient times. In the long centuries between, it had dwindled to a fishing hamlet.

VILLAGE FOUNTAIN, source of water for most of the houses. Running water at home is a luxury out in the country, and buckets must be filled every day.

THRESHING TIME and the whole family and their beasts join in to beat out the ripe grain. Greek farms are usually small, less than ten acres.

PHOTOS, MAYNARD WILLIAMS FROM SHOSTAL

THE GUY ROPES of boats seem to web the old houses clinging to the water's edge at Hydra. It is the port of the rocky little island of Hydra, about four or five hours by steamer south of Athens. The colorful port attracts many artists.

GAY RUGS lie on historic ground—Delos, the smallest island of the Cyclades. It was sacred to Apollo, in Greek myth, and in ancient times was a proud independent city-state.

THE THEATER AT EPIDAURUS, in the northeast Peloponnesus. The structure was part of the famous sanctuary of Asclepius, the god of healing. Besides the theater, the sanctuary included a temple and a stadium, crumbled stones today. Northwest of ancient Epidaurus is a later town, Nea (New) Epidaurus. Greek independence was proclaimed there in 1822; complete freedom was won in 1829.

EWING GALLOWAY

14

won, however, after much toil. The people sum up this contrast in their lives in the saying "Poverty requires having a good time." They have had long schooling in frugality. Their daily bread *is* bread, with a few olives, onions, goat cheese, yoghurt, beans, salted or fresh fish, eggs and milk (usually goat milk) and green salads. Meat is a rare treat. Moreover, the Greeks have a quality of resignation, if not stoicism, coming from a belief in what sometimes seems a stern Providence.

The Greeks are family people. Throughout their lives, family bonds remain very close. They love children but prefer boys to girls, for the simple reason that the girls, when they grow up, must be provided with a dowry.

In the small communities, everyone knows everyone else. Consequently, strangers are conspicuous. They awaken interest rather than hostility, however. The Greeks are warmly hospitable to visitors.

Salamis, Aegina, Poros, Hydra

The islands provide many of the sailors on the nine million or so tons of shipping owned by Greeks. Modern Greece, like ancient Greece, is a seafaring country. Though some of the islands are but a few miles apart, they might almost be oceans apart, so different are they. Let us visit a few of those in the Aegean Sea. South of Athens is Salamis, famous for the naval battle that took place close by, in 480 B.C., when the Greeks defeated the invading Persians. Salamis is a low, pine-covered island with a few vineyards. Towering by contrast is nearby Aegina. This island is known for its flourishing farms, pistachio trees, and fishermen. It is they who bring tasty fresh fish to the markets of Athens. A few miles south of Aegina a conical hill emerges from the sea, dotted with small white houses. This is Poros. One hour's sailing south and on the horizon looms the abrupt, bare, rocky island of Hydra. Like its green, idyllic neighbor, Spetsai, Hydra was the home of seamen of 1821 who emulated their forebears of Salamis by scattering the ships

of another Asiatic foe, the Ottoman Turks.

Still farther south comes the group that forms a sort of circle on the map: the Cyclades. All have poetic names, such as Andros, Delos, Mykonos. On one—Melos (or Milos)—the famous marble statue known as the Venus de Milo was found in the last century. Mykonos is windswept and treeless, except for one miserable fig tree. Nevertheless, Mykonos is the delight of summer visitors from Athens and abroad. On the shimmering waters of its semicircular harbor, fishing boats, motorboats and caïques (Levantine sailing vessels) ride at anchor. Reflected in the water are the dazzling white of cube-shaped houses, their painted red wood doors and brown balconies. About three hundred chapels are scattered over Mykonos. They are expressions of

CORINTHIAN COLUMN (cut down) and entablature from ancient times in the museum at Epidaurus.

RUINS OF ANCIENT CORINTH, which in olden days was the most prosperous and one of the fairest of Greek cities, dot the slopes beneath the rock of the Acrocorinth or citadel. The seven columns that we see in the center of the photograph are all that remain of the once splendid temple of Apollo, now surrounded by other ruins. A few miles away there has sprung up a new city of Corinth which, although its trade brings it considerable prosperity, does not enjoy the commercial greatness that belonged to the ancient city visited by St. Paul.

16

THE TEMPLE OF APOLLO at Corinth, which we saw in the distance on the page opposite, is the most impressive ruin now standing among the remains of that ancient city. Even these seven battered columns, each of which is carved from a solid block of stone, enable us to imagine the splendor of the temple as it originally stood. Situated on the narrow isthmus that joins the Peloponnese peninsula to the Greek mainland, ancient Corinth was the most convenient centre in the Mediterranean for trade from the east and the west.

17

GREEK EVZONES, king's guards, in summer uniform. The fustanella (skirt) is of white linen or cotton, finely pleated. Black embroidery adorns the white jacket. The winter garb is dark blue, trimmed with red braid and with a straight fustanella. The men are chosen for soldierly qualities and good looks. Most of them are at least six feet tall. A proud corps of light infantry, the evzones are usually recruited from mountain areas.

18

gratitude by Mykonian women for the safe return of their men from voyages on which it had been feared that the men were lost.

In the Cyclades exists the only live volcano in Greece. It is close to dark-cragged, earthquake-ridden Thera (Santorin). This island is really the remains of the volcano's circular crater. After a catastrophic eruption, thousands of years ago, the rest of the volcano was submerged.

Off Turkey lie several larger islands: Chios, Lemnos, Samos, Mytilene. Farther south lie Rhodes and the group of twelve islands known as the Dodecanese. Sponge fishermen live on this group. Some sail all the way to the northern coast of Africa to dive for sponges. Others have gone even further afield. There is a settlement of sponge divers from the Dodecanese at Tarpon Springs, Florida. These people still follow many of the customs of their native land.

Modern Greeks, of course, do not wear the flowing white robes of the ancients. Most of them dress very much as other Europeans or North Americans do. In the mountains, however, shepherds often wear a kind of kilt called a fustanella. The king's guards—the evzones—wear it too. As part of their woolen winter uniform, the fustanella is straight and dark blue, with dark red braid. The summer fustanella is white, of linen or cotton, with myriad pleats which make it stand out like a ballerina's skirt. The short jacket of the summer uniform is also white, with black embroidery. White wool hose, red leather shoes with pompons on their upturned tips, and a cocky red beret with a long black tassel hanging down to the shoulder complete the guards' picturesque costume. These men are handsome six-footers, selected partly for their good looks and height. Their ballerina skirts to the contrary, they are first-class fighting men. Many an enemy has flinched in the face of a whirlwind attack by the evzones.

PALACE AT ATHENS. The severely simple gray limestone building was completed in 1838. Only five years before, Athens had become the capital of the newly established Greek kingdom. The mansion faces on a large plaza, sunk below the level of the street.

BOISSONNAS

VILLAGERS OF ZEMENON, led by priests, walk slowly homewards over the winding hill path in the calm evening. All the women and children are dressed in their holiday clothes—brightly colored dresses and hoods—and one of the men wears the white fustanella or short linen kilt of the Greeks. The bearded priests, who are of peasant stock, are permitted to marry. The curious, tall hat with the brim at the top instead of round the head, worn by the one who is second from the right is part of the conventional garb of the Greek priests.

20

NEMEAN PEASANTS drive a team of horses and mules yoked together over the wheat to separate the grain from the ears. Behind them are three pillars, all that remain standing of the famous old temple of Zeus, "ruler of the universe." These peasants may not have heard the legend, but a story runs that a ferocious lion once ravaged the Nemean valley until it was slain by Hercules, who afterwards wore its skin. In ancient times, famous games were held every two years at Nemea, and athletes came from all over Greece to compete in them.

At the beginning of the twentieth century, almost every village and every island still had its own costume, with a distinctive design and embroidery. Then country women wore three or four skirts, overlaid with a pretty apron, and an embroidered blouse and short jacket. Today such costumes are seen occasionally at village festivals. At Megara, for instance, on Easter Sunday the girls and women don their traditional clothes to dance in the square or on the threshing floor. Their headdresses glitter with gold pieces; and there is the gleam of gold or silver from their large belt buckles.

Greek folk dances may be quite intricate and the pattern varies from place to place, though some dances are common to the whole country. A few, it is believed, go back to classic times.

The Greek mountains breed fine soldiers; and the islands, daring and skillful sailors. The valorous deeds of the klephts, the Greek outlaws who fought the Ottoman Turks for more than two centuries, live on in the folk songs of the Pindus mountain range, in the northwest. Thanks to men such as these, the country became free. The struggle for independence began in 1821 and during the eight years that it lasted caught the imagination of many men in other lands. Some came to help, such as Lord Byron, the English poet. With the success of the rebellion in 1829 the history of the modern Greek nation begins.

The Road Back after War

The Greeks were the first of the Balkan peoples to gain independence. At the time the country was but a third of its present size and its population about one tenth of what it is today. Since about 1900, the Greeks have fought for their country seven times, some eighteen years of war in all. Most of the fighting took place on Greek soil. In World War II and afterward in the struggle against the Communists, many villages were laid waste. The most tragic aspect was that thousands of children were maimed or slain or died of starvation. Since 1947, however, when help from the United States was forthcoming, Greece has gradually been recovering.

So recent ruins, as well as ancient, dot the land. Yet when the Greeks look at the still beautiful though broken columns of classic temples, the domes of medieval churches, they have a deep sense of pride. From countries thousands of miles away, visitors come just to gaze at the crumbling stones. These are symbols to the Greeks that though Persians and Romans, Goths and Huns, Slavs and Bulgars, Venetians and Turks have passed and fought over the land for more than three thousand years, the spirit of ancient Greece as well as the Greeks themselves have endured.

Few places were more famous in ancient times than Delphi, a city on the south slope of Mount Parnassus, in central Greece. Wealth flowed into Delphi and it was adorned with marble temples, painted and gilded, and numerous bronze monuments. The latter commemorated the victories of the various city-states.

Ancient Delphi's Oracle

Delphi's great lure was the oracle. The word means both the person through whom hidden knowledge was revealed, with the gods' help, and the place where the revelation was uttered. There were many oracles in ancient Greece but none as powerful as the Delphic oracle. There the person was a woman.

Let us imagine the scene so long ago. Entering Apollo's temple, we see the oracle seated on a golden tripod. She is chewing laurel (bay) leaves, sacred to Apollo. The tripod spans a chasm, from which strange fumes arise. Like our neighbors in the temple, we believe that the fumes come from the bowels of the earth. The vapor puts the oracle into a trance, and in this sleeplike state, she mumbles. Nearby are priests, listening. At last, in verse, they announce the prophecy. We are awed and shiver a little as we step out of the hazy temple into the sunlight.

Visitors still go to Delphi, no longer to hear the oracle but to see the place that once so captured men's minds. Today the site blends into the mountainside.

ROCKY, EARTHQUAKE-RIDDEN THERA (Santorin), southernmost of the Cyclades group, in the Aegean. The island is the remains of a volcano that ages ago erupted violently.

One can hardly tell its man-carved, time-tormented stones from natural rock. Yet something of the old grandeur lingers.

For somewhat similar reasons, visitors are drawn to Olympia, the city in the western Peloponnesus where the first Olympic games were held. Today Olympia is a serene, pine-shadowed vale of grass-grown column drums, broken tablets, cracked friezes and chipped Doric, Ionic and Corinthian capitals. Time-decayed as they are, they are yet originals of an architectural style copied in many of the world's most admired buildings.

The islands as well as the mainland have their reminders. Crete was the center of a very early civilization, the Minoan. The capital was Cnossus, or Knossus. It is supposed that a strange structure there was the labyrinth of Greek myth. All that is left of it today are the confused traces of a vast ground plan, a handsome stairway that leads to nowhere, and great stone jars in which olive oil and wine were stored. The few walls still upright are gaudy with restored murals of the Cretans of three thousand years ago.

Greece calls up such vivid pictures of

23

PERCIVAL, PIX

A THATCHED WINDMILL, with sails for vanes, dazzling white houses, the Aegean in the distance—at the island of Mykonos, in the Cyclades.

EASTER PARADE in Athens. One giant float bears the figure of Dionysus, the god of wine and revelry to the ancients, riding on a rocket-powered cask.

WIDE WORLD

classic times that its medieval, largely Byzantine, period is dimmed, at least to outsiders. To the Greeks themselves, the later era is, above all, the source of their Church. And other evidences are not lacking. Near Sparta, for instance, you can roam the byways of a romantic medieval fortress, on Mistra Hill. Within the walls are a Byzantine palace and churches.

Perhaps the most famous remnant of Byzantium is at Mount Athos—to the Greeks, the Holy Mountain. This is on the easternmost of the three prongs of the Chalcidice peninsula, in the northeast. On its slopes are some twenty monasteries, many dating back to the tenth century. Neither women nor any female animals, including hens, are allowed on the mountain. The monasteries perch on rocky crags and have high walls, once needed for protection against the cruel pirates who used to rove the Aegean. About five thousand monks live there, following an unworldly, austere routine which has changed little since Byzantine times. As of old, they cultivate field crops, vegetable gardens and orchards. The buildings are treasuries of ancient manuscripts.

Along with the castles on the hill tops there are also towers of steel. They carry the electric transmission lines that bring light and power to many towns and villages. After World War II several dams were built to harness the swiftly running waters of some of the larger streams. In this way the Greeks have begun to enjoy the benefits of twentieth-century technology and science.

Not that there are no factories at all in Greece. There are many textile mills, food-processing plants, cement factories and industries producing chemicals.

Greece needs and wants modern industry but is held back for lack of enough power. The country produces no oil, unlike some of its neighbors. Its coal is brown—low grade. So the beginnings of hydroelectric development are of special importance to Greece. When it becomes possible to get cheap power from atomic energy or from the sun, then Greece will be one of the countries to benefit most. Then industry can expand. And the Greek people will be able to enjoy a better life than they have known in our time.

By STEPHEN G. XYDIS

GREECE: FACTS AND FIGURES

THE COUNTRY

A peninsula lying south of the Balkan States; bounded on the north by Albania, Yugoslavia and Bulgaria, on the east by Turkey and the Aegean Sea, on the south by the Mediterranean Sea and on the west by the Ionian Sea. It includes about 600 islands, the largest of which is Crete. The total area is 51,182 sq. mi.; total population, including that of the Dodecanese Islands, about 8,000,000.

GOVERNMENT AND CONSTITUTION

Constitutional monarchy based on constitution of 1911 as amended in 1951. There is a one-chamber parliament, elected for four-year terms, and a cabinet. Women have the right to vote and to stand for election.

COMMERCE AND INDUSTRIES

Agriculture is the chief industry and the land is largely in the hands of small proprietors. Of the total area only 1/5 is cultivable. Chief crops are tobacco, currants, wheat, corn, barley, oats, olives, grapes, figs and cotton. Leading industrial products are flour, olive oil, textiles, cigarettes, leather, machinery, chemicals and building material. Mineral resources include lead, salt, lignite, emery and crude magnesite. Chief exports are tobacco, currants, wine and raisins; imports: cotton goods, woolens, coal, iron and steel, and machinery. Monetary unit, the drachma.

COMMUNICATIONS

1,672 mi. of railway; canal 4 miles long cuts the Isthmus of Corinth; highway mileage, 17,696; air service; merchant fleet, 541 vessels; 545,000 radio sets; 151,466 telephones.

RELIGION AND EDUCATION

Greek Orthodox is the state religion but there is freedom of worship. Education is compulsory between the ages of 7 and 12 though attendance is not well enforced. There are trade, agricultural and technical schools. Athens has many schools including a half dozen of university rank. Two universities, at Athens and Salonika. The Ministry of Education has charge of the Service of Antiquities.

CHIEF CITIES

Greater Athens (including seaport, Piraeus), 1,379,000; Salonika (Thessalonica), 297,000; Patras, 79,000; Volos, 55,000; Candia, 52,000.

Athens

... ancient splendor and modern capital

WHEN Athens became the capital of a newly independent Greece in 1834, only the ruins of classic grandeur atop the Acropolis set it off as different from any other poor Greek hamlet. Today Athens is again the heart of Greece, in commerce, banking, transportation and, not least, the arts.

Considering the inspiration at hand—above all, the Parthenon, rosy and serene in the clear light—it is hardly surprising that Athens is an international center of archaeology. France, Germany, Great Britain, Austria, Italy and the United States all have schools of archaeology there. Partly through their efforts and more recently with the active participation of the Greek Government, many of the city's classic structures are being either restored or entirely reconstructed. This is easier to do in Greece than in Rome. Unlike the Romans, who used concrete cores, the ancient Greek builders used solid blocks of limestone or marble. Such stone is still quarried in Greece and Greek masons retain the skill to carve and fit it. Besides this, the rules of classic Greek architecture are so specific and well understood today that almost every detail can be duplicated. When resto-

ration of the Acropolis buildings was begun in the early 1900's, Pentelic marble was used. It came from quarries on Mount Pentelicus, the source of the original stones. Unfortunately it was a glaring white against the ancient stones weathered to pink and cream and brown. Consequently Pentelic marble was not used in the 1928 restoration of the Parthenon. In fact, one of the caryatids (draped female figures) on the porch of the Erechtheum was reconstructed in terra cotta.

In the 1950's the authorities returned to Pentelic marble for the reconstruction of the Stoa of Attalus II. Little of the ancient structure remained. It is an arcade 324 feet long, with two stories of colonnades, which runs along one side of the agora, the ancient market and assembly place at the foot of the Acropolis. A glistening white when erected, the stoa is slowly mellowing. Its balustrade is painted a brilliant blue with touches of red, like the original stoa. As the visitor strolls in the shade of the massive colonnades he may reflect that he is treading the same ground that Socrates did.

Many other plans are going forward,

THE STOA OF ATTALUS II as reconstructed in the 1950's. Its gleaming grace and serenity give us a glimpse of how Athens must have appeared to the citizens of antiquity. Left, waterspouts are carved for the roof of the stoa. When it rains, water gushes from the lions' mouths.

not only to beautify Athens and rid it of unsightly buildings but also to ease traffic, a problem there as elsewhere. One project involves the area around the ancient theater of Herodes Atticus, on the flank of the Acropolis. The theater, used for summer concerts and plays, is getting a new approach. The Acropolis itself will also be easier to reach. Constitution Square, the center of the modern city, and Kalfthmonos Square are also being redesigned, each with an underground garage. New avenues radiate from the city to the growing suburbs.

Yet for all this twentieth-century bustle, Athens still keeps something of a village air. A short walk in almost any direction brings one within sight of fields or mountains or sea. Athenians live mostly in the open air. Whole families sit in cafés precisely as if they were in their own living rooms. The true Athenian goes home only to sleep. Discussion, more rivalry in wit and logic than true argument, is his favorite pastime. Housewives and peddlers bargain with all their lung power. They sound as if they'd fly at each other's throat any minute but each really enjoys the exchange as part of an endless game.

The peddler and his donkey (in spite of motor traffic) is one of the most typical sights in Athens. First to appear, early in the morning, is the vendor of tomatoes, eggplants, vegetable marrows, singing their praises in a lyrical chant. A little later, donkeys laden with grapes appear. Last come the flower sellers. Only their donkey's long ears are visible above the great heaps of lilies, carnations, chrysanthemums, roses and sometimes whole loads of violets, the "crown of Athens." In pleasant weather the flowers and the sidewalk cafés give the Western visitor the illusion of being in Paris. Athens is almost equally gay and sophisticated.

Festivity reaches a height twice a year, usually in October and February, which mark the beginning and end of the Mediterranean winter. In October it follows on the "treading of the grape"—wine making—and in February on the "roasting of the young lamb"—lambing time. Theaters and movie houses are thronged then. While the Greek National Theater relies on the classics such as Sophocles, other theaters draw on international sources: Shakespeare, Ibsen, Molière, Shaw, Tennessee Williams, Bertolt Brecht. The National State Orchestra gives weekly concerts, and foreign ballet companies are welcomed. Race meets at Phaleron and elegant, formal balls add to the gaiety of these peak social seasons.

We could, if we so desired, approach Athens by train. We should jolt into a

AN EVZONE on guard. The evzones are an elite corps, who are recognized at once by their picturesque uniform—tasseled cap, short kilt, and shoes with huge pompons.

THEATER OF DIONYSUS. Its tiers rise on the slope of the Acropolis. The plays of such great Greek dramatists as Sophocles were first performed here.

RICHARD JOSEPH

THE TEMPLE of Olympian Zeus is today only a cluster of lovely Corinthian columns. In classic times, it was the largest temple in all Greece.

A SPONGE for your bath, Sir? Sponges of excellent quality are plucked from the waters of the Aegean.

MODERN ATHENS AND LOFTY LYCABETTUS FROM THE STADIUM

The white marble stadium and its colonnade, built in the classical style in the nineteenth century, add a touch of old Athens to a panorama of the new city's parks and buildings.

TRANS WORLD AIRLINES

THE LIGHT BOATS OF FISHERMEN IN THE HARBOR OF PIRAEUS

Five miles from Athens is the ancient port of Piraeus, the capital's outlet to the sea. Precious little of the classical past remains in this thriving center of industry and trade.

vast modern station at the end of our journey in so commonplace a manner that it would be exceedingly difficult to believe ourselves actually in the famous city whose history is as glorious as that of the greatest empire. But let us rather make part of the journey in a steamer, which we shall imagine is now churning through the bright blue waters of the Saronic Gulf. We pass a tiny green islet crowned with the ruins of an ancient temple. Beyond is Mount Hymettus whence, long ago, honey was brought to the Athenian market—honey so fragrant that poets wrote in praise of it.

Let us keep our eyes fixed on the land for presently we see in the distance, across dull green trees, the ivory-tinted pillars of the Parthenon standing on the huge flat rock of the Acropolis. At its base are the white buildings of the modern city of Athens. Before long our ship is in the harbor of the Piraeus, the port of Athens, and we are ready to disembark.

Much that we see is modern and familiar. There are steamboats and tugs, wharves and warehouses, for the Piraeus is itself a large and bustling town. Many of the ships moored to the quays are small, gaudily painted boats with large sails. These remind us that, in about 500 B.C., ships of much the same type traded with the Piraeus, for even at that

time it was the port of Athens.

But we cannot delay any longer by the waterside, for a car is waiting to take us to Athens—a distance of about five miles. In the ancient days, these two cities were connected by massive walls, sixteen feet wide and thirty feet high, running along each side of the road. Portions of them are still visible.

The modern Athenians are not very different in appearance from the inhabitants of any other great city of western or southern Europe. The short, voluminous kilts that constitute the Greek national dress are not commonly worn by the Athenian men, except perhaps on feast days and by some soldiers, for whom they are part of the regimental uniform. A fez may be seen occasionally and serves to remind us that we are on the threshold of the Middle East. So do the many street merchants who try to sell us sweetmeats, flowers and an endless variety of cheap wares. Everybody munches from little bags of pistachio nuts.

This Oriental atmosphere is especially noticeable in the side streets. Here we may see tinsmiths, cobblers and blacksmiths at work in their booths or in the open air. Cookshops abound, and we see that the food is often prepared in the streets. These establishments are very popular, and when a Greek from some country district visits Athens, he does not

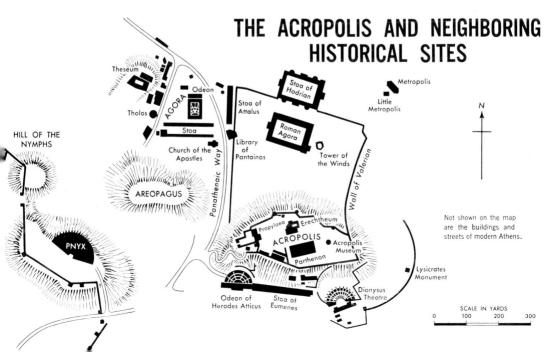

THE ACROPOLIS AND NEIGHBORING HISTORICAL SITES

THE ACROPOLIS, or Citadel Hill, dominating the surrounding plain made an ideal spot to the early Greeks for building temples to their deities. In the centre background is the Parthenon, dedicated to Athena with Mount Lycabettus at its right, while to the left is the Temple of Erechtheus. Farther to the left is the Propylæa, which was the ceremonial approach to these

temples. Beneath the Acropolis are the ruins of the Odeum, or Concert Hall, where Athenian playgoers gathered to witness dramatic performances. In the building, erected by Herodes Atticus, a wealthy Athenian, the seats rose in semi-circles up the side of the Acropolis, giving accommodation to 5,000 spectators.

ATHENS, MOTHER CITY OF GREECE, REFLECTS A GLORIOUS PAST

Modern Athens spreads out in a jumble between the Acropolis, heart of the ancient city, and
Lycabettus, the nine-hundred-foot summit that looms up in the background.

GENNADIUS LIBRARY, AT THE CENTER FOR AMERICAN STUDIES OF GREEK ARCHAEOLOGY AND CIVILIZATION

At the foot of Mount Lycabettus and facing Speusippus Street, in Athens, is the library of the American School for Classical Studies. The ground on which the beautiful building stands was donated by the Greek Government. Completed in 1926, the gracious structure was made possible by contributions from America. Its most striking feature is the slender columns with Ionic capitals. Within the library there is a valuable collection of rare manuscripts relating to the Byzantine Empire and to ancient and modern Greece, the gift of Dr. and Mrs. Johannes Gennadius.

© E. N. A.

THE PROPYLÆA, viewed from the northwest, seem to command the Acropolis. On the right, standing on a bastion flanking these imposing and stately ruins, is the temple of Athena Nike. Its date is uncertain but it was reconstructed in 1835 with the fragments of the original building. Like the Propylæa it is of Pentelic marble, and the sculptured frieze depicts a council of the gods. The Propylæa were begun in 437 B. C. on the foundations of an older gateway and are composed of a series of vestibules and doorways, which gave entrance to the Acropolis.

AROUND THE PARTHENON, lie shattered columns and weather-worn stones, each of which could tell a romantic story of the vanished glory of ancient Athens. In the central aisle of the Parthenon is a space paved with dark-colored stone, on which formerly stood a famous gold and ivory statue of Athena of colossal proportions, probably designed by Phidias.

usually stay at a hotel, but at a rooming house that supplies him only with sleeping accommodation, for he prefers to buy his meals at the eating place that looks the most attractive.

In the more prosperous districts there are splendid stores and handsome offices, apartments and mansions. The streets are lined with trees unfamiliar to us, and there is an abundance of excellent cafés. To them the Athenians flock to discuss the latest political news and to argue interminably over affairs of state. It is this love of arguing and freedom of speech that has much to do with the political unrest in Greece.

As might be expected in a city so full of remains of the past, there are exceedingly interesting collections of antiquities in Athens. Many glorious works of art are to be seen in the Acropolis Museum, which has a collection of sculptures found on the Acropolis, and the National Archæological Museum is a vast treasurehouse of all that throws light upon the ancient history of Greece. These ancient monuments are kept in repair by a special department of the Greek government while institutions supported by the French, Americans, British, Italians, Germans and Austrians aid in archæological research so that we are coming to know more and more about the ancient Greeks and their culture.

It must not be thought that where learning is concerned Athens is always looking back to vanished glories. It is not only the capital of Greece and the seat of government, but it is also the national center of learning. There are six schools of university standing which provide for advanced education and there are numerous schools for special training. A walk along University Street will soon

EWING GALLOWAY

IMPRESSIVE REMAINS OF THE SHRINE OF THE DELPHIC ORACLE

In a grotto nearby the oracle sat upon her tripod stool. When asked for advice, she stroked a laurel branch, inhaled a vapor and chanted messages inspired by the god Apollo.

THE THESEION, STAINED BY WEATHER AND AGE TO A GOLDEN HUE

On a small rise north of the Areopagus, meeting place of the ancient court of Athens, the Theseion stands out as a reminder of the architectural genius of the Greeks. Like the Parthenon, it is in the Doric style and its beautiful marble is from the Pentelic quarries.

convince us that the modern Athenians have a love for culture and are certainly progressive.

Their good taste, too, is shown in the architecture of the Academy of Science— a really noble building of classical plan, faced with gleaming white Pentelic marble such as was used in the ancient buildings. This institution does all in its power to encourage scientific studies in Greece. Another imposing building, constructed on the same lines, is the well-equipped National Library which has a very fine reading-room. Very different in outward appearance, however, is the University, which is gaudy in the bright sunlight and not at all in harmony with its surroundings.

Some of the schoolboys are educated for the Church, and these we easily recognize, for they look very like young monks. Their hair is long but is usually bunched under their hats.

As we stroll past the schools and colleges of modern Athens, we remember that the city was famous for its learning more than four hundred years before Christ. Here the great philosopher, Socrates, taught. Here, too, his most famous pupil, Plato, also a teacher of philosophy and one of the most profound thinkers that the world has known, established his school, the Academy, early in the fourth century B.C.

But the history of Athens is not altogether a record of peace and the advance of enlightenment. Time has not been the only destroyer of the splendors of ancient days. The Persians took and sacked the city in 479 B.C., but they were driven out, never to return to Greek soil. As a protection from further invasions, the Athenians built strong walls about the city and then proceeded to construct new buildings. Many of the fine temples, which we can see in ruins to-day, were erected. Pericles was then the head of the Athenian state and this period (445 B.C. to 431 B.C.) has come to be known as the Golden Age, for he did all in his power to make Athens

THE PORCH OF THE CARYATIDS (Maidens) on the Erechtheum. There are six such figures, in classic pose. Five of the marble originals remain and one is a copy in terra cotta.

THE ERECHTHEUM, a temple built in the fifth century B.C., is the best-preserved building on the Acropolis. Because of the uneven surface of the ground, part of the exquisite structure is nine feet higher on two sides.

the intellectual leader of the city-states. The other states were jealous and this brought about the Peloponnesian Wars which resulted in the defeat of Athens. Although Athens was occupied by the Romans after their conquest of Greece in 146 B.C., they did not prove destructive. It was after the capture of the city by the Turks in 1458 that most damage was done.

The Parthenon's Enduring Beauty

Let us climb the Acropolis to the Parthenon, a ruined temple of the goddess Athena. We can easily imagine how majestic it must have been when the huge ivory and gold statue of the goddess stood in its place.

The statue is gone. Much of the sculpture has been broken or removed to museums, and the pillars have suffered. Yet the plan of the building, the height and symmetry of its columns and the power and beauty of such of its reliefs as remain, convey an impression of incomparable magnificence.

The Parthenon was the holiest shrine in the city, but not by any means the only splendid one. On the Acropolis are also the remains of the Erechtheum, a temple adorned with lovely statuary; the Propylaea, the old ceremonial approach to the Acropolis; and an exquisite temple (restored) to Athena Nike.

From the Acropolis we notice the fifteen tall columns of the Olympieum that are still standing. It is later in date than the Parthenon and was one of the largest Greek temples ever built. According to legend, it stands on the spot where the waters of the Flood disappeared into the earth.

Other remains tell us something of the different aspects of ancient Athenian life. There is the Panathenaic Stadium, for example, in which athletic contests were held. It is interesting to remember that it was here that the first modern Olympic games were held when they were revived in 1896. But, however popular the sports in the stadium might be with the people of ancient Athens, they were not nearly so important to the Greeks as the per-formances in the theaters, in the open air.

In ancient Athens, as in all the Greek states, the drama had a religious significance. Greek drama, in fact, developed in connection with worship of the god Dionysus, and this explains why the greatest theater of ancient Athens is named for the god.

Two Theaters of Ancient Athens

It lies at the base of the Acropolis and we can still survey the ruined stage and vast, semicircular orchestra from one of the many tiers of seats, although these features date from Roman times. They are of limestone—except the seats of honor, which are of marble, richly carved. (The original seats were of wood.) Here throngs of eager citizens watched the tragedies of Aeschylus, Sophocles and Euripides, today famous throughout the civilized world, when they were performed for the first time. We may visit another immense theater, too, the marble odeon, or music hall. This was erected at a much later period (after A.D. 160) by a wealthy friend of the Roman Emperor Hadrian, Herodes Atticus, in memory of Herodes' wife, Regilla.

As we walk about the city we pass the Tower of the Winds, where observations of the weather were made in ancient days. Not far away is the site of the agora, already mentioned, where Athenian municipal affairs and much business were transacted. Beyond it, again, is the Street of the Tombs, once lined from end to end with monuments to the dead. Some magnificent examples still stand to-day, but alas! how few. Here we will leave Athens with the thought that if these commemorate private individuals, the city itself might be considered as one vast monument commemorating all the unknown Athenians, by whose aid so much beauty was created. Modern Athens, with a situation that rivals even that of Naples on its famous bay, is truly charming. We cannot fail to enjoy, too, the unaffected manners and real hospitality of the true Athenian, but the glory of this Greek city remains some of the most sublime works ever erected by man.

TANGERINES SPREAD UPON PALM LEAVES TO TEMPT THE PASSER-BY

A wrinkled fruit vendor of Greece waits patiently at the edge of the curb for customers to purchase his freshly picked and juicy merchandise. Tangerines are also called mandarins.

THE ANCIENT TEMPLE OF ATHENA STILL RISES ABOVE ATHENS

The marble columns of the beautiful Parthenon high on the Acropolis once sheltered a huge statue of the mythical goddess. Modern Athens has widened out from the base of its famous hill.

43

Albania

...communist outpost

THE few Westerners who have managed an inside look at modern Albania have not been impressed. One reporter wrote: "Only in distant areas of Siberia or Central Asia is one likely to see so many ragged, destitute persons." Most of these visitors are prone to blame the Moscow-directed communist regime which has been in power since 1946. The truth, though, is that Albania's handicaps existed before Moscow took charge and will probably continue long after it has relinquished control. In fact, the Albanians have Soviet aid to thank for what little improvement their country has seen since World War II's end.

None of the several nations that have taken turns as Albania's overlord has been able to solve the age-old problems. In the first place, Albania's mountainous countryside is divided sharply in two by the River Shkumbi and this division has hardly aided national unity. To the north, where winters are cold and the land largely barren, live the Ghegs, a stern, hardy race. To the south, where the weather is much milder, live the Tosks, a lively, affable people, largely converted to the Muslim faith. The Ghegs and the Tosks each speak a separate dialect, and like many isolated mountain people, they often feud among themselves and with each other.

In the second place, that mountainous countryside effectively limits Albania's ability to feed itself. When the Communists took over in 1946 birth rates were high, disease rates higher and starvation common. This despite the fact that before World War II 99 per cent of the people were engaged in agrarian and rural pursuits. Only a small portion of the land is arable and the native farmers employ lamentably primitive methods of tilling it despite communist efforts to the contrary. Starvation no longer slays large numbers of people, but the plain fact is that Albania must import foodstuffs to

44

ALBANIA

EUROPE

L. Scutari
Adriatic Sea
NORTH ALBANIAN ALPS
Drin R.
Bojana R.
COASTAL LOWLAND
DINARIC ALPS
Shkumbi R.
Semeni
Vijosa
L. Ochrida
L. Prespa

live, and there is little native industry to provide the cash for them.

A third factor, particularly crippling in this century, has been the high illiteracy rate, which has kept Albania in a semi-feudal state for centuries. The Communists here have done yeoman service, even if not to the extent they claim (from 85 per cent illiteracy in the 1930's to 10 per cent today).

Clearly, Moscow is up against no easy task. It is finding that the cost in rubles and effort of maintaining a Mediterranean outlet for its empire is high. Since Albanian industry was practically nonexist-

ent, new plants had to be installed from the ground up. Among the new structures are a film studio at Tirana, a sugar refinery at Maliq, a 150,000-ton oil refinery at Cerrik, a 40,000-ton cement factory at Valona, the Stalin textile plant at Tirana, two cotton gins, a tannery, two tobacco factories and a hydroelectric plant.

Moscow assumed its burdens early in 1946, following an election late in 1945 that placed the Albanian Party of Labor in control of the Government. On January 2, 1946, exiled King Zog I was deposed and on January 11 a republic proclaimed. At first, Albania worked hand in hand with neighboring Yugoslavia, but Tito's defection from Stalinism returned the control of Albania directly to the Kremlin. The Kremlin, in its turn, has found the Albanians difficult to teach but not to lead. Of all the iron curtain countries, Albania is the most enthusiastic about the Russians. The Albanians are even loud in praise of Stalin, long condemned in other Sovietized states, and his picture appears everywhere. One American newsman observes: "Albania seems not a little like a distant colony of the Roman Empire that still holds out, unaware and unbelieving that the barbarians have stormed the citadel." Their martial zeal is impressive. Sixty thousand men out of a population of little more than 1,500,000 bear arms. Their trigger-fingers are not slow, either, as "incidents" involving English and American planes testify.

The cultural level in Albania, predictably, has never been very high. The Soviet crash program in education, therefore, is proving of considerable benefit.

Before World War II the country's two newspapers scraped for every reader. Today, their circulations have each shot up to a respectable 70,000. Krasto Algi, editor of Albania's satirical monthly *Hosteni* (Pitchfork), is translating Shakespeare, Byron, Whitman, Pushkin and some contemporary Russian poets into the native tongue. The State Theatre has among its repertory *Othello*, Schiller's *Intrigue and Love* and Molière's *Avarice*, as well as Russian plays. American cultural influence, aside from Whitman, would hardly be represented at all were it not for Tom Mix. The old cowboy hero dominates the country's 160 cinemas and frequently appears on hand-woven velvet tapestries in Albanian homes. To date he is one of the few ambassadors from America to be received warmly.

The small country occupies a portion of the territory along the eastern coast of the Adriatic Sea. It is only about 11,000 square miles in area, and has been a completely independent nation only in this century. After long years of domination by the Turks, Albania secured her independence in 1912. In 1939, Italian troops marched into Albania. Five years later the guerrilla leader Enver Hoxha seized control. He set up the communist dictatorship in 1946, subservient to Moscow.

Rugged Land and Tumbling Streams

Albania, or Shqipni, is an oblong country, as the map shows, with many rugged mountains, especially in the northern part. Some of the peaks of the Albanian Alps, the "accursed," reach over eight thousand feet in height, and the scenery is equal in beauty to any in Europe. These, as well as the mountains of the east, form a natural frontier between Albania and its neighbors, Yugoslavia and Greece. There are mountains, too, in the south, though not so high or so continuous as those of the north. The narrow coastal lowland alternates between bare rocks and marshy plains. Numerous rivers rise in the mountains and flow toward the sea, but of these the only one navigable is the Bojana (or Boyana) which connects Lake Scutari with the Adriatic.

Except for Durazzo, whose docks can handle ocean-going freighters, the harbors of Albania are little developed. Valona is largely a haven for fishing boats. There are two single-track railroads, one connecting Tirana and Durazzo, and the other, Durazzo and Elbasan. Towns are linked by rough roads, perilous in the mountain passes, though they are being improved slowly.

The Eagle's Brood

The Albanians, or the Eagle's Brood, as they like to call themselves, are no doubt one of the oldest peoples on the Continent. It is likely that they are the descendants of Illyrians, a very early people already there, and Thracians. The latter were driven from Greece in ancient times and settled in the mountain fastnesses. Over the years they and the Illyrians mingled.

The territory was part of the Roman Empire when, in the fourth century A.D., it broke in two. Albania was assigned to the Eastern, or Byzantine, Empire, whose capital was Byzantium (Constantinople). It was the Byzantines who gave the Albanians their present name.

There followed a period of invasions by Goths, Slavs, Bulgars and Sicilians, in turn. Through it all, the Albanians held fiercely to their own identity and their customs and language.

In the fifteenth century there was a brief period of independence under a Gheg ruler known as Scanderbeg, or Skanderbeg (George Castriota). He is Albania's only national hero. After his death the country fell to the Turks, who governed it rather slackly for five centuries. The unruly Albanians were inclined to make trouble if there was much interference. Finally, in 1912, the Turks were thrown over. Complete independence came in 1917, when Turkey was going down to defeat in the first World War.

Influence of Islam

Under the Turks, many of the Albanians came to accept Islam. Some were taken into the Turkish army and a few, such as Mehemet Ali who became famous as a

WEATHER-WORN CHURCH OF THE GREEK ORTHODOX FAITH

The tile roof and heavy stone walls, so typical of the Mediterranean region, offer protection against the hot summer sun; and the interior offers comfort to the followers of the Eastern Greek Church. The building has a look of repose and quiet endurance though it shows the scars of centuries. A rather unusual feature is the many-sided tower that crowns the top.

LIKE A NEEDLE piercing the sky, the slender minaret of a mosque rears above a crowded byway in an old quarter of Tirana. Many sections of the city have an Oriental aspect.

48

viceroy of Egypt, made places for themselves in the history of Turkey or of Turkey's vast dominions.

During this period of Turkish domination the people were slowly developing a national feeling which did not make itself felt very strongly until the whole northern part of the country blazed out in revolt. For three years, from 1909–12, they fought for their freedom, and finally proclaimed their independence. They were recognized by the European powers. Having no outstanding person for a ruler, the place was offered to Prince William of Wied who had held his regal position for a few months only when World War I broke out and he was forced to take refuge in another country. Albania, then, with no one at its head, fell into a state of anarchy, and at the same time several contending armies were making use of the land as a battleground. The Albanians fought on both sides with equal enthusiasm, for they were concerned more with the actual fighting than with the interests involved. The end of the war saw them with an independent country but it also saw their land desolated. The process of reconstructing their villages and endeavoring to make the soil produce sufficient food

THREE LIONS

TAKING A MOMENT OF REST OUT OF LONG HOURS OF TOIL

Workmen relax on top of a load of produce they have been handling. In the background forest-clad mountains come down to meet the waters of Valona harbor, on the Adriatic Sea.

CARRYING THE DAY'S PURCHASES HOME FROM THE MARKET

The sure-footed donkey is a highly valuable means of transportation in Mediterranean countries where streets are roughly paved and often too steep or narrow for any wheeled vehicle.

for their needs is occupying them even today.

The people have never produced a surplus of food. In fact, each family usually looks after its own needs, as most of them are engaged in agriculture of a primitive sort. It is the women who do most of the work, such as getting the firewood, carrying water, weaving, cooking and taking the small surplus to market.

The regard for women is higher than in most Mohammedan countries. A woman is safe in every way from the clans with which her family may be at feud, and safety is even accorded a man who may be accompanying her. In the country districts they often go unveiled, and some of them are very good to look upon. They are also much brighter and quicker witted than most Moslem women. Those who can afford it adorn themselves with embroidery and gold braid. Their

apparel, like that of the women in most Mohammedan countries, consists of pantaloons (of silk if possible), which are gathered in at the ankles with gold-embroidered ankle bands. With these is worn a blouse made with wide flowing sleeves, and this costume is further embellished by a jacket or bolero richly embroidered in gold thread and studded with imitation stones. Some of the embroidery which comes from Albania is very fine. Most of it is used at home, however, and very little ever reaches the world's markets.

A marriage in Albania is an interesting event. Children are betrothed when very young and marry as early as thirteen years. On the day of the wedding the bride, in apparent protest, is taken screaming and struggling from her father's house, and is carried by her brothers to the husband's family, who come to meet them at a place between the lands of the two tribes.

SOVFOTO

ALBANIAN FARM GIRLS GATHER A CROP OF WARM-CLIMATE MELONS

The mountains in the background show how rough and rugged the terrain of the little Mediterranean country is. Only a small portion of Albania's land can be used for crops and pasturage.

51

REFRESHING PAUSE IN THE DAY'S OCCUPATIONS

A street vendor gives two Albanian workmen an opportunity for a brief respite. From his rough cart, he is dispensing what appears to be milk and bread—energy-giving foods anywhere.

52

It is not the custom for two people within the tribe to marry. On arriving at her husband's house, she takes a place in the corner and stands for three days and nights with her hands folded on her breast, her eyes downcast and without food or drink. In this way, the bride is a suppliant for the gift of fire, of life and of the mystery that continues the race. For six months, she must obey the commands of her elders and speak only when addressed and then some day when it is convenient she and her husband will go to the priest to be married.

A birth is none the less interesting for some ancient customs are still in use—customs that may be two thousand years old. When a child is born, cakes made of a mixture of flour, water and olive oil are fried and sent to the relatives and friends. Then etiquette requires that the relatives must call within three days. On the third day a banquet is given and pres-

ents are brought to the mother. According to a legend, on the third night after the child is born, three fairies appear carrying with them the skein of fate. The first spins the thread, the second measures it off on the spinning-wheel and the third cuts the thread with the scissors. Thus the destiny of the child is determined.

Due to the influence of the Turks, many of the Albanians, as we have said, became Moslems. Now about two-thirds of them call themselves Moslems, although they are not very strict about their religion, and have a tolerance for the Christians, as the Christians have for them, that is not found elsewhere—certainly not in the Near East. One will find the Christians using a prayer rug, and Moslems observing Roman Catholic feast days. But the Albanian is first of all an Albanian and no religion interferes with his own standard of right and wrong. Taking revenge when revenge is due is a matter of necessity to an Albanian,

SOVFOTO

"LIQUID GOLD" GUSHES FROM A PIPE IN AN OIL FIELD

The mountainous little Balkan country has been able to produce enough petroleum for its own use in recent years. There is a pipeline from its principal fields to the seaport of Valona.

and this has often brought about feuds among the various tribes.

In the old days Albania had a peculiar legal system called "the law of Lek." Lek was a fifteenth-century tribal chieftain who wrote down the unwritten laws of his people. The law of Lek placed great emphasis on the virtues of hospitality and of keeping one's promised word. Most of the law, however, was concerned with rules for conducting the feuds. By a certain kind of pledge, for instance, some persons were granted protection during the quarrels. This applied especially to boys under sixteen years of age and to women. A man accompanied by a woman would be safe.

Up until the early 1900's, the beys (Turkish governors) were the aristocrats of Albania. They lived in the hills in feudal splendor. King Zog, who reigned from 1928 until 1939, was the only Albanian monarch the country ever had.

The Albanian language, which has survived so many centuries, has ever been a puzzle to philologists. Unlike the Greek or Slav of the neighboring countries, it is thought to have come from the primitive Illyrian, the language of Macedonia in the time of Alexander the Great. All attempts of the Serb, Greek and Turk have failed to destroy the Albanians' love for it. Once, in southern Albania, where some of the people are Greek Orthodox Christians, the priests taught that it was useless to pray in Albanian for God could not understand it. The Turks forbade giving instruction or printing books in the language but books were printed abroad and smuggled in.

What education the people had was chiefly gained in the schools started by the

SOVFOTO

A JEEPLIKE TRUCK RECEIVES CARGO FROM A COASTAL STEAMER

The ship is docked at Durazzo, Albania's chief port, which is on the north shore of the Gulf of Durazzo, a little arm of the Adriatic. Most of the city's trade is with ports of other Balkan countries—offering olive oil, grains and tobacco in exchange for manufactured articles. Durazzo has a beautiful location, on a rocky promontory just south of Mount Durazzo.

Austrians and the Italians, each of whom had an eye to annexing the territory. Students who could afford it were sent away to Vienna or Paris or to the American School in Constantinople for advanced training but a vast majority of the people were totally illiterate. In the few years following her independence Albania set up several hundred primary and a few secondary schools. Primary education was free and compulsory, but there were not enough schools for the people within the age limits and the law was not enforced.

Albania's industries are little developed, each family generally providing for its own needs. Cattle-raising is the most important activity, and receives special attention. In the mountain pastures, goats and sheep graze. The chief dairy product is cheese. It is a staple of diet and an item of export. Tobacco is grown in sufficient quantity for shipment abroad.

Mineral resources, excepting oil, have been largely neglected. But Albanian crude-oil production was the sixth highest in Europe before 1940.

Between the two world wars, Italy had a strong influence on affairs in Albania. Italian businessmen built up the petroleum industry and financed other plans. But Italy wanted mostly to rule the Balkans. In 1939 she invaded Albania as a first step in this direction. For five years thereafter Albania was occupied by either the Italian or the German army.

After liberation in 1944, the new Communist Government turned to Yugoslavia for the help that Albania once had received from Italy. In 1948, however, when Yugoslavia broke with the Cominform (Stalin's international propaganda organization), Albania chose to side with Russia and abandon her treaties with Yugoslavia. As a result, Albania has been in a precarious position. Though dominated by Russia, she is outside the iron curtain and cut off from sources of food and raw materials.

ALBANIA: FACTS AND FIGURES

THE COUNTRY

A communist republic since the end of World War II, Albania is bounded on the north and east by Yugoslavia, on the east and south by Greece and on the west by the Strait of Otranto, the Adriatic Sea and Yugoslavia. The area of the country is 11,099 square miles, and the latest estimate of the population is 1,650,000.

GOVERNMENT

For centuries a semifeudal state under Turkish rule, Albania proclaimed its independence in 1913 and was a principality or aristocratic republic from then until 1928, when the President made himself King Zog I. His government included an elected chamber and a Cabinet. Zog was driven out by Italian invasion in 1939, when the King of Italy became King of Albania. German occupation replaced Italian in 1943, and a regency was set up. Albania was proclaimed a republic in 1946, and an all-communist Government fashioned a Soviet-type Constitution. A unicameral legislature.

COMMERCE AND INDUSTRIES

Before World War II, the country had but 10% of its land under cultivation; animal husbandry was the principal industry. Number of livestock—mostly sheep and goats—is nearly 3,000,000. Principal crops are corn and wheat. Like other East European communist countries Albania has emphasized the development of manufacturing. The Government claims large postwar increases in the production of food, textiles, leather footwear, building materials, tobacco, chemicals and electric power. Considerable mineral resources include deposits of copper, oil, chromite, bitumen and salt. The greater part of Albania's foreign trade is with Russia and with the countries of the communist bloc. Monetary unit, the lek.

COMMUNICATIONS

There are about 75 miles of railways; 2,500 miles of roads; but the mountain districts are mostly inaccessible by road. There are about 2,000 telephones. Durres (Durazzo) is the chief port; the merchant marine consists of 6 coastal vessels. Two foreign airlines (Hungarian and Russian) service the country.

RELIGION AND EDUCATION

About 70% of the people are Moslems, 20% Orthodox Catholic and 10% Roman Catholic. Clergy and church leaders have been forced to submit to state control. Adult education is encouraged as part of state effort to reduce illiteracy; 10% to 20% of the people are now literate. There are about 3,500 primary, secondary, teacher training, medical, trade, agricultural, art and technical schools and one university.

CHIEF TOWNS

Tirana, the capital, has a population of 110,-000; Scutari, 38,000; Koritsa, 33,000.

Yugoslavia

... land of

the southern Slavs

THE face of modern Yugoslavia amply reflects the surprising changes that have taken place there since 1946. Along Belgrade streets roll Mercedes Benzes, Fords, Chevrolets, Volkswagens, Simcas, home-produced Fiats, even some Moskwiches made in Bulgaria. The roads, always a headache to tourists, are being improved. Several four-lane highways have been built—one running from Belgrade to Zagreb, another down the scenic Adriatic coast. Yugoslavia's cities, furthermore, are expanding rapidly.

This growth is not only due to a population rise, either. The Yugoslavs were long a rustic people, content with the simple joys of their rocky countryside. Today, drawn to the cities by opportunities in industry, they are finding life there unexpectedly pleasing. Most important of all, perhaps, the intellectual climate in Yugoslavia is freer, more relaxed than at any time since before World War II. Eyewitnesses find the Yugoslavs free to criticize their Government in every medium except the large-circulation newspapers. The midnight visits of the Security Police, apparently, are a thing of the past. The Government has even displayed a lenient attitude toward the Catholic Church of late. One Politburo official explained: "It is an illusion to believe that religion and worshiping can be abolished." Some observers think that Belgrade will restore diplomatic relations with the Vatican.

The upturn of the national economy is partly responsible for this relaxation. After long years of sacrifice to the goals of communism, the people are finally beginning to reap a few profits. The Government, quite naturally, need fear the expression of minor complaints no longer. Recently, the Government claimed that gross national production under Tito had increased 11.9 per cent a year and personal consumption 10.1 per cent. Certainly there is some exaggeration here. Yet the fact remains that the Yugoslavs are somehow finding the wherewithal to buy creature comforts they never had before—refrigerators and vacuum cleaners as well as automobiles. The gains in agriculture, furthermore, are substantial. Modern techniques have increased the yield of the land. Wheat, corn and fruit crops are mounting. The number of tractors, always a telling statistic, has increased from 6,250 in 1950–51 to about 30,000 today.

None of these changes could have been safely predicted in 1946, when the Allies handed over control of the country to Marshal Tito and his Partisans. Nor could they have been predicted in 1947 and 1948, while Moscow was superintending Yugoslavia's conversion to communism. The Russians planned to turn Yugoslavia into an agricultural supply center for its industrial satellites in Eastern Europe. The Yugoslavs balked at this, among other things, and since then have gone their own way.

Of course, not all is sweetness and light in present-day Yugoslavia. Coal and power shortages continue. The housing problem in most of the cities, particularly Belgrade, is acute. The prices of those beloved appliances, complicated by inflation, are high—so high that most citizens must go into debt to buy them. Despite the open air of discussion, finally, the people still complain that travel abroad is unnecessarily limited and controlled by the Government. Worse, Milovan Djilas, a former party official, was ruthlessly treated upon the publication of his anti-communist book, *The New Class,* in 1957.

ELECTION TIME in Yugoslavia. Citizens preparing to vote are flanked by Communist Party flag (left) and Yugoslavian national flag (right).

His prison term was immediately increased from three to ten years.

But there is always tomorrow to rectify today, and Yugoslavia's special brand of communism has done enough with yesterday to merit optimism. Furthermore, that brand apparently allows more elbowroom for individual initiative and enterprise than might be expected. Yugoslavian industry, for example, is run on an amazingly decentralized basis. The Government decides where a given plant shall be located and what it will produce, and then builds it. All else is up to the work-

ers, who in a very real sense staff and run the plant *in competition* with others like it. The employees elect a workers council, which in turn elects a manager (whom they may fire if they choose) and have the final say on all policy, including prices and wages. "The plant is built by the state," the Yugoslavs say, with pride, "but it is owned by society." This "enterprise" system, as they call it, does not characterize Yugoslavian agriculture, but then neither does collectivization. Roughly 90 per cent of the farms are privately owned. Most of them are quite small, and their buying and selling are facilitated by the local *zagrudas*—voluntary-member co-operatives which, again, are manned and run by the farmers themselves. Clearly, the economic practices of Yugoslavian communism differ a good deal from those practiced by the Russians. There is less bureaucratic control over the workers and more direct competition for markets.

The Yugoslavs maintain the same independence in their international relations. They have declared themselves firmly in favor of peaceful coexistence between the communist and noncommunist world; they are friendly, therefore, with both East and West. To be sure, relations with Russia are often strained, no doubt because Yugoslavia's continued success is distinctly embarrassing for the Russian empire. (Khrushchev, in his 1956 speech denouncing Stalin, recounted that Stalin once said, waving a letter of complaint from Tito, "I will shake my little finger—and there will be no more Tito. He will fall." Khrushchev's comment: "We have paid dearly for this shaking of the little finger.") Still, the Yugoslavs trade and barter with the Soviets. In 1959, for example, under a continuing agreement for the peaceful use of atomic energy, they bought most of the equipment for a new experimental atomic reactor from Russia. Trade relations with America are no less important, to say nothing of the near $1,500,000,000 of United States aid pumped into Yugoslavia since 1950.

Politics at home are much less exciting. The elections are by and large cut-and-dried affairs, with the Government's list of candidates usually receiving over 90 per cent of the vote. Most of the votes are sincerely cast, too. The Yugoslavs grumble loudly about government inefficiency and waste but not about Tito or the system he represents. Tito's 1952 marriage, his third, to a Serbian working woman who had fought with the Partisans in World War II, moreover, hardly damaged his already imposing popularity.

The Six "People's Republics"

The 1946 constitution divides Yugoslavia into six "people's republics": Slovenia, Croatia, Bosnia and Herzegovina, Serbia, Macedonia and Montenegro. The northernmost of the republics is Slovenia. It is also the wealthiest and most industrious: with 8 per cent of the total population, the Slovenes produce 20 per cent of the national income. Their incomes are proportionately high, too, thus accounting for the attractive agricultural and mining communities that dot the landscape. The main source of its wealth is a 700,000,000-ton lignite reserve, one of Europe's largest.

Croatia, which includes the ancient province of Dalmatia, located on the lovely Adriatic coast, lies just below Slo-

GREATER TRAFFIC demands modern highways. This smooth road runs between Karlovac and the lovely Plitvice Lakes, in Croatia. Here it spans the Korana River on Y-shaped piers.

HOUSING PROJECTS erected in Belgrade to meet the needs of new city dwellers. The Yugoslavs are hard pressed for housing everywhere. Towering, modernistic apartment units like these are the most noticeable answer.

venia. It boasts three important towns: Zagreb, its capital, an important communications center; Rijeka (Fiume), which is besting Trieste in the battle for northern Adriatic trade; and Split, an industrial town to the south of Rijeka.

Bosnia and Herzegovina, pocketed in the middle of the country, is a stronghold of the Muslim faith. Many of the towns, like Jajce and Sarajevo, retain a strong Turkish flavor. Sarajevo, the capital, for example, has sixty-seven mosques.

Serbia and Macedonia

Serbia, the largest of all six, borders Rumania and Bulgaria. Primarily agricultural, Serbia is famous for its pigs and plums. Some copper ore is mined at Bor, however, and chrome in southern Serbia. Belgrade, the fast-growing capital of Yugoslavia, is also located in Serbia.

Macedonia, the southernmost "people's republic," is the economic antithesis of Croatia, to the north. It is a land of mountains interspersed with broad level valleys which are tilled by the most primitive methods. The Government, much to the dismay of richer areas, is diverting almost 25 per cent of the national budget to the improvement of backward republics like Macedonia. Nearly $600,000,000 has been invested there in new factories since 1947.

Montenegro

Macedonia's closest rival for sheer poverty is Montenegro, another rocky stretch of land, which fronts the Adriatic. The Montenegrins have special resources of their own, though, particularly spirit and color. For many centuries they held the Turks at bay while their neighbors collapsed to the left and to the right of them. The brightly colored native costume of the Montenegrin gentleman reflects this vigor. On his head he wears a black *kapa* with a crimson

THE REPUBLIC OF YUGOSLAVIA

top, symbolic of the blood shed for freedom. The peasants dress similarly, only the materials are much coarser.

The Montenegrin is seldom to be seen without his gun, the symbol of his hard-won freedom. The late King Nicholas of Montenegro often used to stop one of his subjects in the street in order to examine his rifle, and if it were dirty, which was very seldom, the punishment would be severe. When a Montenegrin is happy or excited he discharges his gun into the air, which is naturally rather alarming.

Cetinje, the capital of Montenegro, has no port of its own, but does its shipping through Cattaro, on the coast, a town which possesses a wonderful natural harbor of indescribable beauty. The harbor is land-locked except for a narrow opening into the Adriatic Sea. There are several of these beautiful lake-like inlets along the coast, and they have been compared with the fjords of Norway.

The port of Cattaro itself is full of interest. It is so closely ringed by the mountains that it can scarcely find room beside the waters of the gulf. In the streets we may see Montenegrin peasants who have brought their market produce down the long zigzags of the "Stairs of Cattaro," a road carved out of the face of a mountain and the only way into Montenegro from the west.

Cetinje is really not very interesting, except from an historical point of view. There are no imposing buildings and we see no crowds in the streets. The market square is a feature of Cetinje, as it is of all Montenegrin towns, but there are no shops as we know them—in fact there is not a large glass window in the whole town. One sees many cafés and everywhere the colorful clothes that the people love to wear.

A characteristic of the Montenegrins is their absolute honesty. To be called a thief is a terrible insult, second only to being called a coward. They are a strong and hardy people, although they exist on a frugal diet of salted fish, called scoranze, potatoes, heavy bread made of rye or corn, and cheese.

On this simple fare, however, the Montenegrins perform wonderful feats of endurance and never show fatigue. Unfortunately, however, the men despise all manual labor and are content to sit about and dream of their victories. We may see old women and young girls toiling up a rocky path with buckets of water—which is sometimes more precious than wine for the spring may be a two hours' journey away—while near by may be sitting two handsome warriors who will never attempt to help these tired women, not even if they be their own sisters or mothers.

Christmas is a great festival in Montenegro. On Christmas Eve ivy branches are hung over the doors in order to bring good luck. Everyone is gay, songs are sung and revolver shots fired all day long. Easter is also a great festival all over Yugoslavia, and there is much rejoicing and feasting.

The Montenegrins are fond of family life and are devoted to their children, who are brought up very strictly and are taught to be brave and manly. Girl babies are counted as a misfortune because they are unable to fight. Once women were not counted in the census, which included only those able to bear arms for their country.

The Serbians, unlike the Montenegrins, were unable to hold out against the Turks, and for 345 years, they formed a pashalik, or province, of the Ottoman Empire. However, they had not given up their dream of a nation of Southern Slavs and they were frequently at battle with their oppressors until about 1830 when they became an autonomous state. Their history from then on did not run smoothly for there were constant upsets due to internal politics and there were wars with Turkey

A FARMING SCENE on the broad, flat Posavina Plain of central Yugoslavia. Lying along the banks of the Sava River, this area constitutes some of the country's richest farmland.

ACROBATIC LEAPS with the greatest of ease—Macedonian folk dancers. Macedonia is largely a mountainous region, and the men have the vigor and agility of a mountaineering people.

HORSE-DRAWN CARTS bring in a wealth of fresh vegetables to an open-air market in the heart of Belgrade. The city lies in a fertile valley, in which many truck gardens flourish.

A BROOM-MAKER'S SHOP is to be found in practically every Yugoslavian town and village. Though industries are increasing in the country, artisans still produce many of the articles needed for everyday life.

AMERICAN MUSEUM OF NATURAL HISTORY—J. HALPERN

FRIENDLY GOSSIP is part of the charm of market day in Ochrida. The town is on the lake of the same name on the Albanian border. Behind the women stretches a vivid example of the rug-making art of the area.

BOTH PHOTOS, CHARLES J. BELDEN

AT TREBINJE, resort town, a modern inn welcomes visitors for a stay beside the Trebisnica River. Farther along its course, the stream vanishes and makes its way through miles of underground passages.

63

ARGOSIES OF OLD SET OUT FROM THE HARBOR OF DUBROVNIK

Broad beaches and architectural riches attract tourists from all over the world to this loveliest of spots on the Dalmatian coast of the Adriatic. Known through most of its history as Ragusa, Dubrovnik was long a republic and the port for overland trade to and from Constantinople. Modern docking facilities make it one of Yugoslavia's busiest ports.

again, resulting in complete independence in 1878. Wars with their neighbors, the Bulgarians, followed, then came the Balkan wars and the murder of the Archduke Francis Ferdinand at Serajevo, which touched off the World War of 1914-18. After these years of struggle, Serbia finally came to realize the "Great Serbian Idea" upon the establishment of the new state of Yugoslavia, land of the southern Slavs.

The population of Yugoslavia has increased at one of the fastest rates in Europe. And about three out of four persons live on small farms, working with very crude implements. Indeed, farmers in some of the remote parts of the country have never used anything more modern than a wooden plow.

Less than one-fifth of the land is really fertile, and the good farming region—the north and east—is the most densely populated section of the country. Consequently, Yugoslavia is always dangerously close to famine. When crops fail, people go hungry.

Yugoslavia has been a communist state since World War II. The Yugoslav Government now invests large sums of money to build heavy industries in the cities. It feels that industry can, first of all, supply the tractors and trucks that are needed so badly on the farms. In fact, Yugoslavia has need of modern machinery in every field of manufacture. Increased production in industry will call for more workers; many young men and women will leave the farms and villages and go to the cities to earn the high wages that are promised them there.

These changes have undoubtedly affected the daily lives of the Serbs, Croats, Slovenes and others who make up the Yugoslav nation. In the old days these groups fought among each other bitterly, but city life has a tendency to break down barriers of prejudice. Though it is at odds with the Soviet Union, Yugoslavia is still a communist country and controls every facet of the lives of its people.

When a young Serbian goes to ask a girl to marry him he takes two friends and brings a flat cake made of wheat and a bunch of flowers. One of his friends

64

MACEDONIAN MOSLEMS GATHER ROUND THE FOUNTAIN OF A MOSQUE

At the entrance to a mosque in Skoplje, capital of Yugoslav Macedonia, several fezzed loungers pass
the quiet time of day.   More than one Yugoslav in ten is of the Mohammedan faith.

65

THE LOVELY EXPANSE of Lake Ochrida, deepest lake in the Balkans and noted for its exceptionally clear water. Topping the cliff are mellowed buildings of a tenth-century monastery.

66

HORNS AND A BIG DRUM signal the beginning of a dance high in the mountains above the Vardar River. The girls wear gay embroidered aprons that may have been their grandmothers'.

PEACE to the village. In a Sunday procession, the statue, rising from a mass of flowers, is reverently carried from the church. Before it an altar boy, in scarlet, swings a censer.

ST. LAWRENCE TOWER, hoary with time, stands guard near Dubrovnik on the Dalmatian coast. Lapped by the ultramarine Adriatic, the coast is unsurpassed for magnificent scenery.

THE HORNS AND DRUMS OF THE GIPSY BAND SERENADE A BRIDE

A wedding party is not a wedding party in the western Macedonian village of Galicnik without the gay music of the gipsy bandsmen who are ever willing to lend their talents. Galicnik is on the Radika River in the high cattle-raising country near the border of Albania. The principal occupation of the villagers, aside from herding, is the making of cheese.

carries a pistol, for any joyful event is announced by the firing of rifles or pistols. After every convention has been carefully observed, the young man is encouraged by the father of the girl to come and ask for his bride. If he is successful, he pays a sum of money to show that he has bought her.

The marriage service usually takes place on a Sunday, but the celebrations often begin as early as the preceding Thursday, when special wedding cakes are prepared in the bride's and bridegroom's houses.

On Saturday the dowry is taken to the bridegroom's house. On Sunday the bride is decked with orange blossoms, and a coin is hidden in her hair, to prevent her ever wanting money in after life. The couple are presented with crowns of flowers or metal; they then walk with the priest three times round the altar, while the guests sprinkle them with raisins, sweets and nuts. Although the Serbs, Croats and Slovenes are not rich, there is always plenty of food at the wedding feast.

The costumes of the peasants are picturesque although in most parts of Serbia they do not display the desire for color seen throughout the Near East. White or gray linen clothes are worn by both men and women, and during the cold weather, they put on tweeds or woolen clothes and thick sheepskin coats with the fleece inside. The national costumes vary according to religion and locality. The Mohammedan men, for instance, wear a fez and the women wear baggy trousers.

There is beautiful scenery in Serbia, especially along the Danube, and a large part of the land is covered with splendid forests. We may sometimes come upon a gipsy camp, but though the gipsies occasionally settle down, forming separate camps or villages, they usually prefer a wandering life. They are generally admirable musicians, and almost every town possesses a gipsy band.

Croatia and Slavonia were freed from the Turkish rule in 1718 by the Austrians and, except for a brief period during which they were under French rule due to Napoleon's conquest, they remained as Austrian possessions until the end of World War I.

A GREAT INDUSTRIAL PLANT THAT CONVERTS COAL INTO COKE

Only brown coal is mined in Yugoslavia, and some is imported from other lands. In large, modern factories, such as the one shown here, the coal is made into coke, one of the most important fuels of the twentieth century. Much of Yugoslavia's coke is consumed by the country's rapidly expanding iron, steel and allied industries.

CROATIAN LOVERS are seen here wearing their holiday best to celebrate a feast day. Then both men and women array themselves in bright-colored clothes, often of silk, on which much hand-work has been lavished. The Croats, like the Serbs, are mostly Slavs by race, but differ in their modes of living and in their religious beliefs.

THIS YUGOSLAVIAN GIRL is posing in a gaily colored peasant costume typical of those which were once worn in her native Serbia, today a part of the Federation of Yugoslavia. After posing for this picture she returned to her work in the fields. There is still little industrialization in Yugoslavia, and farm women must work hard, raising crops by primitive methods.

71

SERBIAN WOMEN DRAW WATER FROM AN OLD VILLAGE FOUNTAIN

Serbian housewives fill earthen jugs, metal pots and a sprinkling can at the village fountain. It is their chief source of water for all washing, cooking and drinking needs.

LUMBER WAITING TO BE PUT ABOARD SHIP AT SENJ

The small harbor town is on the Adriatic Sea in western Croatia. Senj is said to be the oldest town in the region, dating back to the Romans, and was once a hiding place for pirates.

HOUSEWIVES STOP FOR A MOMENT OF GOSSIP IN A SERBIAN TOWN

The houses of Galicnik follow the road that winds up the side of a steep hill. There is good pasturage on the slopes; and the making of cheese is a profitable occupation in the town.

Racially, they are the same as the Serbs but most of them are Roman Catholic by religion, while in other parts of Yugoslavia, the larger number are Greek Orthodox or Mohammedan. The peasants occupying Croatia and Slavonia are perhaps less prosperous than those of Serbia as the climate is more severe. Among the Karst Mountains they have sudden and violent climatic changes, and at times the "bora," a fierce northeasterly wind, sweeps over the land. The riverside districts are barren, monotonous steppes which are somewhat unhealthy, especially beside the River Sava, where marsh fevers are prevalent.

The Croatian homes are more primitive than those of the Montenegrins and Serbians, for many of them are merely rough huts of wood with thatched roofs. As in Serbia proper, there is no middle class between the peasants and the very few educated people, and those who do the little trading that there is are mostly foreigners—Germans, Italians or Jews. Numerous gipsies wander from village to village, selling and buying horses.

The Croatian farmers produce corn in abundance and also cultivate wheat, oats, rye and barley, but much of the land is not fit for cultivation. The plum orchards of Slavonia are wonderfully beautiful when in blossom. Most of the fruit is dried, but some of it is made into a kind of homemade brandy which the peasants love. Many of the estates are planted with mulberry trees for feeding silkworms. Parts of both Croatia and Slavonia are covered by forests, and herds of swine feed in the oak and beech woods.

Dairy-farming and bee-keeping are other occupations, and horse-breeding is a flourishing industry. The farmers are constantly trying to improve their livestock by importing purer breeds.

KOSTICH

A SUNNY HARVEST MORNING IN A FIELD OF FLAX

The mist is rising in wispy clouds from the mountains beyond the meadow as the morning sun warms the ground. These women are at work early, gathering the flax and tying the stems in bundles. Flax plants must be harvested carefully by hand, for the fibers lose something of their spinning value if they are cut by a sharp instrument.

KOSTICH

GOTHIC SPIRES OF THE CATHEDRAL OF ST. STEFAN IN ZAGREB

The magnificent fifteenth-century edifice, which stands in the Main Square, is viewed from the Strossmayer Promenade in the old part of the city. Zagreb is the capital and cultural center of Croatia and is the second largest city in Yugoslavia. It is a trading and manufacturing town located on the abundant agricultural plains of the Sava River.

WHITE GEESE PLAY "FOLLOW THE LEADER" IN A SERBIAN FARMYARD

The geese furnish eggs, down and feathers as well as meat. High above the waddling fowl is an oddly shaped bird house or roost to entice small feathered visitors. For a time the Yugoslavian Government tried to collectivize farms on the Soviet model. In 1953, however, it gave up this plan and announced that Western types of agricultural co-operatives would be formed.

KOSTICH

TROUT-FISHERMAN'S DELIGHT

Lake Ochrida (or Ohrid), in southern Yugoslavia and eastern Albania, is twenty-five miles long and as much as 938 feet deep in some portions. Nestled high in the mountains, this lake is breathtaking in its scenic beauty. Its waters abound with rare fish, notably salmon trout. Fishing nets can be seen hanging to dry from the poles on the beach at the right.

North of Croatia, parts of the former Austrian territory of Carniola, Corinthia and Styria have been united to form Slovenia, so named because it is inhabited by Slovenes. Here, these Slavonic people have lived since the seventh century and have retained a language quite distinct from that of their neighbors although it is related. They are mostly peasants, but they produce some tannin, and bentwood furniture is manufactured to a considerable extent.

Dalmatia, the most beautiful province of Yugoslavia, consists of a strip of coastland running down most of the eastern shore of the Adriatic Sea. No part of the Mediterranean shore, except the coast of Greece, is so deeply indented as the Dalmatian coastline, with its multitude of rockbound bays and inlets sheltered from the open sea by a barrier of beautiful rugged islands.

In calm weather the channels between the islands and the mainland resemble a chain of lakes. All along the cliffs are half-

ruined castles and monasteries, which seem to cling to the rugged rocks and add to the beauty of a scene not easily forgotten. Although it is not so rocky as Montenegro, the country is everywhere mountainous.

The highlands of Dalmatia are composed of dry, barren limestone which is honeycombed with caverns and underground watercourses, into which all the rain immediately goes. Even the few surface rivers often suddenly disappear underground and do not reappear for many miles. Owing to this strange geological formation the peasants are only able to cultivate about one-tenth of their land.

The once famous forests of Dalmatia were either burned by pirates or were cut down to provide timber for shipbuilding, and all attempts to replant them have failed owing to the lack of soil and rain. The peasants rival those of Montenegro in courage and stature and are like them, too, in having an olive skin with dark hair and eyes, although sometimes

77

one sees the fair type with blue eyes.

The people of Dalmatia are hardy fishermen, their fleets taking in large catches of tunny, lobsters and sardines. Dalmatia's coastal waters are also rich in coral and sponges.

Across the Dinaric Alps from Dalmatia stretch the rugged limestone plateaus that form the region of Bosnia and Herzegovina, two states with long histories of subjection to a number of countries. They were finally united as one province by Austria-Hungary in 1878 and became a part of Yugoslavia in 1918.

The Hard Lot of the Farmer

Herzegovina and western Bosnia are poor farming lands. The valleys cut out by the Bosna and Vrbas rivers are fertile, but the yield of crops is low. Methods of cultivation are ancient. The poor mountain roads have kept the peasants from contact with the outside, and very near starvation year after year.

The northern and eastern parts of Bosnia are more fortunate. Here broad plains watered by the Sava and the Drina make farming easier and more productive.

There are also large mineral deposits scattered throughout the highlands of Bosnia-Herzegovina, and the tumbling mountain streams are great potential sources of hydroelectric power.

The greatest city of Yugoslavia is Belgrade—often called the northern gateway to the Balkans. Situated at the junction of the Danube and Sava rivers and commanding a rising bluff, it has been the center of trade for a rich region and a strategic site for military installations.

Building and Rebuilding

During World War I the city was occupied by Austrian troops. At the end of that war it became the capital of the new state of Yugoslavia. In the next twenty years the city was transformed and its population increased more than three times. Belgrade received a terrific bombing when the Germans occupied Yugoslavia in 1941; many buildings, such as the national library and the state theater, were destroyed or damaged. Most of them have been restored since or replaced with parks and houses.

We have seen that Yugoslavia has many problems. A high rate of farm production, for example, is a persistent requirement that is seldom met. Farm regions are overpopulated, and poor transportation makes the introduction of scientific methods and the distribution of goods extremely difficult.

During the 1920's improvement was hampered by hostility between the Croats and Serbs, who could not seem to work together in Parliament. Strong measures were taken by the King to control the situation. He closed Parliament and imposed military rule, which forbade the printing and reading of pamphlets likely to inflame regional ill will. Eventually the King restored order and brought the Croats and Serbs together. A period of recovery at the close of the decade was the result of this co-operation.

The Effects of Depression

Yet prosperity was cut short by the great depression of the 1930's. Yugoslavia, like all the countries of Europe, could find no markets for the products of industry. There was widespread want and unrest. In order to keep the country from complete collapse, the Government was forced to borrow money from Germany.

Later, however, Germany made Yugoslavia pay heavily for this indebtedness. In 1941 the Germans needed to send troops and materials to Africa, and demanded passage through Yugoslavia. When the Yugoslavs refused, Hitler ordered the invasion of the country and air raids on Belgrade. The entire country was occupied within ten days.

During the four-year occupation that followed, two groups—one led by the Serbian patriot Mihailovitch; the other by Josip Broz, or Tito, a Croatian Communist—waged telling warfare against German and Italian troops. Yet because the resistance groups differed in political ideals they could not present a united front to the enemy. Indeed, part of their time was spent in attacks upon each other. In 1944 the Allied governments openly supported Tito rather than Mikhailovitch, upon the assumption that Tito waged more effective resistance to Hitler's troops.

Tito fought alongside Russian troops when they invaded Serbia in 1944 and also helped repulse the forces of Mikhailovitch. When the war ended Tito set up a communist government. In 1946 he enacted a constitution modeled after the Soviet pattern. Mikhailovitch was executed for collaboration with the Germans, and church leaders were imprisoned.

As time went on, Tito balked at Russian leadership. In 1948, his Government was banned from membership in the Cominform, the Soviet propaganda agency. From then on Yugoslavia was forced to go ahead without Soviet help.

Tito's regime has been marked by considerable progress in education. The illiteracy rate is down from 47 per cent to 20 per cent today. The compulsory period of education has been expanded from four to eight years and thousands of new schools have sprung up. Universities have multiplied also. Even so, both school and university facilities are overcrowded (in Belgrade, for example, every fifteenth resident is a college student).

Tito's greatest feat, however, may well have been the ease with which he has welded the disparate peoples that make up his realm into a unified nation. Among the separate ethnic strains recognized in Yugoslavia are the Slovenes, Croats, Serbians, Montenegrins and Macedonians, and there are three official languages—Slovenian, Macedonian, Serbo-Croatian. Under Tito's rule, though, the petty racial and religious quarrels of the past have largely disappeared.

YUGOSLAVIA: FACTS AND FIGURES

THE COUNTRY

Yugoslavia has been both a monarchy and a republic since the end of World War I. At the end of World War II, it became the Federal Peoples Republic, composed of the 6 republics of Serbia, Croatia, Slovenia, Montenegro, Macedonia, and Bosnia and Herzegovina and the autonomous regions of Vojvodina and of Kosovo-Metohija. It is bounded by Austria and Hungary on the north, by Rumania and Bulgaria on the east, by Greece on the southeast, by Albania on the south and the Adriatic Sea and Italy on the west. Its area is 99,380 sq. mi. and the population is 18,500,000.

GOVERNMENT

Country is administered under a constitution adopted in 1946, amended in 1953, which provides for a federal people's republic. The National Assembly comprises a Federal Council and a Council of Producers, representing various sectors of the economy. A Federal Executive Council has replaced the old Cabinet and in 1954 a president of the Republic replaced the Presidium. The Government is communist but independent of Russia.

COMMERCE AND INDUSTRIES

Agriculture occupies about 70% of the population. Besides corn, wheat, oats, barley and rye, there are grown large quantities of grapes, plums, apples, pears, olives, sugar beet and tobacco. Cocoon production is important. Fishing and the raising of livestock are carried on extensively. There is a large forest area. Minerals include bauxite, lignite, iron, copper ore, gold, lead, chrome, antimony and cement. Oil is found to some extent. Chief industries are flour milling, brewing and distilling, cotton spinning and weaving, tanning, bootmaking, pottery and iron working. Meat packing is a growing industry as is also cardboard and paper making. Chief exports: copper, timber and livestock; chief imports: cotton and cotton goods, metals, machinery, chemicals and mineral oil. Monetary unit, the dinar.

COMMUNICATIONS

Railways, 8,675 miles; roads, 40,000 miles; navigable waterways, 1,300 miles. Telephone subscribers, 200,000. Domestic and international air services.

RELIGION AND EDUCATION

Roughly 13% of the population claim no religion. Of those who do, 50% are Serbian Orthodox, 37% Roman Catholic, 11% Muslim, the rest miscellaneous. Primary education is free and compulsory. There are 16,500 primary and secondary schools; 1,100 technical schools; 85 teacher-training colleges; 108 workers' colleges; 175 art, music and dramatic schools; and 110 faculties, academies and high schools for higher and specialized education.

CHIEF TOWNS

Belgrade, capital, 510,000; Zagreb, 350,000; Skoplje, 160,000; Sarajevo, 158,000; Ljubljana, 148,000.

THE Russians began to wield real power in Bulgaria during 1947. It was then that anticommunist political leaders began to be "eliminated." It was then that a Soviet-style constitution was adopted by the National Assembly. One year later a twenty-year treaty of friendship, co-operation and mutual assistance between the two countries was signed. In 1950 the extent of Russian domination was rudely rubbed in when the assembly voted special status for Russian citizens residing there. They were given equal status with the Bulgarians (including the right to hold office). Moreover, the Russians have made efficient use of their power. Three of their major objectives were achieved quite early: the cutting of Bulgaria's relations with the West, the collectivization of the farmers and their land, and the conversion of a primarily agricultural economy into an industrial one.

The anti-West campaign began as soon as the Communists were in firm control. Bulgarian institutions with foreign ties were destroyed; Western correspondents were barred; Bulgarians employed by the American Embassy were tortured. All of these acts were accompanied by vitriolic anti-American editorials in the Bulgarian press. Finally, in 1950, the United States broke off relations with Bulgaria. Relations with Turkey and the Vatican were hardly less strained, due to Bulgarian treatment of the Muslim and Catholic minorities. Some 250,000 Muslims were expelled by the Government in 1950. In 1952 a Catholic bishop and three priests were sentenced to death on charges of treason and espionage (twenty-eight other priests were imprisoned). Bulgaria, at that time, displayed all the characteristics of an advanced police state. The number of political prisoners before Stalin's death amounted to about one per cent of the entire population.

Apparently, collectivization was pushed forward with the same ruthlessness of purpose. Today, virtually all of Bulgaria's arable land has been collectivized

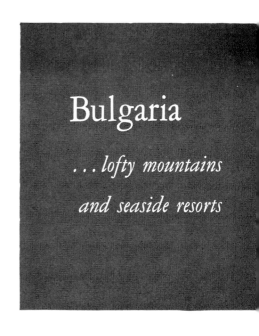

Bulgaria

... lofty mountains and seaside resorts

—that is, it is worked in common by farmers under the direction of agricultural experts appointed by the Government. Most of the collective farms are quite large and some are quite successful. The Perevenetz farm, on the outskirts of Plovdiv, for example, occupies 6,620 acres and has a population of 8,500 persons, most of whom are housed in attractive, newly built villages. Nonetheless, reports persist that brutal enforcement has accompanied the collectivizing process. It is hard to discount them, because Eastern European farmers everywhere have resisted the system bitterly, and nowhere save Bulgaria have the Communists had so much success—and so quickly.

State economic planning in Bulgaria began under Soviet direction in the spring of 1947. By 1952, private ownership and enterprise had largely disappeared. Three five-year plans have so far been completed. The last, ending in 1960, called for a 60 per cent increase in industry, a 30 per cent increase of farm produce, a doubling of the power capacity, and a coal output of 10,000,000 tons. Clearly, the Kremlin here, as elsewhere, is thinking first in terms of heavy industry, something that is fairly new to the Bulgarian economy. Imports and exports of industrial products

RED STAR on Communist Party building towers above citizens strolling home in Sofia. A large store is on left, hotel on right.

have soared above pre-World War II records. The Russians have been especially successful in developing the Bulgarian chemical, textile and coal industries.

Of late the Bulgarians have been striking out into economic paths more natural to them (with the Kremlin's blessing, of course). Long famed for its truck farming, Bulgaria is once again turning to the cultivation of tomatoes, other fresh vegetables, fruits and vineyards. Furthermore, the Government is pouring money into tourist and resort facilities on the Black Sea that have no counterpart elsewhere behind the iron curtain. The heart of the project is a resort called Golden Sand on the Black Sea, near Varna. Here there are 21 hotels, 520 beach bungalows, 9 restaurants, a theater and a gambling casino. The Bulgarians hope to draw visitors not only from their communist allies but from the free-spending West as well—America included. Bulgaria could well use some tourist revenue. Despite Soviet aid, it is one of the more underdeveloped countries in Europe.

For this and other reasons, American-Bulgarian relations have improved of late. In 1959 the two countries restored diplomatic relations. Early in 1960 the United States legation in Sofia was reopened to receive the first American ambassador to lodge there in almost ten years. Meanwhile, trade with noncommunist countries, particularly those in Western Europe, is expanding all the time. A relatively freer day seems to be dawning for a country that has been long isolated from the rest of the world by the dictates of Moscow.

A glance at a map of Europe shows that Bulgaria forms a part of the Balkan Peninsula. It is wedged in between Greece and Turkey on the south, Rumania on the north and Yugoslavia on the west. The eastern boundary is formed by the waters of the Black Sea.

Sofia, the capital and largest city, lies between two mountain ranges in the heart of the Balkans. It has a population of about 700,000 people. It is the economic, cultural and education center of Bulgaria. The city is the home of the world-famous University of Sofia. Yet despite its prosperous appearance, Sofia gives unmistakable evidence of being the capital of a war-weary country that has been on the losing side too many times. It is no longer the spruce capital of the early twentieth century. Its shops and restaurants have lost their sparkle; its air of buoyancy is gone.

In 1912 Bulgaria, flushed with successes in the first Balkan War, was at the height of her power. She had united with Greece, Serbia and Montenegro to throw off the Turkish yoke. But after their victory, they were not able to come to any agreement about the division of the territory newly acquired from Turkey.

Serbia especially was disappointed with the division of territory as it was now cut off from the Adriatic by the newly independent Albania. As a result, Serbia demanded that Bulgaria cede the greater part of Macedonia. Thus the second Balkan War broke out, in which Rumania, Greece and Turkey joined Serbia in attacking Bulgaria. It ended in utter rout for Bulgaria, which lost territory to all its enemies. The intense nationalism aroused by these wars paved the way for a greater conflict.

Then, in 1914, came the first World War and its ruler, King Ferdinand I, again failed to justify himself as one of the wisest of the Balkan sovereigns. After a year's hesitation and intrigue, he suddenly threw in his lot with the Germans and Austrians. The Bulgarian people paid heavily for the two errors of royal judgment. Not only did they lose several thousand square miles of their fertile lands but they were faced with a crushing war debt which took years of hard work to lift.

Unable to cope with the rising discontent, Ferdinand gave up his crown, and was succeeded by his eldest son, as King Boris III, who assumed the powers of a dictator. But whether they had king or dictator was of little concern to

Wheat grows in northwest and north-central Bulgaria; corn, north of the Balkan Mountains; livestock is raised in the north, south and west; lumbering goes on in the mountain areas.

L Lignite coal
A Copper
M Manganese
G Graphite
S Salt
Chemicals
Tobacco
Truck farming
F Food processing
Textiles
F Flour milling
Metal industries
M Tobacco manufacturing

most of his subjects. Boris died under somewhat mysterious circumstances in 1943, after a conference with Adolf Hitler. When the war ended, Bulgaria acquired a Soviet-model government. Since Stalin's death and downgrading, however, Bulgaria is copying the Soviet pattern less slavishly. There is less emphasis on heavy industry. Many fields that were planted with wheat and corn are once again orchards and vineyards. With an eye on the tourist trade, Bulgaria is investing considerable money in resorts on its lovely Black Sea coast.

Wild Riders from the East

Like other peoples of eastern Europe, the Bulgarians have a melodramatic history, with barbaric Eastern overtones. The original Bulgars were Turkic tribes, who came from Asia. Superb horsemen, they rode west of the Ural Mountains as early as the fourth century A.D. So fierce were they that the very sight of their turbans, aflutter with horse tails, caused terror.

In the seventh century one tribe seized upon lands north of the Danube River. Soon the tribe spread south, into the Balkans, and conquered the Slavs already living there. Conquerors and conquered mingled in time, and the Bulgars adopted the Slav language and culture. However, they kept their Asiatic system of government, and the land was ruled by khans (chiefs) and boyars (nobles).

Conflict with the Byzantine (Eastern) Empire was constant. The emperors, taking shelter behind the mighty walls of Byzantium (Constantinople), trembled at the sound of the Bulgar war horns. The Emperor Nicephorus was slain in 811 by the Bulgar Tsar Krum. It is said that the barbaric Krum fashioned his enemy's skull into a drinking cup.

Tsar Simeon I

In 865, Tsar Boris I introduced Christianity into his domains. A son of Boris', Simeon I, became, for a time, the most powerful ruler in eastern Europe. Skilled in the arts of peace as well as of war, Simeon was a civilizing influence on the country. Nevertheless, he was just as jealous of Byzantium as earlier Bulgar rulers had been. Three times the silver armor of his soldiers appeared before the walls of Byzantium, and he exacted toll of all the riches passing between Europe and Asia. As was written at the time, "Greece sends her silks, her wines and her fruits; Asia, her dyes and her perfumes, her precious stones, her white peacocks with gilded feet; Bohemia, her swan-necked steeds; Russia, her furs and her wax, her honey and her slaves."

Bulgaria fell to the infamous Byzantine Emperor Basil II in 1018. Some two hundred years later, Bulgaria was the victor and, under Ivan II, controlled all of the Balkan Peninsula except Greece. New foes now appeared; first the Serbs and then the mighty Ottoman Turks. In 1395, Bulgaria became the first European country to be overrun by the Turks. Not until 1878 was their iron grip on Bulgaria relaxed, and then partly by the intervention of Russia. The Tsar's troops "liberated" Bulgaria—and lingered on for almost twenty years. Full independence was achieved only in 1908.

There have been great changes since, though there is still little love lost

EASTFOTO

THE CAMELS, a massive stone gate built by the ancient Romans in south Bulgaria.

IT WAS ROSES, ROSES, ALL THE WAY

The rose garden in which this girl stands probably covers many acres. From the petals of the blossoms is distilled the oil, or attar, of roses that is exported to perfume makers. Formerly, many billions of roses were produced each year in Bulgaria, but the industry has declined since synthetic perfumes have largely replaced flower scents.

INTO THE BOILING KETTLE GO MILLIONS OF ROSE PETALS

Making attar of roses is an important industry in the Sofia region of Bulgaria, and thousands are employed on the rose plantations. Attar, a fragrant oil that comes to the surface when the petals are boiled in water, is a costly ingredient of perfumes and cosmetics. More than two hundred pounds of petals may be used to produce only an ounce of the attar.

CATHEDRAL COMMEMORATES RUSSIAN HERO-SAINT

Sofia is the site of the new Cathedral of St. Alexander Nevski, consecrated in 1924. The Russian hero received his surname to commemorate his victory on the Neva in 1240. The Russian church canonized him. Peter the Great honored his patron saint, in the 18th century, by building a monastery on the battle site and by creating the order of the Knights of St. Alexander Nevski.

between the various Balkan nations. In both World Wars these countries have neither aligned themselves against a common enemy nor remained neutral, but have fought among themselves. Border territory is likely to change hands during periods of international crisis, and the Balkan map does not remain fixed for very long.

Through all this welter of fighting the Bulgarian farmer has gone on driving his team of slow oxen or buffaloes across his fields. Before collectivization, he most commonly tilled a small farm of from one to six acres.

The Bulgarian farmer has all the peasant virtues and defects. Though he and his forefathers have worked on the land for centuries, he has taken a long time to discover that the old ways are not always the best. Until quite recently his farming methods were as primitive as his great-grandfather's, but, nevertheless, he has always raised fine crops of wheat, corn, barley and oats. Tobacco, too, is cultivated to a great extent and forms a

most important article of export. Around Sofia, where there are sugar refineries, the sugar-beet is grown.

The Bulgar, though he is quite a picturesque person, has not such a lovable nature as have others of the Balkan peoples. Frugal and taciturn, he has not the cheerful air of the Rumanian nor the expansive hospitality of the Serb.

As someone has said: "Put a Bulgar and a Montenegrin in a palace, and the Bulgar will look the peasant he is, while the Montenegrin, who has never bowed his neck to a conqueror, will look like a nobleman." But put them in a desert and the Bulgar will make it a garden of roses, while the other watches him work.

Elementary education in Bulgaria is free and obligatory for the youth but two-thirds of the population are peasants, who mostly live far away from the towns and are too much occupied with work to send the children to school regularly. Nevertheless, these hard-working farmers are the backbone of the Bulgar republic.

86

THE IMPOSING HOME OF OPERA IN BULGARIA'S CAPITAL CITY

Late in the nineteenth century, Sofia was rebuilt almost completely and the opera house dates from that period. It is a copy of the ancient classical style, with Ionic columns and a triangular pediment above the entablature. The building is embellished, however, in accordance with the rather fussy taste that frequently prevailed in the 1800's.

AN EQUESTRIAN STATUE DOMINATES A SQUARE IN SOFIA

To the right of the statue is the Moscow Cinema, which features Russian films. There is a star near the roof and the upper stories are probably offices for Soviet Union representatives.

AN ORNATE PUBLIC BATH IN SOFIA IN THE MIDST OF A PARK

Public baths are quite common in cities and towns of Europe, a custom left over from the days of ancient Rome. The conveniences of modern plumbing are lacking in many old buildings.

MOHAMMEDAN ARCHITECTURE AT ITS SIMPLEST—SOFIA'S MOSQUE

Recalling the long rule of the Ottoman Turks over the Bulgarians is the Banya Bashi mosque at Sofia. The single minaret has a dramatic effect, lending distinction to a simple design.

89

MONKS OF BULGARIA are known as the "Black Clergy," because they wear long robes and tall caps of dead black. Those we see here dwell in a beautiful flower-decked monastery near Tirnovo, the ancient capital of the kingdom. Most Bulgarians are, by religion, members of a national form of the Orthodox Eastern Church.

THE ISKER VALLEY is for a considerable distance a dark and gloomy gorge through the mountains. At other parts it is wider and in the north, near the junction of the Isker River and the Danube, it is about two miles broad. The surrounding hills afford pasture for many sheep, whose wool is converted by the peasants into brightly-dyed cloth.

FASHION NOTE IN MILLINERY

The holiday costume in northern Bulgaria features a hat made from a kerchief smartly draped and tied and wreathed with flowers. Blouse and jacket are richly embroidered.

If we go on a railway journey through the Rhodope Mountains, which lie to the south of the Balkan Range, we shall see some magnificent scenery. These Rhodope Mountains are extremely beautiful and thrust their peaks above the forests and the vineyards that grow on their slopes. There are great gorges through which the rivers dash headlong to the sea, and in the dark pine forests that cover the hillsides we might expect to find those lost princes and green-winged dragons that figure so largely in the romantic old folk tales and ballads the Bulgarian shares with the Serbs and other Slavic neighbors.

Harvest Songs and Dances

In the autumn, when the grain has ripened, the Bulgarian peasant and his whole family almost live in the fields until the harvest is in. Then the harvest songs and dances enliven the villages. Young and old join in the fun. Dances are of various kinds, but the chief one is the *hora,* the national dance of Bulgaria. Any number of people can take part in this. Dancers join hands, or else each dancer places a hand upon the shoulder of his neighbor in front. A step is taken to the left and then three to the right. To the drone of a *gaida,* or bagpipe, the mass of dancers assumes the form of a serpent that coils and uncoils.

It is interesting to note that the bagpipe is a very ancient instrument, known to the Greeks and Romans. It has long been a favorite of Balkan peasants for whom it renders plaintive notes or stirring military airs or wildly gay melodies.

When the winter winds howl about the little lonely mountain cottages, the Bulgar peasant, snug by the fire, whiles away the long evenings telling old tales to amuse his children. Some of these stories are about peasants who marry beautiful fairies, only to see their brides vanish up the chimney on the wedding night. Others are of princes who fly as eagles and of women who are changed into swallows.

Prince Marko, Superman of the Slavs

Many wonderful tales are told about Prince Marko, son of a Serbian King. Marko actually lived in the fourteenth century; but the Serbs and Bulgarians and other Slavs have made him a legendary figure. In the stories, he resembles King Arthur, the English hero, or, perhaps, more exactly Paul Bunyan, early American Superman. Marko, in story and poem, lives for three hundred years; he rides a horse that is a hundred and fifty years old; his feats of strength and valor are prodigious if not supernatural; and he always uses his powers to comfort the sorrowful and free the oppressed. His great enemies are the Turks, and many of Marko's storied exploits are against Turks trying to bring Slavs under their yoke.

In spite of all the glamour that surrounds him, Marko is always a sad figure, a prince cheated of his throne.

There is not sufficient space here to tell

BULGARIAN WOMEN PLANTING FLOWERS ALONG THE PUBLIC STREET

In Bulgaria, it is up to the women to keep their towns beautified. This picture, taken in Karlovo, shows a group hard at work cultivating beds of flowers in the public square.

THE FOUNTAIN used to play an important part in many customs of Bulgarian village life. Into it, for instance, a bride would throw a coin as an offering to the water nymphs. But such quaint customs, like the peasant costumes of the past, are gradually being discarded under the changes imposed by the communist-dominated Bulgarian Government.

THIS FRUIT-GATHERER is returning home with her baskets full to overflowing. There are many types of Bulgarian national dress. This is the one that is worn round Kostenetz, a village in the south-west, at the foot of the Rila Mountains. The two young girls, whom we see on the opposite page drawing water are near neighbors of this girl.

AT TROYAN, QUAINT APARTMENTS OVERLOOK THE GENTLE OSAM

Ducks waddle in the rocky headwaters of the Osam as it flows beneath the bracketed tenements of Troyan, a health resort and woodworking center on the slopes of the Troyan range.

100

A SUNNY PAVILION AT VARNA, A SEASIDE RESORT

On a narrow sandy stretch between the Gulf of Varna and the Black Sea is the busy port of Varna.
Its mineral baths and pleasant beaches make it a Mecca for Eastern Europeans on holiday.

TRADITIONAL SHIRTS are worn proudly by the Gulsa National Choir. Each embroidery design indicates the man's region.

Another important production is silk. There is considerable mineral wealth, most of it now being exploited by the Communists. Among the more important industries are the weaving of textiles, flour milling and the making of pottery, wines and cigarettes.

The defeat of Bulgaria in the second Balkan War and in World War I left the state impoverished. World War II proved to be no less disastrous to the Bulgarians. Though neutral at first they soon joined Germany in the fight against the United States and Britain. When Russia declared war on Bulgaria in 1944, Bulgarians immediately begged for an armistice, which was granted in September of 1944.

After the defeat of Germany the Communists in Bulgaria began their drive to control the country by gaining a hold on the Fatherland Front, the leading political coalition in the country. Parties outside the coalition were at first represented in Parliament but in very small numbers. They had no cabinet positions. In 1945 the Western Allies demanded that democratic elections be held before they would make a peace treaty.

But Bulgaria ignored the demand. A plebiscite in 1946 abolished the monarchy. In the elections for Parliament that followed the Communists gained virtual control of the Government. Yet there was a semblance of democracy; the opposition was allowed a few seats in Parliament. Britain and America signed the peace treaty in September 1947. The Communists then held trials and executions of opposition-party leaders. After the Soviet-type constitution was drawn up, the assembly soon passed laws taking over banking, industry and agriculture.

It can be seen that the story of Bulgaria since World War II has been much like that of other iron-curtain countries.

CHIMNEY SWEEP on a Sofia street, a sign of the Bulgaria that is passing.

BOTH PHOTOS, DENNIS STOCK, MAGNUM

HARVESTTIME on a collective. Even the women must pitch in.

BULGARIA: FACTS AND FIGURES

THE COUNTRY

Became a communist People's Republic in 1946. It is bounded on the north by Rumania, on the east by the Black Sea, on the south by Greece and Turkey and on the west by Yugoslavia. As a result of the treaty of Craiova, signed with Rumania on September 8, 1940, Bulgaria gained Southern Dobruja, increasing both her population and area. The total area now is 43,047 sq. mi.; population, 7,700,000.

GOVERNMENT

According to constitution of 1947, highest organ of Government is the unicameral National Assembly, consisting of 253 deputies. When not in session, assembly is represented by the Presidium. Actually, political power is vested in the Politburo, an organ of the Central Committee of the Communist Party. In its government organization, Bulgaria follows the U.S.S.R. pattern. There are two parties—the powerful Communist Party and the closely allied Agricultural People's Union. The country is divided into 12 provinces.

COMMERCE AND INDUSTRIES

A large percentage of the people still engage in agriculture, despite rapid industrialization. Nearly all the arable land is collectivized. Wheat and corn are the principal crops but fruit, wine, cotton, tobacco, sugar beets, roses and sunflowers are also important. Stock raising is carried on extensively. Industrialization has been aided by the building of new power stations. Products include coal and lignite, cement, pig iron, cotton and woolen fabrics. Copper, manganese, lead and zinc are also available and greater efforts are being made to develop them. Exports include tobacco, wines, iron, wheat, hides, and attar of roses; imports are textiles, metals, machinery, hardware, chemicals, motor vehicles, mineral oils and cereals. Monetary unit, Bulgarian lev.

COMMUNICATIONS

Railway mileage, 2,670; roads, 15,870. One domestic and three foreign airlines serve the country. There are 61,000 telephones.

RELIGION AND EDUCATION

Most of the people belong to the Eastern Orthodox Church. There are some Muslims and Roman Catholics. Elementary education is compulsory and free between the ages of 7 and 14. There are special factory schools and vocational courses, and 11 universities and colleges, including Sofia, Stalin and Plovdiv. Education is patterned along Soviet lines.

CHIEF CITIES (with Populations)

Sofia, capital, about 592,000; Plovdiv, 163,-000; Varna (called Stalin City, 1949-56), 120,-000; Ruse, 84,000; Burgas, 73,000; Dimitrovo, 60,000; Pleven, 58,000; Stara Zagora, 55,000.

Rumania

... Balkan state on the Black Sea

AFTER generations of foreign domination, the Rumanians entered this century in full control of their own destinies. But the results were unexpectedly disastrous. Both industrial and agricultural output sagged. The monarchy earned the enmity of the people by its dissolute behavior and dictatorial policy. Then came World War II and Rumania's unfortunate alliance with Hitler. The country suffered still another blow when Russia occupied the devastated land, in 1946. All of this needs to be kept in mind when the Rumanians are criticized for their "passive" acceptance of Russian rule. As one aged Rumanian told a visiting reporter: "You have a way of forgetting what went before and of making heroes out of everyone kicked out by the Communists. I am not a Communist but they are not heroes to us, those people that were kicked out."

Moreover, the Rumanians have been fully as effective as some of their neighbors in resisting communist ideas. Farmers have refused to co-operate, often to their own detriment, since small plots of land tilled by primitive methods can hardly provide adequate livings. Nonetheless, they do not want to give up land they consider their own. The Government, plagued by poor harvests, agreed recently to revise its original program.

A new form of co-operative farm has been introduced, for example, in which a farmer is compensated in kind for the land he contributes to be worked in common. Clearly, the Communists are now more than willing to modify ideological objectives in order to curb farm discontent.

Rumanian agriculture has also suffered from a dearth of machinery and equipment. The reason for this seems to be the Kremlin's familiar fixation on heavy industry. Most of the funds available for investment have been spent on industrial development—on refineries, natural-gas fields, hydroelectric plants, steel and paper mills, chemical plants and so on. The results have been especially good in the oil industry. New equipment has revitalized the Ploesti oil field, and more strikes have been made south of the Carpathians. Rumania's oil wells are now producing at a rate well above prewar records. The Rumanians complain, however, that this budding industrial system is doing them little good. As elsewhere among the Eastern European satellites, the patience of the Rumanians is wearing thin over the shortage of consumer goods in the face of all this heavy industry. Trade with the West, foreshadowed by some recent agreements, may be the ultimate answer.

Before the war, Rumania, despite her poverty, was a gay, cosmopolitan place. "Bucharest," John Gunther wrote in 1936, "is a tinselly sort of Little Paris where the main street, the Calea Victorei, flutters with silken shirts and the leather trappings of gay carriages." Western influence was strong. Wealthy citizens traditionally sent their children to be educated either in Paris or in one of the several French-run private schools at home. Western literature, architecture and fashions were avidly adopted. Rumanian education, based on the liberal-arts ideal, emphasized the humanistic disciplines.

When they took over the country the Russians immediately set about changing the Western slant of Rumania's education and culture. In a famous 1948 speech, Teohari Georgescu, then minister of the interior, told a group of university students: "In our epoch, the light comes not from the West but from the East." A massive educational reorganization followed. Traditional courses and their teachers were tossed out. Some 80 per cent of the faculty at Bucharest University's School of Letters and Philosophy were eliminated. New courses, new teachers, nay, a whole new system took their place. Rumanian education is now organized around four levels: pre-schooling (optional; ages three to seven); elementary (required for seven years); medium (for those qualified; this lasts three years and is subdivided into college preparatory, pedagogical, technical and trade schools); and, finally, superior (university level; here again, there is a considerable variety of schools, mostly technical, to choose from). Above the elementary level, specialization, the very opposite of the liberal-arts ideal, is the heart of modern Rumanian education.

The Western spirit is far from dead, however. Bucharest still resembles Paris more than it does Moscow. It is clean, colorful, unmarred by the worst excesses of Russian architecture. "Arriving from [Moscow]," one American writes, "the newcomer is plunged into a different world, of electric signs, honking automobiles and functional office buildings." This individuality does not extend to the political sphere, however, and its benefits are paid for in economic exploitation as well as loss of independence. The previous rulers were not "heroes" either, as the old man said; they didn't bother, as the Russians have, to provide the people with the essentials of a modern industrial system.

VARIETY in Bucharest —bearded priests, a balloon seller and a sign announcing a Russian film in "Cinemascop."

105

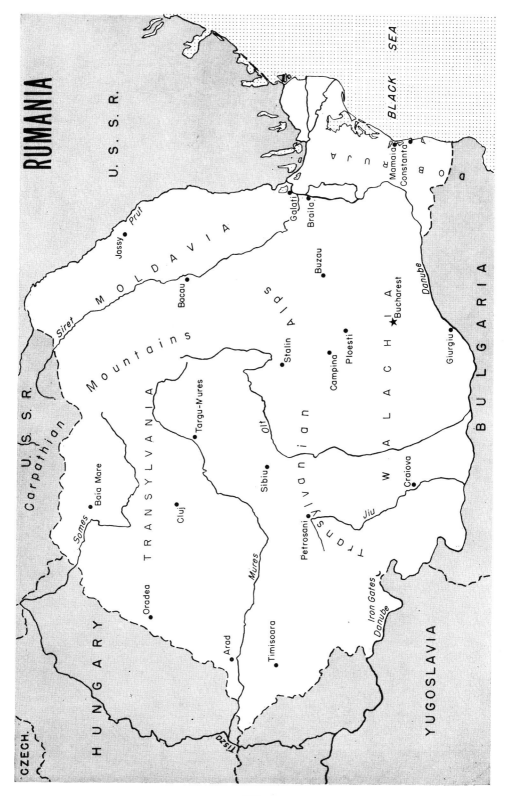

RUMANIA

U. S. S. R.

BLACK SEA

Danube

Mamaia
Constanta
Galati
Braila

Buzau

MOLDAVIA

Bacau

Jassy

Prut

Siret

Bucharest

Ploesti

Campina

Stalin

Alps

WALACHIA

Giurgiu

BULGARIA

Mountains

Targu-Mures

Olt

Transylvanian

Craiova

TRANSYLVANIA

Sibiu

Cluj

Jiu

Baia Mare

Carpathian U. S. S. R.

Somes

Petrosani

Iron Gates

Danube

Oradea

Mures

Arad

Timisoara

Tisza

HUNGARY

CZECH.

YUGOSLAVIA

THRESHING TIME IN TRANSYLVANIA

The great Transylvanian plain is a rich, well-watered area; but the people have been backward in adopting modern farming methods. The scene above is typical—the grain is hauled by a team of slow-going oxen to an old-fashioned thresher in the field. The Rumanian Government has promised to mechanize the country's agriculture.

TIMBER FROM THE CARPATHIAN SLOPES

Though agriculture is the mainstay of the country, Rumania has many other fine resources. There are wide forests, rich oil and gas deposits, gold, silver, copper, iron, lignite and salt. Since Rumania became a satellite nation of the Soviet Union (in 1948), the people of the Western world have not been able to learn very much about her.

107

EASTFOTO

BRINGING TO THE SURFACE THE RICHES THAT LIE UNDER RUMANIAN SOIL: AN OIL FIELD AT PLOESTI

Rumania's most important source of mineral wealth is oil, although production has slackened in recent years. Ploesti, second city of Rumania, is an important center of the oil industry. During the early years of World War II, the rich Ploesti oil fields fueled the German war machine.

The Romans' Dacia Felix

The beginning of Rumania is usually dated from the expeditions of the Roman Emperor Trajan against the Dacians in A.D. 106. The Dacians (the Greeks called them Getae) were a Thracian tribe who had settled between the Carpathian Mountains and the lower Danube River long before. Many Roman colonists established themselves in the fertile new territory, and Dacia Felix (Happy Dacia), as the Romans called it, flourished. The people were Romanized, Latin became the Dacian tongue and the Dacians were proclaimed Roman citizens in A.D. 212.

In the next half century, however, Roman power began to wane. Barbarians from the north, aggressive Teutonic tribes as well as the Huns bursting forth out of Asia, started to sweep down on the empire's outposts.

From that time on, this land fronting the Black Sea was subject to a series of continuing raids, by Goths, Huns, Avars, Slavs, Bulgars and, finally, Turks. In time two large principalities developed, Walachia and Moldavia. Separately, each tried to free itself from the Ottoman Turks, who had gained control in 1526. Not until 1859, however, did Walachia and Moldavia unite and give the area its present name. Independence from Turkey was declared in 1877.

Rich in timber, rich in minerals and especially so in petroleum, Rumania normally is one of the greatest grain-producing regions in Europe. The soil is fertile and there is plenty of rainfall. Large quantities of wheat and corn are grown.

Danube River Trade

The main artery of trade is the Danube River, by which cargoes—mostly petroleum, grains and timber—are brought down to be loaded on sea-going vessels at Brăila and Galati, the two most important river ports. The Danube has one serious disadvantage for trade, however; it is either frozen or in danger of freezing during most of the winter. Then transportation, especially of bulk freight such as timber, must rely on the network of railroads and highways.

Rumania's only port on the Black Sea is Constanta. It has a modern harbor that can accommodate the largest ocean vessels. It is also the end of a pipeline that brings petroleum from the oil fields, which center about Ploesti, about 140 miles northeast of Constanta. Near the port are two seacoast summer resorts, Mamaia and Eforia, as well as the famous mud baths, which have long been credited with medicinal properties, of Takir-Ghiol.

Historic Regions

The Rumania of today is considerably smaller than it was yesterday. The Southern Dobruja has been returned to Bulgaria; and Bessarabia is a part of the Soviet Union. The loss of these two regions cost Rumania almost half its coastline on the Black Sea, though neither the wide mouth of the Danube River nor the port of Constanta. Toward the west, however, Rumania has kept the southern part of Bukovina, and Transylvania, a high, fertile plain. Many of the people of Transylvania are Rumanian; about a third speak Hungarian. Both Rumanians and Hungarians claim Transylvania on historical grounds. The country's present-day neighbors, therefore, are the Soviet Union, on the north and northeast; Hungary, on the west; Yugoslavia, on the southwest; and Bulgaria, on the south.

The Iron Gates

The Danube is the joy and pride of the people, although they can claim only its lower course. It is truly a marvelous river. It is said to take its rise "in the courtyard of a gentleman's house in Germany," and it receives many tributaries as it flows through several other countries before it reaches the Kazan Pass, where it rushes through the Iron Gates and so into Rumania. It is at its narrowest and deepest in this pass. The submerged rocks that gave rise to the name of the Iron Gates have been cleared by dynamite to make a safe channel through which ships may go.

Although the Danube is not "blue," as the song describes it, it is far more mag-

BLACK STAR

SUNDAY AFTERNOON IN TRANSYLVANIA

Tidy main street in Rucar, a village in the Transylvanian Alps. The Sunday costume has a white
kilt over tight trousers, a bell-sleeved blouse and sleeveless overjacket. Since the second century,
when the Emperor Trajan conquered it, Transylvania has had a checkered career. Invading
Romans, Slavs, Magyars, Saxons and others have left their imprint.

nificent and imposing than even the Rhine
because of its stillness and breadth. It
expands to a width of between two and
three miles near Belgrade, and has islands
and lovely reaches that give variety to it.
The most famous bridge over the Danube
in Rumanian territory is that at Cerna-
voda, which was completed in 1905. It
carries the railway line from Bukarest,
or Bucharest, to the Black Sea port, Con-
stantza. The bridge is itself over twelve
miles long, as it has to cross vast tracts
of marshy land as well as water. Three
arches of it were blown up by Rumanian
soldiers in 1916 to prevent the advance of
the enemy. We can imagine the grief

they felt at having to destroy it. The restoration took five years. Work is underway on a Danube–Black Sea canal.

But let us leave the Danube to carry its huge burdens of timber and grain at its own dignified, if rather lazy, pace and fly northward. We shall pass over the capital, Bucuresti, which is also spelled Bucharest and Bukarest.

The city's favorite drive crosses Kisilev Park, which is styled after the Champs Elysées in Paris. It is typical of the

SOVFOTO

POSING IN FRONT OF AN OLD CHURCH IN A TRANSYLVANIAN TOWN

The church's roof of straw is the kind found on peasant houses in villages of the Rumanian province, and the gaily colored embroidery of the man's blouse is a sample of the needlework for which Rumanian women are noted. On the garments of men, women and children, even on sheepskin coats, they like to work rich, intricate patterns in red, gold, blue and black.

MODERN INDUSTRY IN RUMANIA. The Carbochim plants in Cluj supply electrodes, grindstones and silicon carbide to the nation's metallurgical and oil enterprises.

DYNAMO PLANT WORKERS in Bucharest. Rumanian industry is nationalized, and the Soviet Union makes decisions on plant capacities and distribution of their output.

A RUMANIAN GIRL DISPLAYS THE COTTON SHE HAS BEEN PICKING

She stands knee-deep in the midst of the ripened cotton plants to gather the valuable fiber fluffs. The field she has helped to tend is not far from Bucharest, in the flat, fertile lowlands of southern Rumania below the Transylvanian Alps. When the cotton has been carefully picked by hand it will be shipped to the city's textile mills to be processed into cloth.

113

TENDING A BUSY TEXTILE LOOM WITH SKILLFUL HANDS AND EYES

Textile mills are among the important enterprises in Bucharest, a manufacturing city as well as a capital. Extensive Rumanian farmlands furnish the mills with cotton, flax and wool.

114

TRIANGLE

THE SUN MUST DO ITS SHARE IN BLEACHING NEWLY WOVEN LINEN

In Rumania, where a vast majority of the people are engaged in agriculture, flax is one of the profitable crops, and processing and weaving its fibers into cloth is a gainful industry.

115

EASTFOTO

A TALENTED PLAYER OF RUMANIA'S FOLK MUSIC

Wearing the hand-embroidered blouse of his Transylvanian village, he is eager to interpret the traditional songs of his country. Rumanians are devoted music lovers.

roads and the chief terminal of the Rumanian air lines.

Burcharest lies in the midst of a vast plain, which swelters in the heat of summer and is lashed by bitter winds in winter. It is a fertile region, however—three-fourths of the Rumanians live on farms—and today maize (corn) has taken the place of wheat as the principal crop.

As far back as 1918, large land holdings were slowly being broken up and redistributed among the peasants. This process was speeded up after 1945, when the Communists gained control, and by 1949 all the great estates had disappeared. The Government then began to organize "Centers for Agricultural Machines and Equipment," similar to the machine-tractor stations of the Soviet Union. (The plain lends itself to large-scale farming, for which modern farm implements are necessary.) It is thought, however, that this plan has not been entirely successful and that production has suffered. Every phase of agriculture is subject to strict control under Rumania's masters, who work in close co-operation with the U.S.S.R.

wide boulevards crossing the city. The principal one is the Calea Victorei. Most of the streets would look familiar to Westerners, but here and there are curious little byways lined with bazaars which point up how close Rumania is to the Middle East.

Before World War II, Bucharest was a gay, cosmopolitan capital, with many theaters, motion-picture houses and cafés. Its gaiety and luxury vanished with the rise of the Communists, of course. Nevertheless, it remains one of the most important cities in this part of the world behind the iron curtain. It is the center of a network of at least eight rail-

On the small farms and in the little villages, the families usually occupy houses of a simple and hardy construction.

Upon four posts driven into the ground the builder places the roof. The walls are of clay and straw, and whitewashed when dry. Walls are brightened by gay bands of red or blue. The mud floor is as hard and smooth as timber. The cabin is divided into rooms. There will be a veranda gay with creepers, so that the home is quite picturesque outside and in.

The interior is bright with gay rugs and painted furniture and often with home-made embroideries and polished metals. It is only the better cottages, however, which are so charming for there are others so poor as to be hardly fit to live in. Each village has a church and school and post office, and a well, which is the meeting place of the gossips and of sweethearts.

There is a great love for children in Rumania. An old proverb says: "A child is a blessing to any man's roof," and a large family is the pride of the parents. Children are useful, of course, as they start to work in the fields at a very early age—the girls gather the flax and fetch wool and the boys help with the plowing and reaping. Attendance at school is, however, steadily increasing.

Young and old are very fond of dancing. The young people will walk miles to a dance in a neighboring village, and the public dancing ground is of earth beaten smooth and hard and clean as a board. The girls wear ribbons, flowers and a smart though home-made dress. The young men a long, snow-white blouse, with a border richly worked in color, a sash of scarlet or embroidered leather and a sleeveless coat. They keep on their hats while they dance. All wear heel-less sandals. There is invariably a master of ceremonies, whose duty it is to see that the girls have partners—and no "sitting-out" is allowed. Music is usually furnished by the gipsies, or *tzigani,* of whom there are a large number in Rumania. They are quite distinct in race from the other people and although some live in settlements, they are mostly nomadic. The haunting strains of their melodies have an immense popularity with the Rumanians both in the country and in the towns.

The Rumanian peasant has no fear of having his house robbed. When he goes out he props a stick against the door to show he is not at home. It would be a serious breach of good taste to disregard this and enter. On the other hand it is not a crime to help yourself to his fruit or his grain, provided you do not take more than you need for yourself. It is

THREE LIONS

VIVID BALLS OF YARN DANGLE FROM A HAND LOOM

Several weavers work together on what will be a large carpet. Rumanian crafts are influenced somewhat by the Middle East. This shows in handwoven rugs, which may rival the true Orientals.

SHARING HOUSEHOLD TASKS on a Transylvania farm. One woman winds newly spun linen thread on crude bobbins, while the other weaves linen into cloth for the family's needs.

118

recognized as the right of the hungry to be fed, whether the host is at home or not.

The Rumanian woman has a busy life, especially after she is married. In addition to her housework, she has to collect and prepare all the material for spinning flax or wool. She spins and then weaves it on a hand loom, making the most beautiful materials in both light and heavy textures. The articles are also dyed and embroidered. The native love of color and design is clearly shown in this work. Many of the best pieces are taken to the towns for sale, but every home will be abundantly supplied with rugs and hangings, and the people are very fond of elaborately embroidered clothes. Everything, even pottery, is most lavishly decorated.

As we go north and cross the Carpathians, we come into quite a different type of country and to a people of quite an opposite character. On the farther side of the range the land is pastoral, of wild beauty and great charm. It is German, judging by the buildings, which are of stone and set in walled courtyards, and all as like one another as peas in a pod. The people are all alike, too, sturdy, stolid, not given to speech, but thrifty and most industrious. This is quite a contrast in disposition to the lively Rumanians we have left behind. It is a stretch of country surrounded by mountain peaks, called the Siebenburgen—the land of seven burgs or forts, or Transylvania, the land across the forest—that we come to now.

EASTFOTO

SEARCHING THE HORIZON FROM ATOP THE CARPATHIAN MOUNTAINS

Mountain-climbing vacationers in the southern Carpathians of Rumania examine the faraway valley with their field glasses. Their ascent was made easier by the cable chair that carried them up into the bracing air. This picturesque range of mountains is frequently called the Transylvanian Alps; some of its peaks are more than eight thousand feet in height.

EVERY RUMANIAN VILLAGE HAS ITS TRADITIONAL DRESS

Saliste, a Transylvanian village, was once well known for its elaborate costumes, its folklore and handicrafts. In times past needle arts and hand spinning took up much of the time of the women who created intricate embroidery designs and wove exquisite fabrics. The trousers of these men are of sheep wool; and the women's aprons, a fine black broadcloth.

HIGH IN THE BRACING AIR OF RUMANIA'S TRANSYLVANIAN ALPS

A vacationers' hotel, at an altitude of nearly five thousand feet and well above the winter resort town of Sinaia, looks out over the rolling, picturesque countryside of central Rumania. The Transylvanian Alps are really a part of the Carpathian range that extends into Rumania from the north. Some of its peaks rise eight thousand feet into the clouds.

121

THE GREAT DANUBE collects the drainage of an immense region, and flows in hollows between the Alps and the Jura, the Alps and Bohemia, the Alps and the Carpathians, and the Carpathians and the Balkan range. Between the two last is that famous section of the river known as the Iron Gates. The Danube has also created land where once was sea, for it has a wide delta, formed by the deposition at its mouth of sediment— the stones and soil it carried away when cutting through the mountains— picked up during its course of nearly 1,800 miles.

A RUMANIAN PEASANT FAMILY in the doorway of its thatched, wooden cottage. Changes in government mean little in the daily lives of farming people such as these. They live close to the soil in a yearly rhythm of sowing and harvesting. Flocks of sheep provide them with wool and sheepskin coats for the bitter cold of winter.

MODERN ARCHITECTURE IN BUCHAREST

Bucharest, nicknamed "City of Delight," used to be a gay city, full of color and life. Its people loved to be called "Little Parisians." Today such innocent frivolities are frowned upon. The modern street we show here, Calea Victorei, Street of Victory, received its name after the Battle of Plevna, in 1877, by which Rumania freed itself from Turkish rule.

124

Many of these settlers are Saxons, although where they came from is a mystery. In fact, it is so mysterious that legend has it that the founders of this "tribe," if we may so call them, were those children whom the Pied Piper decoyed from Hamelin town, and who, you will remember, entered the mountain after him and were seen no more by their parents and townsfolk. It is said that they came through the tunnel out into this fertile plain and have remained here ever since, self-supporting, producing everything they want, from nails to embroideries. They are their own carpenters and shoesmiths and tailors, their own weavers and potters and farmers. Truly, Transylvania has been richly endowed by nature. In consequence, the story-book atmosphere is slowly giving way to the gradual inroads of industrialization.

This "land of a thousand beauties and a hundred hopes," as someone has styled Rumania, is a country full of the quaintest superstitions. Many of the peasants live in dread of "The Little People," or, as some call them, "The Good People." Many spells and incantations are practiced to induce these spirits to be merciful.

It would seem that "The Little People" have not lent kindly ears recently to the inducements of the Rumanian people, for their country has been beset with many difficulties both in war and peace. Forced to enter World War II on the side of the Axis, the Rumanians suffered heavy losses. After the war's end the country came under the domination of the Communists and today forms a part of the Soviet bloc of nations.

In times of national joy and national sorrow, too, the mountains are dear to the country folk of Rumania. They know and deeply love the passes, the mountain pastures, the secluded valleys and the defensible gateways to the plain.

RUMANIA: FACTS AND FIGURES

THE COUNTRY

Lies in southeastern Europe on the Black Sea. It is bounded on the north by Soviet Russia; on the east by Russia and the Black Sea; on the south by Bulgaria; and on the west by Yugoslavia and Hungary. Divided in 18 administrative districts. In 1940, Rumania was forced to restore Bessarabia and Northern Bukovina to Russia and they are now recognized as part of Soviet Russia. Southern Dobruja was ceded to Bulgaria. Area, 91,700 square miles; population, 17,150,000.

GOVERNMENT

With the abdication of King Michael (Mihai) in December, 1947, Parliament voted to abolish the monarchy and have a Constituent Assembly draw up a People's Republic constitution. It elects a Grand National Assembly (parliament) for a four-year term. When not in session, it is represented by a Presidium. There is universal suffrage, but only one (Communist) party.

COMMERCE AND INDUSTRIES

Agriculture is the chief occupation, and the main crops are corn, wheat, barley, oats, rye, beets and tobacco. Forestry is carried on extensively especially in the Carpathians. There is much livestock. Petroleum wells and salt mines are worked, and other minerals include lignite, iron and copper ores, lead and antimony. Salt mining is a state monopoly. Since 1954 most other industries have also been socialized. The chief exports are cereals, petroleum, timber, hides, wool, vegetable oils, wood manufactures, and the imports are manufactured goods (mostly textiles), machinery, automobiles, vehicles and chemicals. Monetary unit, the leu.

COMMUNICATIONS

Miles of railways, 7,636; roads, 43,363. Telephones, 135,000 instruments, 91,327 miles of wire; 226,000 radio receiving sets. Airlines connect with European cities. Both the Black Sea and the Danube are important for commercial navigation.

RELIGION AND EDUCATION

Most of the population belong to the state church, namely Rumanian Orthodox, with the liturgy conducted in Rumanian. Eight per cent of the population is Roman Catholic. There is state control over all church administrative and educational activities. Education is free and compulsory. There are special schools, including commercial, agricultural and polytechnic institutes, and universities located at Bucharest (Bucuresti), Iasi (Jassy), 2 at Cluj, and Timisoara.

CHIEF TOWNS

Bucharest, the capital, population, 1,250,000; Cluj, 118,000; Timisoara, 112,000; Ploesti, 96,000; Braila (and suburbs), 95,600; Iasi (Jassy), 94,100; Galati, 80,500; Constanta, 78,600.

A PEASANT GIRL of Rumania returning from the well with a jar filled with water, greets with a smile any chance wayfarer she may meet for she believes she will bring him good luck. But should she meet anyone as she carries an empty jar to be filled, she is sad and ashamed for then it is ill-luck that she brings. Such is the old superstition.

THE CALUSARE, one of the national dances of Rumania, is usually performed by men. In gay costumes, decorated with fringe and tinkling bells at their knees, they dance in the open air at fairs and festivals to the music of the flute, the lute and the violin, played by ragged gypsy musicians. In another dance, the Hora, women also take part.

The Soviet Union

...leader of the

communist world

"NEVER underestimate a rival" is an old adage that, in the contest between the free and the communist worlds, has particular application to the Union of Soviet Socialist Republics. The picture of a sullen, shabby people, cowed by constant fear of secret police, has been altered radically since Stalin's death in 1953. As might be expected the change is most vivid in Moscow. Today the Kremlin, grimly forbidden territory when Stalin presided there, is open to the public. On a pleasant day the grounds are thronged with happy crowds, who cluster around souvenir booths and jam the inexpensive cafeteria. When the House of Christian Dior exhibited Paris fashions at the French Embassy in Moscow in 1959 the showing had enthusiastic audiences though the later American exhibit was even more popular. One Russian official boasted: "Often you cannot tell from their [Moscow women's] dress whether they are Americans or Russians, especially in the summertime." Gorki Street is so brilliantly lighted (for Russia) at night that Muscovites proudly refer to it as "Brodvay."

This is not to say that the Soviets have retreated one iota from their belief that communism is the best system of government ever devised. Khrushchev's famous remark "We will bury you" is evidence. He—and quite obviously the majority of Russian people—is supremely confident that communism will eventually win out over capitalism all over the globe. The triumph, so the Russians imply, will not be won by war. (*Mir miru*—"peace to the world"—is the phrase that visitors to Russia hear most often.) Rather, it will be an economic victory. The flaw in this belief is that the average Russian, never abroad, is convinced that Marx' description of the horrible working conditions in England in the early 1800's still holds good for Western Europe and America. In Russian periodicals the favorite photograph of the United States shows long bread lines of unemployed. Western visitors, trying to correct this impression in casual conversation, are constantly frustrated by the bland implication that they must be lying.

Stalin, secretive and distrustful of the people, ruled by terror. Khrushchev, apparently fearless and a far more astute psychologist, has striven to erase discontent and fear. His authority is no less absolute than Stalin's was but it appears more benevolent. Khrushchev seems to have learned that robust morale is as important to an advanced industrial nation

128

RED SQUARE between St. Basil's Cathedral (left) and the Kremlin (right). The group is being led to Lenin-Stalin tomb.

as regulations. Yet early in 1960 the party leaders deemed it necessary to order a propaganda drive to educate the people "in the spirit of patriotism and national pride." The real aim, however, seems to have been to strengthen adherence to Russian communist ideology.

Economically, the emphasis is still on heavy industry. In 1958 it represented almost three fourths of total production. According to the latest plan, it is to be increased 88 per cent by 1965. The 1965 goal for the lagging consumer goods is a 68 per cent increase. Meanwhile the desire for modern clothes, furniture, home appliances grows apace. One difficulty here is the government quotas. For bookkeeping it is easier to set a quota as so many rubles' worth. In a furniture factory, say, the result is likely to be a few, massive, expensive pieces instead of numbers of simple, light, cheap ones. The ubiquitous symbol of this problem is the

fringed Victorian lamp shade, usually orange, a dust-catching horror. Khrushchev has said it must go. Indeed, planning is likely to improve as modern analytical and programing techniques, borrowed from American business, are applied. For all the opening of new lands beyond the Urals, agriculture remains a weak spot.

There is reason to believe, though the figures are in dispute, that the U.S.S.R.'s Gross National Product (GNP)—the value of everything produced per year—has been growing at least twice as fast as the United States'. Thus the Soviet Union just might catch up in fifteen years or so—providing the American rate remains static. However, whereas the United States, in 1959, with a population of almost 180,000,000 had a GNP of $400,-

129

IN THE KREMLIN—a forest of "onion" domes crowns the four cathedrals on Cathedral Square.

A COLOSSAL STATUE, in stainless steel, of farm youths, at the Agricultural Exposition, Moscow.

JULIEN BRYAN

EXHIBIT of various kinds of machinery. In the foreground are chassis for farm vehicles; in the background, buses.

SPORTS DAY, a gala event to the sports-loving Russians, in the enormous Moscow stadium. It can seat 100,000 persons.

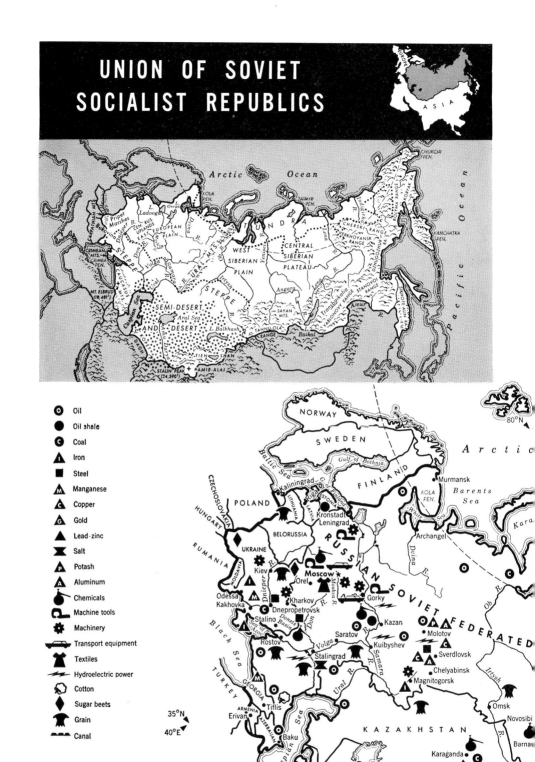

UNION OF SOVIET SOCIALIST REPUBLICS

Map legend:

- ◉ Oil
- ● Oil shale
- Ⓒ Coal
- ⚠ Iron
- ■ Steel
- Ⓜ Manganese
- Ⓒ Copper
- Ⓖ Gold
- ▲ Lead-zinc
- ✕ Salt
- Ⓟ Potash
- Ⓐ Aluminum
- Chemicals
- Machine tools
- ✿ Machinery
- Transport equipment
- Textiles
- Hydroelectric power
- Cotton
- Sugar beets
- Grain
- Canal

Meat and dairy products are found everywhere; lumber coincides with forest belt between steppes and tundra.

SCALE OF MILES
0   200   400   600   800   1000

35°N
40°E

132

000,000,000, the U.S.S.R., with a population of 208,000,000, had a GNP of $200,-000,000,000.

Russian education has impressed many Western observers profoundly. Schooling is thorough and begins at an early age in such fields as science, mathematics and languages. In addition it is turning out far more professionals such as engineers and doctors (most of the latter, women) than American education is. Soviet education is better adapted to the Soviet system and where it is not it is being modified. Certainly it is producing first-rate physicists and technicians, as the sputniks and Luniks testify. Russians have always had a flair for mathematics. In chemistry and biology the system seems to be weaker. In a few instances, stand-ard universities have dropped specific courses on Marxism-Leninism. The humanities are infused with Soviet ideology.

That the Russians have superb creative gifts is well known. They ebbed under Stalin's insistence on "socialist realism"—in effect, that a novel, a symphony, a painting must glorify the state. This is still the official line though by all accounts Khrushchev is on the side of somewhat greater creative latitude. After the initial uproar over publication of Boris Pasternak's *Doctor Zhivago* in the West, Pasternak was left free. In fact there are hints that the controversial novel may be published in Russia in the 1960's. Though much of the fiction and poetry issued in the U.S.S.R. hews to the line—and is woefully dull—a growing number of works

133

FANTASTIC LANDMARK in Moscow: St. Basil's Cathedral, on the south side of Red Square, begun in 1554 by Ivan the Terrible.

KRESHATIC, the main thoroughfare of Kiev. It was reduced to rubble during World War II and the buildings are largely postwar.

THE TSAR'S BELL, in the Kremlin, which has never sounded. When the 175-ton monster was raised, a two-ton chip fell out.

SNOW softens winter's harshness on the plains around Moscow. Many Soviet officials have dachas—country houses—in the suburbs.

shows freshness, honesty and daring.

The fresh air in the arts is most noticeable in architecture. Stalin's ornate, expensive "wedding cakes" are gradually yielding to functional designs. In music, composers are beginning to write more freely, drawing on Western ideas though modifying them to suit the Russian taste for fireworks. Painting and sculpture are also experimenting though the most advanced creations thus far are shown only in private. In technique, Russian ballet has few peers but it has long been tied to the heavy hand of the past. Experiment has now begun.

International Relations

In international relations, the Soviet Union is vying with the United States in aid and trade—economic penetration. Its targets are the countries committed to neither East nor West. The United Arab Republic, for example, is receiving substantial help to build the Aswan High Dam. In such countries as Italy, where the Communist Party is strong, the strings are tugged to harass the Government. Nevertheless, there are many signs that while the Kremlin doesn't hesitate to make use of Communist Parties abroad it hasn't much respect for them—except in mainland China. No outsider knows exactly what the relations are between the U.S.S.R. and Red China except that after Khrushchev jaunts to the West he sometimes hurries off to Peking. The Soviet authorities cannot be altogether easy about the growing might of their vast neighbor. As the 1960's dawned the chief conflict between the West and the Soviet Union still focused on Germany. At least some easing of tension had been hoped for from the May 1960 summit conference. This hope was dashed when Khrushchev broke up the conference almost at once, seizing as his excuse an American spy plane that had been downed in Russia.

The European Area

Russia in Europe is mostly plain. Its only mountains are the Urals and the rugged Caucasus ranges. It stretches from beyond the Arctic Circle to as far south as Italy. The southernmost part, the Crimea, has quite a mild climate. Elsewhere, the climate is extremely rigorous.

Little is known of the early history of the vast land. About the year 862 certain Slavic tribes came under the leadership of Norsemen (called the "Men of Rus"). They established numerous independent principalities and built Kiev, Moscow and other cities. Some 350 years later the land was invaded by hordes of Tatars, or Mongols, who ruled for more than two hundred years.

Mongol power weakened and the Russians under the leadership of the princes of Moscow threw off the Tatar yoke. Gradually the rule of Moscow became absolute, the boundaries of the kingdom were much extended, and serfdom was established. Yet the country remained a half barbarous, Oriental despotism far behind the remainder of Europe. Finally the royal line of Moscow ran out and there was a period of disorder. Then Michael Romanov was elected czar. It is with his grandson, known as Peter the Great, that modern Russia begins.

This energetic ruler extended the boundaries, moved the capital from Moscow to the new city of St. Petersburg (Leningrad) and attempted to make Russia a European rather than an Oriental state. It was a difficult task and success was not complete, though Russia never fell back to its former condition. Some of his successors were strong men and women and the power of Russia increased.

Storm Clouds Appear

With the spread of education, discontent with autocratic rule grew stronger during the nineteenth century. Many who were suspected of plotting against the Government were exiled to Siberia, but riots and assassinations continued. Finally Czar Nicholas II established a legislative body, the Duma, which met for the first time in 1906.

The story of Russia in World War I is sad. Though the soldiers fought bravely, they were often badly led, and usually lacked the most necessary supplies.

Finally in 1917 both people and army had become war-weary, and revolution broke out. The tsar abdicated but the provisional government was unable to maintain order and later the control was taken over by the Soviet of Workmen, Peasants and Soldiers, which declared for peace and the abolition of private property. Under Nicolai Lenin and Leon Trotsky, the new government was set up. Lenin died in 1924 and was succeeded by Josef Stalin. Trotsky was exiled and was assassinated in Mexico in 1940.

At first, the new Russia in Europe was considerably smaller than the old. However, the Russia of today, called the Union of Soviet Socialist Republics is a huge country which has expanded and extended its influence until it now covers more than half of Europe and an immense portion of Asia. Since World War II, many smaller countries of Europe have become parts of the Union, including Latvia, Lithuania and Estonia.

When the monarchy was overthrown and the Soviet government was established, naturally great changes took place. All power was placed in the hands of the workers and the property of the former business and professional classes was confiscated, and many of them fled the country. The cities, particularly, were

Sovfoto

A TRAVELING SHOP FOR BUSY HOUSEWIVES

The truck is fitted out as a regular store, with display windows at the rear. Halted in a near-by park, this shop serves people in Dnepropetrovsk, a large city in the east-central part of the Ukraine. Dnepropetrovsk is at the rapids of the Dnieper River, above the Dneprostroi Dam, one of the largest sources of electric power in the Soviet Union.

A MAIN STREET IN KIEV, CAPITAL OF THE UKRAINE

Kiev, on the Dnieper, is known in Russia as the "Mother of Cities," because of its great age. It was settled before the fifth century; by the thirteenth century it had become rich and powerful, and it was long the religious center of the Empire. Today Kiev is a bustling industrial town and a shipping port on the Dnieper, which flows into the Black Sea.

transformed, though the changes on the land have been hardly less striking Never before, perhaps, in the entire history of the world has so complete a transformation of an entire people taken place in so short a time.

For several years after the revolution Russia was engaged in wars with her enemies at home and abroad. When the Soviets had finally established their rule they found themselves masters of a country in ruins. Millions had been killed or had starved to death. The government controlled the country's resources, but commerce and industry were at a standstill.

During the first years food, clothing, and other goods were very scarce, and not until 1928, with the inauguration of the first "five year plan," did the real turning-point come. This plan and those that followed it were something new in national policy. Every detail of industry and agriculture—even of cultural life—was planned in advance. It was laid down just how many factories should be increased, what crops should be sown. The whole population was put to work with a will to transform a huge but backward country into a modern industrial nation. Since the Russians lacked technical skill and experience, many foreign engineers and experts—among them many Ameri-

Sovfoto

A TROIKA IS STILL USEFUL IN DEEP SNOW

Russians call any kind of vehicle drawn by three horses abreast a "troika." It may be a sleigh or a carriage. Automobiles have taken the place of the old-time carriages; but when the heavy snows of the bitter winters come, sleighs still glide over country roads. This troika is coming through an evergreen forest in the Ivanovo region, northeast of Moscow.

cans—were imported during the early years. As time went on, the Russians gradually took over the work of designing and operating their own machinery.

Though in many respects the plans fell short of the mark set, the results on the whole were astonishing. Entire new industries were created. A network of electric power began to cover the land. Much-needed canals and other important public works were constructed, often with the labor of political prisoners. In some fields of production the improvement was very great. A tremendously powerful, mechanized Red Army was developed. Education was greatly extended. Where formerly the vast majority of the people had been unable to read and write, to-day illiteracy has been much reduced.

The People Tighten Their Belts

In order to make these things possible, the Soviet Government, dominated by the Communist Party, ruled the country with an iron hand. For many years the people had to tighten their belts and endure many hardships. All enemies of the regime were ruthlessly punished; but the Russian people had undergone centuries of oppression and poverty. Now they were made to believe that the sacrifices demanded of them were in their own interest, for the purpose of building up a better order of things.

There were several five-year plans, with goals set for industry, transportation and so on. However, the planning was interrupted by World War II, in which Russia suffered great damage. After the war, the Soviet Union threw all its efforts into restoring the shattered areas. When the United Nations was set up, Russia became a member with a permanent seat on the Security Council. Unhappily for the world, it has not been a co-operative partner. Disputes and deadlocks have been the rule, aggravating international tension. Even as the carefully selected spokesmen of the Soviet Union have talked "peace" loud, Communists have seemed bent on making any real peace impossible. The most flagrant example, of course, is Korea, where the Chi-

nese Communists have prolonged the conflict—evidently with the approval of the Soviet Union.

Though Russia has become a highly industrialized country, agriculture is as vital as ever it was under the tsars. For a long time, the peasants were the weak link in Soviet economy and not until after 1932 was there any real improvement in the agricultural problem.

The revolution gave land to the peasants, but farming was carried on by individual small land-holders, according to age-old, primitive and generally inefficient methods. Moreover the peasants could not sell their crops to the highest bidder. The government collected the entire surplus, often by forceful methods, paying far below the real value. As a result many peasants refused to raise anything beyond their needs, thus seriously endangering the country's food supply.

The Soviet plan for applying the revolution to the land was called the "collectivization of agriculture." It met with tremendous opposition, especially on the part of the moderately prosperous peasants called "kulaks." Not until there had been bloodshed and hundreds of thousands of these kulaks had been exiled did success begin to come.

Trouble in Agriculture

By the 1940's more than 90 per cent of Russian agriculture was being carried on in collective farms, where 10 to 30 families would work about 600 acres of land. A few years after World War II, the Government launched an even more extreme plan, the creation of agricultural "towns." Each was to contain several thousand persons and to be run by a bureaucratic caste. However, the "town" plan never got very far. According to the most reliable reports available, even the old collective-farm system was breaking down.

When Stalin died, in 1953, a severe crisis was brewing in agriculture. The chief causes seemed to be a shortage of manpower, poor condition of livestock, inefficient Machine and Tractor Service stations, and a tremendous burden of taxes on the farm workers. Letters smuggled

UNDER THE SOLEMN FACE OF THE SOVIET UNION'S FOUNDER
The occasion is the celebration of a Russian communist anniversary. Behind the children sit Soviet leaders; Nikita Khrushchev is at the inner end of the second row on the right.

APARTMENT HOUSES ON THE OKTYABRSKAYA, A STREET IN STALINGRAD

This view of Stalingrad, taken since the second World War, gives little indication that the city was reduced to a heap of smoking ruins in one of the most prolonged and fierce battles of all time. Stalingrad is on the lower Volga River, where it bends to the west; and the Germans hoped to cut the vital supply artery of the river at this point. The battle lasted from August 1942 until February 1943. Defeat of the Germans here marked the beginning of their decline in military power. The Russians took pride in rebuilding Stalingrad as quickly as possible.

out indicated that some areas were close to starvation. A soldier who had returned to a collective near Moscow wrote that "90 per cent of the farmers had no bread and lived on frozen potatoes and pancakes

its way through a field of wheat, while only a mile away women are flailing grain as their ancestors did, centuries ago. Not far from Orel, in central Russia, a truck garden has water pumped to it through

SOVFOTO

WHERE NEVSKY PROSPECT CROSSES ANICHKOV BRIDGE, IN LENINGRAD

Nevsky Prospect is one of the principal thoroughfares in Leningrad and the most famous. For a time after the Revolution it was called October 25 Prospect. Some of the most imposing buildings of the days of the tsars still stand along this street, among them the baroque Stroganov Palace, and the Anichkov Palace. The latter is now called the Young Pioneers Palace.

made of minced grass with a small addition of flour." This situation may have been one of the reasons why the Malenkov regime was so quick to promise better living standards.

Russia is still a land of extreme contrasts. Jet aircraft fly over roads where an oxcart is the usual vehicle. The most modern kind of harvester may be eating

high-pressure nozzles, like lawn sprinklers. Yet the women who live there must draw water, for household use, from a well and carry the buckets home suspended from a wooden shoulder yoke.

In the cities, numbers of apartment houses were hurriedly put up after the war. But conveniences such as electric lights and telephones are rather rare.

RIVER-BOAT PIER ON THE VOLGA AT KUIBYSHEV

At this point in its course—called the Samara Bend—the Volga is joined by the Samara River and is very broad. Along the water front of the city there are many wharves and extensive shipyards. Traffic on the river is heavy, and Kuibyshev has a large share in this activity. River boats leave its docks laden with grain, livestock and many kinds of manufactured goods.

HOUSES FROM TSARIST DAYS FACE REVOLUTION SQUARE

Like many other Russian cities, Kuibyshev (formerly called Samara) was made over in some ways and given a new name after the Communists came to power. Its modern development, beginning around 1900, was due to the fact that it was on the line of the railroads then being built into Asia. Today it is a center of heavy industry, with aircraft, locomotive and tractor factories.

144

HEAVY-DUTY TRACTORS lined up outside a manufacturing plant are part of the Soviet plan to mechanize agriculture. The tractors will be shipped to Russia's collective farms.

Stalingrad and some other badly destroyed centers got modern department stores that quite dazzle the eye. The average Russian, however, was much more likely to be found shopping in the old trading arcades that go back to tsarist days, with little choice of wares.

For years Russia paid little attention to foreign affairs. In August 1939, however, a non-aggression pact with Germany was signed. When Germany broke down resistance in Poland, Russia annexed over half of that state, and compelled the three little Baltic States, Latvia, Estonia and Lithuania, to allow the establishment of naval bases in their harbors. Next it was claimed that Finland was a danger to Russia and cession of territory was demanded. The Finns refused and for over a hundred days resisted the might of Russia, but in the end lost considerable territory. In 1940 Russia took complete control of the Baltic States and also took over Bessarabia and part of Bukovina from Rumania.

In spite of the non-aggression pact, Germany launched a sudden attack against Russia, in June 1941, which brought the Soviet Union into World War II on the side of the Allies. The high-water mark of the German invasion was the Battle of Stalingrad, where the Nazis were turned back after a fierce struggle. Eventually, in the closing days of the war in Europe, Red Army soldiers met Western Allied troops in Berlin. Germany was divided into four zones, with Soviet troops occupying the eastern zone. Here Communist influence became dominant. In Poland, Bulgaria, Rumania, Hungary and Czechoslovakia, the Communists also gained.

Before the Bolshevik revolution of 1917, religion played a great part in the life of the Russian people. The prevailing creed was that of the Russian Orthodox Church. Almost every cottage or house contained a corner with a small sacred picture or image, usually of the Virgin Mary or of one of the saints. Churches and chapels dotted the land.

145

REINDEER EAT LICHENS THAT GROW BENEATH THE SNOW

Reindeer can live where the land is always frozen, and in arctic places like northern Russia they are of great worth. They can draw sleds for long distances and can carry men or heavy loads on their backs, their sharp, cleft hoofs giving them firm footing on ice or in snow drifts. They also provide milk, meat, wool and leather for the people of these northern lands.

146

THEATER IN ARCHANGEL, NEAR THE WHITE SEA

Just below the great port city of Archangel the River Dvina empties into the White Sea. The Arctic Circle is only one hundred and fifty miles to the north, and the harbor at Archangel is frozen for a good half of the year; but it handles a great volume of traffic during the months when it is ice-free. Above is the Civic Theater, at the river's edge.

After 1918, the Communists separated the church from the state and the school from the church, and appropriated most of the church property. Freedom of worship was guaranteed in the constitution of 1936, but no church member may have a part in the Government. Atheism is taught in the schools. Among churchgoers the Russian Orthodox Church has the largest following. Its two branches have headquarters at Moscow.

Peter the Great began to build his city in 1703 upon land taken from the Swedes. The ground was marshy and it was necessary to build the houses upon piles. Thousands of people from all parts of Russia were brought to the spot and forced to labor. So many died that there is an old saying that the city was really built upon bones. Under the succeeding tsars the city grew until the population was about a million and a half at the beginning of the first World War. The name was then changed to the Russian form Petrograd instead of the German St. Petersburg.

In 1918 the Soviet Government transferred the government to Moscow, and the former capital declined. In 1924 the name was changed to Leningrad, after Nikolai Lenin, founder of the U.S.S.R.

There was a general exodus from the city after 1918, and the population was at one time estimated as hardly more than half a million. However, between the two World Wars, the tide turned, and Leningrad is now the second largest city of the Soviet Union, with well over 3,000,-000 population. It is a busy port and shipbuilding center.

A number of railroads converge at Leningrad, and the city is connected with Kronstadt, a port on the Gulf of Finland, by a sixteen-mile canal. Another canal system connects Leningrad with the White Sea, 141 miles away.

Russia is full of museums of every sort. In some, are works of art. In others, the life, customs and dress of every era are shown. There are exhibits of industrial processes and methods. All works of art in private hands all through Russia have been confiscated and placed in museums already existing or in others founded since the establishment of the communist regime. One of the most famous of Russia's museums is the Hermitage, in Leningrad; it contains a magnificent art and archaeological collection.

147

Originally built by Catherine II, it was reconstructed in 1840–50.

Moscow is connected by rail with Leningrad, the old capital of Russia, first known as St. Petersburg, then as Petrograd. We are told that this particular railway affords an example of the autocratic rule of the tsars. The railway was under construction when Nicholas I was on the throne. Difficulties arose as to the line it should follow; marshes were in the way and thick forest had to be penetrated, so that a very winding route seemed necessary. As the engineers were unable to agree upon the best route, the matter was referred to the Tsar who, it is said, called for a map, a pencil and a ruler. Taking the map, he drew a line from Moscow to Leningrad and stated that that was the route to be followed. This is why the railway runs so very straight.

Eastern Domes and Western Subway

During its history Russia has had five capitals, and Moscow has had that honor again since 1918. However, it is a very different city from what it was in the days of the tsars, though still a curious mixture of East and West. The onion-shaped domes of the old churches have a Moorish look; and at the other extreme is a modern subway, one of the Communists' showpieces, with marble stations decorated in stainless steel.

Just when Moscow was founded is uncertain. However, its 800th birthday was celebrated in 1947. It is first mentioned in the Russian Chronicles in 1147. It grew up on the main trade routes that led from Europe to the Orient and from the Baltic to the Caspian Sea. Mongolian hordes sacked it again and again. The Russians themselves set fire to their beloved city—"Little Mother Moscow"—in 1812 in order to prevent Napoleon from setting up winter quarters there, after his capture of the city.

Moscow is in the center of the great Russian plain, and is situated on seven low hills, rising in terraces from the high banks of the Moscow River, which winds across the city. The main part is on the north bank. Overlooking the river from Borovitzky Hill, in the very center of the city, is the vast Kremlin, or "Fortress." Wide streets radiate from it to the city's suburbs.

The ground on which the Kremlin stands is an irregular triangle, surrounded by a wall about 1¼ miles in circumference and from 14 to 20 feet thick and from 30 to 70 feet high. In the wall are 5 gates, and 19 towers, each one in a different style though all are generally pyramids in shape. The eastern and main entrance to the Kremlin, from Red Square, is the fifteenth-century Spasskiya Gate (Gate of the Redeemer), 205 feet high. Atop this gate is a belfry. For many years after the Revolution, the bells pealed forth the INTERNATIONAL at regular intervals. Napoleon entered from the Borovitzkiya Gate (Gate of the Woods), 62 feet high. Inside the walls are a bewildering number of buildings, including a vast palace, in a variety of styles—Byzantine, Renaissance, Baroque. Towering over all is the high dome of the Cathedral of the Assumption, begun in 1393. There is one thoroughfare, Communist Street.

Red Square, 900 yards long and 175 yards broad, is the center of political life. In front of the Kremlin gleams the polished red and black marble tomb of Lenin and Stalin, a communist shrine. On the other side from the Kremlin is the many-domed St. Basil's Cathedral, now a museum. Red Square frequently echoes to the sound of marching feet in the huge parades staged by the Government.

The Soviet Union in Asia

Let us now turn east and cross the Ural Mountains. The long north-south range marks the dividing line between the European and Asiatic parts of the Soviet Union. Soviet Asia includes Siberia (officially part of the Russian Soviet Federated Socialist Republic, the largest Soviet unit) and, in central Asia, five Soviet Socialist Republics, which we discuss in the next chapter. The name Siberia first came into use in the sixteenth century and was taken from a village, Sibir, on the Irtysh River.

A vast area of about five million square

A STEAMER AND GREAT LOG RAFTS BREAST THE MIGHTY VOLGA

Though most of the timber is destined for sawmills, some of the rafts are permanent and have houses on them. They provide shelter for the men who must keep the unwieldy logs in order.

149

BURIAT SHEPHERD AND HIS STEED

The Buriats live in north-central Asia, on either side of Lake Baikal. They are of Mongol origin, with high cheek bones, slanting eyes and sturdy frame. They gain a living chiefly by stock-raising, their occupation now being under strict Soviet supervision. The land of the Buriats is rugged and beautiful. Lake Baikal contains seals, as well as many kinds of fish.

WAREHOUSE FOR FURS IN THE FAR NORTH

Just across the Bering Strait from Alaska is the Chukotsky Peninsula, Russia's northeastern out-post. It is a chill region, bisected by the Arctic Circle and inhabited mostly by foxes, wolves and bears, and their trappers. Here a quantity of precious skins—polar fox and others—are sorted and processed. Furs are one of the Soviet Union's articles of export.

150

IN KHABAROVSK, EMBROIDERY IS A WORK OF ART

The women of Khabarovsk, in far eastern Asia, adorn their tunics, coats, gloves and even their fur footwear with lavish embroidery. Khabarovsk, on a cliff above the Amur River, has a cosmopolitan population, with Russians, Chinese, Koreans and others mingling on the streets. The city is cold for much of the year and clothing must be warmly padded.

151

miles, Siberia sprawls across the northern third of Asia, from the Urals to the Bering Sea. At least a quarter of Siberia is within the Arctic Circle. Off the desolate Arctic coast are the large islands of Severnaya Zemlya, Novosibirskiye (New Siberian Islands) and Wrangel. On the Pacific coast, practically encircling the Sea of Okhotsk, are the Kamchatka Peninsula, the volcanic Kurile archipelago and the island of Sakhalin.

Tundra, Taiga and Steppes

The Arctic shore is bleak tundra. Toward the south, the tundra merges into a region—called taiga—of swampy, evergreen forests. South of this are steppes—dry grasslands. Some of the world's longest rivers—Ob, Yenisei and Lena—flow north through Siberia, their lower courses frozen for nine months of the year.

Western Siberia—between the Urals and the Yenisei River—is largely a low, flat plain, drained by the Ob-Irtysh river system. East of the Yenisei, the land rises to form a great plateau, watered by the Lena. Eastern Siberia, still higher, is ridged with long mountain chains: Verkhoyansk, east of the Lena River; Cherski, farther east; Yablonovy, east of Lake Baikal; and Koryak, Kolyma, Dzhugdzhur and Stanovoi, guarding the Pacific coast. There are a number of active volcanoes among the mountains of the Kamchatka Peninsula. Siberia's southern frontier also is extremely rugged. Here the peaks of the Altai, Tannu-Ola, Sayan and Sikhote-Alin ranges mark the border with China and Mongolia.

Cold Pole of the World

The climate of Siberia runs to extremes—brief, hot summers and long, bitter winters. At Yakutsk, on the Lena, in summer the thermometer may shoot to above 90°. In the northeast, the region around Verkhoyansk and Oimyakon is sometimes called the world's cold pole. There the average temperature in January is between 60° and 65° below zero.

The earliest known people in Siberia were primitive tribes wandering the steppes. Later many of them were driven north into the taiga by warlike Turkic and Mongolian clans, which thereafter occupied the grasslands. Descendants of these various groups still form the basic population of Siberia. Except when it interferes with the Government's plans, their nomadic way of life as herdsmen seems to be left undisturbed.

As early as the thirteenth century, Russian fur traders, seeking ermines and sables, penetrated northwest Siberia. Actual Russian conquest began in the 1500's and won through to the Pacific by 1640. It was during this period that the tsarist police began to use Siberia as a place of exile; the place itself provided punishment. Siberia acquired a reputation of human misery and brooding mystery.

Settlement under the Tsars

On the other hand, many parts of western Siberia were settled by free Cossacks and today seem little different from Russia proper. During the late 1800's so many gifted Russians were banished to eastern Siberia that such cities as Chita and Irkutsk became lively cultural and scientific centers, though hardly known to the world at large. After the Trans-Siberian Railroad was completed to the Pacific, in 1905, numerous Russian colonies sprang up along the right of way.

Industrial Development

So when the Soviet Government turned its attention east—ever on the search for untapped natural resources—it was not launching a completely new policy. Rather, it was speeding up a transformation that had begun under the tsars. Our information about present-day conditions is neither complete nor altogether reliable, but of one broad fact there can be no doubt: the industrial center of the Soviet Union has shifted east of the Urals. Magnitogorsk (at the south end of the range), with its furnaces and rolling mills, is the metal-working hub of the nation. Throughout Siberia the lifeblood of almost every large town is industry—manufacturing, mining or lumbering. The forests are immense and there is great mineral wealth. The Lake Baikal re-

THE CATHEDRAL OF ST. NICHOLAS in Leningrad. Most such old churches are museums today. However, the wintry scene might be from the pages of a nineteenth-century Russian novel.

153

A ROW OF SMALL HOMES IN A WORKERS' VILLAGE NEAR KAKHOVKA

Kakhovka is the center of a hydroelectric project on the Dnieper River in southern Ukraine. The region is a steppe, rich in the production of wheat, cotton, grapes and vegetables.

A MOSCOW FAMILY AT BREAKFAST IN A MODEST NEW APARTMENT

This family is indeed fortunate to have a new home. There is a continuing shortage of housing in the crowded capital and the growing industrial centers of the Soviet Union.

gion, the Lena and Kolyma valleys are rich in gold; Sakhalin Island has oil. In the Kuznetsk Basin (south-central Siberia), the Tunguska Basin, Lena Valley and Irkutsk and Transbaikalia areas, there are large coal fields. The Kuznetsk Basin and Transbaikalia also have important quantities of iron.

Yakutsk, Gold-mining City

Yakutsk, on the Lena River, may be taken as a fairly typical Siberian city. Around it are gold mines. There, also, intensive research is being carried on to find out how to grow such plants as corn and tomatoes in permafrost soil—below about four feet, the ground never thaws. Because of the permafrost, the city's water supply is limited and sewage disposal is a problem. The old houses, many of them dating from the late 1800's, are made of wood, with the fantastic gingerbread decoration of the period. Yakutsk has electricity, and practically every home has a radio—a necessity in this isolated spot. Otherwise, creature comforts are largely ignored. Perhaps the most striking feature of the city is the number of schools. It has no church.

Transportation Problems

Bicycles and motor bikes are used almost everywhere. Even if they were available, automobiles could hardly take the roads, which are usually muddy, pitted with potholes or frozen in jagged ruts. City streets are rarely paved. The Trans-Siberian Railroad serves only a narrow strip and has comparatively few branch lines, though more are being built and planned. To meet the need for getting over the enormous distances, the civil air fleet has a wide-flung network. A tiny hamlet may have a "hedgehopper" plane, connecting with major air routes.

The rivers, particularly the Lena, carry considerable traffic during the warm months. Then steamboats, on fairly regular schedules, ply the Arctic coastal waters and go far inland up the rivers. Outbound, they are laden with such welcome luxuries as fresh fruit. On the return voyage to northern European Russian ports, they may carry gold and furs.

The need to increase food production is one of the Soviet Government's most urgent problems and it is trying to develop the western steppes as a great breadbasket. In some places, especially along the course of the upper Ob, near Barnaul, the soil is rich. Lack of water is the biggest handicap. To overcome it, dams are being erected, for both irrigation and electric power. One of the largest of the dams is being constructed at Novosibirsk, where the Ob is a wide, muddy stream. This dam is supposed to be completed sometime in the early 1960's.

Secret Atomic-Energy Plants

It is surmised that at least two of the Soviet Union's largest atomic-energy plants are near Novosibirsk and Irkutsk. The latter city is on the Angara River, not far from Lake Baikal, and the water-power resources of the Angara are said to be tremendous. Norilsk, near the Yenisei River and close to the Arctic coast, made a sudden, mysterious leap in population during the 1950's. Always a mining town, there is reason for believing that it has become a center of uranium production.

Norilsk points up the dark side of Siberia that still exists. According to one report, at least 120,000 prisoners are toiling in the mines there. Soviet Asia is, in fact, the domain of the secret police, which "recruits" slave labor. The most notorious camps of which the outside world has heard are in the vicinity of Khabarovsk (on the Amur River, in the southeast), Yakutsk, Magadan (on the Sea of Okhotsk—25 per cent of the U.S.S.R.'s gold is supposed to be produced in this locality), Chita, Karaganda and Balkhash (the last two in the Kazakhstan republic).

Forced Migration

In addition to the miserable inmates of the prison camps, there are *spetsi*—a Russian nickname that refers to people who are forbidden to move from a certain city or area. They are in "forced residence." The *spetsi* include the victims of forced mass migration: a colony of Germans who long ago had their own republic on the

COMMUNITY SAWMILL on a show-place kolkhoz (collective farm) near Kharkov, in the Ukraine. The kolkhoz has more than five hundred farmers and is highly self-sufficient.

A KOLKHOZNIK (collective-farm worker) proudly displays the ripe corn he has helped to raise. The Soviet Union is pushing corn production, especially as feed for livestock.

CRUSTY LOAVES for sale on a street corner in Tiflis. The Russians eat large quantities of bread, much of it made from rye flour. Borsch —beet soup—is another favorite food.

PICKING TOMATOES. Fresh vegetables like these are a luxury in some areas. Russian women, in the cities as well as in the country, still wear babushkas—head kerchiefs tied under the chin. *Babushka* in Russian means "grandmother."

157

PALATIAL ARCHED STAIRWAY OF THE METRO, MOSCOW'S SUBWAY

Polished marble walls, domed plaster ceilings, floral moldings and decorative wrought-metal chandeliers complete the picture of opulence in the Komsomolskaya-Koltsevaya Station.

IZMAILOVSKAYA STATION, A SHOW PIECE OF THE SOVIETS

Supplementing the surface means of transportation—streetcars and busses—the Metro branches out in four lines though it is not very long. It is meant for show.

Volga; Letts, Estonians and Latvians; Caucasus tribesmen; Tatars from the Crimea; Russian intellectuals who failed to follow communist dictates. These groups have been sent to the most lonely, harsh areas of Siberia. Most of them live in little more than hovels. There are also "volunteer" settlers, young Russians given no real choice but to migrate—pawns in the Soviet Government's determined effort to develop Siberia regardless of the cost to individual human beings.

UNION OF SOVIET SOCIALIST REPUBLICS: FACTS AND FIGURES

THE COUNTRY

Occupies the eastern half of Europe and the northern part of Asia. On the north the boundary is the Arctic Ocean, on the east the Pacific Ocean, on the south is China, Afghanistan, Persia (Iran), Caspian Sea, Turkey and the Black Sea; on the west, Rumania, Hungary, Czechoslovakia, Poland, the Baltic Sea and Finland. The Soviet includes the Russian Soviet Federal Socialist Republic (area, 6,569,000 square miles). Armenian Soviet Socialist Republic (11,500); Azerbaijan S.S.R. (33,000); Estonia S.S.R. (17,370); Georgian S.S.R. (29,000); Kazakh S.S.R. (1,042,470); Kirghiz S.S.R. (75,000); Latvian S.S.R. (25,000); Lithuanian S.S.R. (25,000); Moldavian S.S.R. (13,000); Tadzhik S.S.R. (55,000); Turkmen S.S.R. (187,000); Ukrainian S.S.R. (223,000); Uzbek S.S.R. (150,000); White Russian or Bielorussian S.S.R. (80,000). Total population, 212,000,000; total area, 8,536,340 sq. mi.

GOVERNMENT

By constitution of 1936, the U.S.S.R. is a "socialist state of peasants and workers." The highest organ is the Supreme Council made up of two chambers—the Council of Union, elected by proportional representation, and the Council of Nationalities consisting of representatives from each constituent republic, autonomous republic, autonomous province and autonomous district. Executive and administrative power is vested in the Council of Ministers of the U.S.S.R. appointed by the Supreme Soviet.

Greater decentralization in the internal political structure was adopted in 1944 as a means of facilitating admission of new republics into the Soviet Union through the assurance of autonomy in foreign and military affairs. All citizens of either sex over 18 years of age are granted the franchise. A "dictatorship of the proletariat" is maintained through the agency of the Communist Party.

COMMERCE AND INDUSTRIES

Formerly a strictly agricultural country Soviet Russia has become an industrial agrarian country, second only to the United States in its industrial output. Industrial production is organized under a planning system and conducted by state trusts and combines, operated under the supervision of appropriate governmental departments. There are great numbers of industrial establishments for the production of pig iron, steel, coal, oil, etc. Ninety-five per cent of the agricultural output, which includes wheat, rye, barley, oats, corn, cotton, sugar beets, flax, sunflower seeds, and tobacco, is produced on collective and state farms that have been highly mechanized. Mineral resources include coal, peat, oil, iron ore, manganese, copper, zinc and lead, uranium. Forests important. Principal exports are sawn timber, furs, oil, cotton fabrics, pulpwood, grain, and manganese ore; the principal imports, industrial machinery and tools, sheet iron and steel, ferro-alloys, motor vehicles and parts. Monetary unit, the ruble.

COMMUNICATIONS

There are about 70,200 miles of railways and about 66,500 miles of navigable waterways. Road mileage is estimated at about 2,500,000. In May 1952 a 63-mile canal was opened to join the Don and Volga rivers and so link the Baltic and White seas in the north with the Caspian, Black and Azov seas in the south in a single waterway. Air service is maintained between all Soviet capitals and with a limited number of foreign countries. There are more than 6,000,000 radios and 800,000 television sets.

RELIGION AND EDUCATION

Officially, according to the constitution, there is religious freedom in the U.S.S.R. However, the state is supreme in all things and even where a faith is tolerated (such as the Russian Orthodox Church, which was the largest denomination under the tsars), it is controlled rigidly by the Communist Government and, in fact, is far from free.

Education is compulsory and entirely state-controlled. There are special schools with emphasis on trade schools, classes and schools for adult education and various universities.

CHIEF CITIES (with populations)

Moscow, capital, 5,032,000; Leningrad, 2,888,000; Kiev, 991,000; Gorki, 942,000; Tashkent, 911,000; Baku (with suburbs), 901,000; Novosibirsk, 887,000; Kharkov, 877,000; Kuibishev (Samara), 760,000; Sverdlovsk, 707,000; Chelyabinsk, 688,000; Tiflis, 635,000; Stalino, 625,000; Odessa, 607,000; Dnepropetrovsk, 576,000; Kazan, 565,000; Riga, 565,000; Rostov, 552,000; Perm (former Molotov), 538,000; Stalingrad, 525,000; Saratov, 518,000; Erivan, 509,000; Omsk, 505,000.

SUKHUMI, on the Georgian coast of the Black Sea. Subtropical and sheltered by the Caucasus foothills, Sukhumi is a popular resort.

STATION, which is actually a youth center, of the children's railroad near Kharkov. Good school work is rewarded with train rides.

160

PETER THE GREAT, astride a rearing steed, looks out over Leningrad, the city he founded in 1703 to give him a "window" on Europe.

CONSTRUCTION PROJECT on the outskirts of Leningrad. The hard labor of digging and shoveling is being performed by women.

Soviet Republics in Asia

To the Soviet Union the five Asiatic republics represent a frontier, with fabulous resources to be exploited. What is taking place there today has something of the same excitement that accompanied the opening of the North American West in the 1800's. There is, however, a crucial difference. The American West was sparsely populated, by Indians. The Asiatic area is one of the oldest homes of man and has had teeming cities since ancient times. The very names of Samarkand and Bukhara call up exotic tales told of Tamerlane and Genghis Khan.

The area came under the control of Russia during the late 1800's and was generally referred to as Western Turkistan (in contrast to Eastern Turkistan —the Chinese province of Sinkiang). Not until after the Communists came to power in Russia was the territory organized into the present republics. The five are: Kazakhstan (which stretches between the Caspian Sea and Mongolia) and (south of Kazakhstan and bordering on Iran, Afghanistan and China) Turkmenia, Uzbekistan, Tadzhikistan and Kirghizia. Kazakhstan alone is about a third as large as the United States.

For a long time the region seemed re-

A FIELD OF WHEAT stretches to the horizon on what was once wasteland in Kazakhstan. The republic is the focus of the Soviet drive to increase farm production.

... *Kazakhstan and its neighbors*

mote and was almost unknown to the outside world. Thus the Soviet Government deemed it a safe place to ship potentially rebellious groups, uprooted from European Russian soil, as well as individuals fallen from political favor. As the various native peoples of the republics are Asians —Turkic, with some strains of Mongol and Persian—and mostly Muslims, adjustments between them and the Russian immigrants have not always been easy.

There has been an even greater influx of newcomers under Khrushchev. As agriculture is the Soviet Union's most vexing internal problem the effort to bring

more land into production is intensive. Hence Khrushchev's pet Virgin Lands scheme, to put the vast plains of central Asia, particularly Kazakhstan, to the plow. Thousands of young Russians have been lured or frightened into "volunteering" for the pioneer work. In some sections of Kazakhstan there are now more Ukrainians than Kazakhs. In spite of complaints of living conditions—as well as the hazard of drought—the pioneers have made Kazakhstan the U.S.S.R.'s breadbasket second only to the Ukraine.

In mineral production the Asiatic republics are also of vital importance.

163

Kazakhstan is Russia's main source of lead and zinc, second of copper and third of coal and oil. Manufacturing is expanding rapidly as well. Uzbekistan, richest and most advanced of the republics, has steel mills, copper refinery and hydroelectric installations. There are hints that Semipalatinsk, a meat-packing center in Kazakhstan, also produces hydrogen bombs.

Cities, Schools and Culture

Some of the old cities, though more hygienic today than once upon a time, retain a bit of their exotic flavor. In fact the Soviet Government has helped to restore various crumbling historic buildings, including mosques. Originally hostile to Islam, the communist authorities now appear to see it as a helpful instrument in their relations with the Middle East. In such cities as Samarkand, old customs and old ways of dressing are still prevalent.

On the other hand the new cities erected by the Soviets have been called "squalid suburban slums." Public buildings and apartment houses are built to uniform designs, drab and boxlike. Along the streets the pedestrian cannot escape the posters and slogans, plastering every wall, calling on him to work for the glory of communism. Inevitably the center of such a city is a Park of Rest and Culture, with more busts of Lenin and others than grass and trees.

The Soviet Union has made good on its promise of education. Tadzhikistan, for instance, which is still rather primitive otherwise, has 350,000 pupils attending 2,500 schools. In 1919 it had a total of 7 schools with 124 students. In Uzbekistan, where only 2 per cent of the people were literate before the Revolution, there are today 81 Uzbek college graduates out of every 10,000 inhabitants. In addition, here as elsewhere in Soviet lands in recent years, native cultures are being encouraged somewhat. The stress on trying to make all U.S.S.R. citizens exactly alike has softened. Books are being issued in Asiatic tongues though in most cases their alphabets have been Russified. Offsetting this trend, official displeasure has been ex-

pressed against young Kazakh intellectuals. They have been resisting Russian influence on their language and culture. Most annoying, apparently, were their paintings glorifying Kazakh traditions before the Revolution.

The excitement of breaking new ground, the possibilities of tremendous expansion are in the air in the Asiatic republics. There the Soviet Union is also in competition with its ruthlessly ambitious, close ally, Red China. In view of Red China's growing might, little doubt can exist that the Kremlin, while eagerly exploiting the resources of the republics, is also anxious to strengthen them as a bulwark.

This large slice of Asia, with an area of over 1,500,000 square miles, has a history that goes back thousands of years before Christ. The Huns, centuries previous to the time we hear of them in Europe, had an empire in this territory. They were driven out by the Chinese who were in turn succeeded by a people later

❶ KAZAKHSTAN
❷ TURKMENIA
❸ UZBEKISTAN
❹ KIRGHIZIA
❺ TADZHIKISTAN

known as Tatars. The Arabs, making converts to Islam as they came, overran it, as also did the Turks and Mongol hordes.

Turkestan was a fierce battleground for the wild tribesmen of the region. Emir and khan, one after another, rose in power and held sway until a stronger leader came to wrest supremacy from their hands. Genghis Khan became one of the greatest conquerors known to history but greater even than he was Tamerlane. He led his plundering hordes from the Volga to the Persian Gulf, from the Hellespont to the Ganges. Tamerlane was actually on his way to invade China with his victorious armies when death overtook him.

It was at Samarkand that Tamerlane held his court. Magnificent though it had been before, the city attained greater fame and glory under this mighty ruler. His barbaric cruelty is notorious. In the drama *Tamburlaine* by the Elizabethan poet Christopher Marlowe, Tamerlane appears almost as an insane monster. It is

less well known that he gave encouragement to science and the arts and constructed what we would call vast public works. Tamerlane's tomb is still one of the sights of Samarkand.

As Tamerlane's kingdom crumbled away it was parceled out among lesser kings and khans. One group and then another won independence and set up a khanate, or kingdom. Turkomans gathered in the country between the Amu Darya (the Oxus of the ancients) and the Caspian Sea. Elsewhere the petty kingdoms of Bukhara and Khiva were established.

The greater part of this area is desert, but here and there oases occur and the land has extraordinary fertility. The surface of the earth constantly changes, rivers shift their courses or wander off to be swallowed up by the desert sands, lakes dry up and earthquakes sometimes occur.

Uzbekistan is sprinkled with ancient and famous cities planted centuries ago on the oases of this semidesert land. The mere mention of the name—Bukhara—

SOVFOTO

A COTTON PICKER IN THE UZBEK FIELDS

This smiling girl, dressed in the colorful costume of her district, holds an armful of freshly picked cotton.

of this group of present-day Soviet Republics the Turcomans are the most important. Mohammedans by religion, they are akin to the Beduins in the nature of their life, for they have regular camping places and move from one pasturage to another according to the season. Turcomans were always nomads, and because of their fierceness they were always dreaded by their neighbors. They plundered ruthlessly, waylaying the rich caravans of the Persian traders and looting greedily. Out of this arose a great trade in slaves, but the Turcoman's activities in this direction have been checked by the Russians.

The Turcoman is rather a striking figure dressed in his baggy trousers and coarse shirt, which is mostly concealed by an outer garment of colored material somewhat like a dressing-gown. To complete his costume, he wears high-heeled boots, a shaggy high hat made of sheep's wool and a gaudy scarlet sash. This is the ordinary tribesman of the plains. In the case of the better class Turcomans, those who are counted wealthy in flocks and herds, the common garments give place to richly embroidered robes, while the trappings of their horses and camels are splendidly adorned with gold and silver and precious stones.

Their womenfolk like to wear quantities of jewelry and display many bracelets and anklets. In place of the sheepskin or felt hats of the men they cover their heads with cotton cloths, much in the form of a turban, and these headdresses, too, will be plentifully decorated with silver ornaments and coins. It is said that one judges the wealth of a Turcoman by the amount of silver worn by his wife. Like the Beduins to whom they have been compared, this people leave a great deal of

brings memory of gorgeous oriental rugs which have been named after the cities where they have so long been marketed.

But Turkestan is known not only for its rugs but also for its eagles. For the Mohammedans love to train hawks and eagles for hunting. Their eagles will attack even wolves.

Across this country people have sifted through the centuries like sand over a desert. To understand modern Turkestan a brief historical sketch is necessary. The country has altered little since the time when Tatar, Turk and Mongol ranged over its mountains and plains, when "Sultan after Sultan, with his pomp, abode his hour or two and went his way." And in some respects the peoples themselves have undergone but little change. Large numbers of them live by raising horses, camels, cattle and sheep, by growing cotton and wheat and fruit, or by working the rich mineral deposits of the country.

Among the peoples in the western part

manual work to the women for which reason the latter age quickly. The women go unveiled, like the Beduins again, but unlike the women of nearly all other Mohammedan countries.

There are Turcomans who settle in towns and villages, in which the houses are simply built of mud and stone. But the majority, true desert wanderers, live in tents—"kibitkas" they are called— which are made of braided willows and covered with felt. If we look into one of these tents we shall see that the furniture consists of a carpet on the floor and several brilliantly colored rugs hanging on the walls, together with cloaks, embroidered garments, saddlebags, bridles and other articles. In one corner is a wooden chest, which contains the women's clothing and other gear. During the winter time a fire

burns in the middle of the tent, and as there is no chimney and the smoke has to find its way out as best it can, the atmosphere is none of the pleasantest.

Summer time on these western "steppes," or plains, is endurable, though often very hot. In the winter, especially when the weather is severe, the conditions of life are very hard. Terrible blizzards storm across the desert, often destroying flocks and herds and human beings as well. In January the temperature may go down to 40° below zero. We can get some idea of the intensity of the cold from the description given by Colonel Burnaby in his famous Ride to Khiva. The nostrils of the horses, he says, became blocked with ice, and cabbage soup froze solid when it was made. It had to be carried on camelback and broken off as it was wanted.

EWING GALLOWAY

TOWNSMEN AT EASE BEFORE A MOSQUE OF ANCIENT BUKHARA

A water seller sits behind his jugs; a melon peddler is at the foot of the steps to the mosque, a center of social as well as religious life in the Islamic city. Most of the people of Bukhara are Uzbeks, nomadic herdsmen of Turkestan who long ago drove the Persians and Turks from the Kyzyl Kum, the arid region between the Amu and Syr Darya (rivers).

LIEUT.-COL. P. J. ETHERTON

THE ROOF OF THE WORLD is the picturesque name man has given to that huge, bleak knot of mountains known as the Pamirs, lying in central Asia between Afghanistan, Turkestan and Sinkiang (Chinese Turkestan). From it run some of the earth's mightiest mountain chains, including the Himalayas, the Karakoram range and the Hindu Kush. "Pamir" means valley between two ridges. These valleys are nowhere less than 10,000 feet above the sea and the highest peak is over 26,000 above the sea. Through them roam the Kirghiz, the only dwellers in this inhospitable region.

It is desert country, this western region. There are oases, however, and vast tracts are being irrigated. The soil itself is rich. Around the oases, for years, wheat, barley and especially cotton have thrived, along with orchards and vineyards. Today, above all in Kazakhstan, millions of acres of steppe have been plowed for grain growing. This is the heart of the Soviet "new lands" program, begun in 1954.

Iron from Kazakhstan

Kazakhstan also has extremely valuable mineral resources. The iron-ore reserves alone are supposed to be the largest in the whole Soviet Union.

These developments have changed the character of the population. In Kazakhstan—and probably in some of the other Soviet Asiatic republics as well—European Russians are beginning to outnumber the native peoples.

Besides the Turcomans, already mentioned, there are Kirghiz and Uzbeks. The first-named are themselves divided into the Kazakhs, or Kirghiz-Kazakhs, and the Kara-Kirghiz. Their features show plainly their Mongolian origin. They are a short people, with round, dark faces and small, keen black eyes. The Kazakhs are lowlanders, who dwell in the northern and eastern steppe and are shepherds and herdsmen. The Kara-Kirghiz are mountaineers. Their home is in the lofty Pamirs and the mighty Tien Shan, the Celestial Mountains.

By religion the Kirghiz, like other Turkestan peoples, are Muslims though the men shave their heads and allow their beards to grow. Their costume—and some still wear it—resembles that of the Turcomans except that the baggy breeches are made of leather. A coarse shirt, with a wide-striped collar, and an overtunic are worn, together with the usual tall hat of sheepskin.

Noah's Forty Granddaughters

The Persian word *kirghiz* means "forty daughters." In the legends of the people, a son of Noah settled in Turkestan after the Flood, and this son was the father of forty daughters. From these the Kirghiz believe themselves to be descended.

The Uzbeks are lighter in complexion. The men wear turbans of white linen, and their principal garment is a khilat, a long flowing coat dyed in brilliant colors. Occasionally one may still see a Uzbek woman wearing a veil. Among all the peoples of Soviet central Asia, however, Western clothes of a rather drab sort are gradually replacing the picturesque garb of an earlier day.

The Tajiks, or Tadzhiks, who lay claim to Arab descent, originally hailed from Persia. Clever and enterprising, they are merchants by tradition and usually congregate in the towns.

Where Tamerlane Trod

Many of the cities of the region were once strongholds, which witnessed the deeds of such barbaric conquerors as Genghis Khan and Tamerlane. Some other cities, however, began much later as Russian citadels.

Alma-Ata (the name is a Kazakh term meaning "father of apples"), the capital of Kazakhstan, was founded as a fortress in 1854. It has been razed twice by earthquakes, in 1887 and 1910. The city is surrounded by orchards, noted, as the name indicates, for apples.

Frunze, the capital of Kirghiztan, also began as a fortress, in 1873. Then for some years it was merely a sleepy little trading center. But since the railroad reached it in 1924, growth has spurted.

Fabled Tashkent

Tashkent, the capital of Uzbekistan, long stood at the junction of Asiatic trade routes; its markets teemed with the riches of the East. The city's site is dramatic—on a branch of the Syr Darya, the Jaxartes River of the ancients, with great mountains looming in the background. Today Tashkent is the Soviet show place in Asia. In place of the old walled blocks of mud hovels there are tall apartment houses, a system of parks. Even the old Oriental Bazaar has been transformed, with clean, roofed stalls. Though some of its color has undoubtedly been lost, it still displays beautiful rugs, em-

BUKHARA STUDENTS TAKE TIME OUT FOR A JOKE IN THE SUN

The young men are Mohammedans who are studying the Koran. Their setting is appropriate
for the niche is in the Moslem style of architecture. Above the grill is a lovely mosaic.

170

A SHOULDER MAKES A FINE PLACE TO DISPLAY A RUG

The fringed rug, in an interesting geometric design, is the product of a factory in Mary, Turkmenistan. Once called Merv, the city has long been a center of carpet manufacturing.

IN THE BROILING SUN OF THE DESERT, AT TEKKE OASIS, A CARAVAN PAUSES FOR REST AND WATER

So much of Russian Turkestan is desert that caravans of camels are still the chief means of transportation. Most caravans move on regular sched- ules, and there are inns (the Eastern word is "caravansary") at several oases for the convenience of travelers and their beasts of burden.

172

A KAZAKH TRIBESMAN, HIS FACE ETCHED BY TIME AND WEATHER

On his native plains he has endured withering heat in summertime and intense cold in the winter. For Kazakhstan is deep within Asia and has the extremes of a continental climate.

173

A UZBEK COBBLER GRINS CHEERFULLY OVER A WORN BOOT

The soles must be of tough leather for the boots of Uzbek horsemen get hard wear. Instead of settling down permanently in a shop, the shoemaker follows his roving customers.

174

UNIFORMED SCHOOL CHILDREN march beneath the statue of Lenin that dominates the town square of Ashkhabad, the commercially important capital of Turkmenistan.

SCHOOL DAYS IN THE FABLED CITY OF SAMARKAND

Books are a special delight to these boys for it is likely that they are the first members of their families to go to school. Samarkand is deep in central Asia, a region where people speak strange tongues. Even today some of these dialects have no written form. Tamerlane, the fierce four-teenth-century Mogul conqueror, made Samarkand his capital city.

broidered cloths and the delicate silver and brass ware of the skilled workers in metal. Among the frequenters of the bazaars a familiar figure is the sherbet-seller, who goes about in the crowd with a tank on his back and glasses in his hands. He makes his approach known by rattling the glasses together.

If Bokhara is not so large and important as Tashkent, it is, nevertheless, a great commercial centre. Into this old-world city pour the camel caravans from China, India, Afghanistan and Persia, loaded with their precious freights of tea, silk, furs, dyestuffs and other goods. These are the caravans which, in past years, were pounced upon by the rapacious Turcoman. From Bokhara they go out again with

cotton, ironmongery, sugar, coffee and other commodities, which have been mostly obtained from Russia.

As a leading trading centre Bokhara is noted for its carpets. The finest in the world are exhibited here. Another particular feature of its market is "caracul," a fur, which comes from the prepared skin of the Persian lamb, or sometimes kid. We are also familiar with it under the name of astrakhan.

But Bokhara has another claim to distinction besides that of commerce. It is a university town, a home of learning, and has been so for more than a thousand years. At one time the city could boast of 197 mosques and 167 "madrasahs," or Moslem theological colleges, most of which

176

have fallen into decay. There are, however, many state controlled educational buildings in Bukhara that are still in use.

The most famous mosque is the Masjid Kalian, dating back to the tenth century. It was into this mosque that Jenghiz Khan, the great Asiatic conqueror, rode in defiance of the mullahs, or priests. He dismounted, went up into the pulpit, and threw the Koran on the floor, shouting to his followers as he did so: "The hay is cut! Give your horses fodder!" This was the signal for the savage Mongolian soldiery to begin a dreadful massacre and to loot the city.

The Mir Arab is another noted mosque, an ancient seat of Moslem learning.

The architecture of Bukhara, with its domes and minarets, tells the story of the city's past religious and cultural grandeur. Bukhara was once so important a center of Islam that it rivaled even the holy city of Mecca as a place to which young men came to study for the priesthood and to which scholars journeyed from great distances. It is still deeply Eastern in flavor, with its labyrinthine streets and outdoor bazaars.

As has been told, Khiva has been joined up with Bukhara to form a Soviet Republican State. It is an ancient province of Turkestan, for it dates back to the first and second Persian empires and to the days of Alexander the Great whose armies were in the country more than two thousand years ago.

In the town of Khiva are several "madrasahs," for so important a place cannot be without its colleges. Khiva was the capital of the province of Khiva, a distinction which previously belonged to Urgenj, in the markets of which were sold the corn, cotton, rice, tobacco and other products of the rich province, as well as the spendid breed of horses for which it was famed.

Ferghana is another province of Turkestan, and its chief town is Khokan. It

SOVFOTO

A STURDY TILLER OF THE SOIL IN UZBEKISTAN

As a Uzbek, he belongs to a group of people who are Mohammedans and whose way of life was influenced by Persia for centuries. Their language, however, is related to Turkish.

POLO ON THE ROOF OF THE WORLD

The Pamir Plateau is a lofty tableland north of the Hindu Kush range. Much of it is mountainous, but there are flat areas that make good pasture land. The region is sometimes known as "the roof of the world," for its average elevation is about 13,000 feet. Polo is a favorite sport among the Kirghiz who live there and who raise fleet, intelligent ponies.

lies in a fork of the great Tian Shan mountain range and is a very fertile and fair country. Of all places in Turkestan, there is none that appeals more to the imagination than does Samarkand. The town of this name was in olden time the capital of Asia, and its splendors were unsurpassed and were extolled by historian and poet alike.

"Golden Samarkand" could not attain to such a height of glory without paying the usual penalty of those times. It was attacked, destroyed and rebuilt over and over again, and in the course of years much of its beauty and greatness passed. Today it is a city of considerable size, with a trade in horses and asses; but, except for a few open squares, it is composed of narrow, ill-kept streets. Prominent among its buildings are the three "madrasahs," seats of learning, which are still famous throughout the province.

Apart from these survivals of the past, the "madrasahs" and mosques, Samar-kand has scarcely anything to show of its former splendor. In the city where Alexander the Great and Tamerlane in turn held sway are mean-looking houses, some of mud, and the rich trains of merchandise that once found their way thither by horse, mule and camel have long since turned their steps to Bokhara, to Tashkent and to the other newer cities.

These interesting cities with such a long and colorful past are all within the limits of the Uzbek Soviet Republic. In the Turcoman Republic, Merv, situated in an oasis renowned for its fertility, is considered in Hindu, Parsi and Arab tradition as the ancient Paradise. Like Samarkand and Bokhara, it became a rich and splendid city and at one time was the center of learning, but all its glory has passed away and in the nineteenth century, the old town was abandoned for a new site on the Transcaspian railway on which its carpets, long famous, and its agricultural products may be exported.

178

Ashkhabad, the capital, in part owes its importance as a commercial center to its situation on the Trans-Caspian Railroad, the western terminus of which is Krasnovodsk, on the Caspian Sea. Krasnovodsk is the port for the republic. Cotton and dried fruits are the chief exports.

Ashkhabad was founded by the Russians in 1881. It lies in the midst of a fertile oasis, in which vineyards and orchards flourish. For some years its chief manufactures have been textiles and food processing though no doubt it has some heavy industries today. The Turkmen University was established in the city in 1950; and other cultural organizations are a branch of the U.S.S.R. Academy of Sciences and motion-picture studios.

One last feature of Soviet Central Asia remains to be mentioned. This is the great knot of mountains known as the Pamir, "the Roof of the World." From the bleak, craggy heights run some of the mightiest mountain chains on earth, such as the Himalayas, the Hindu Kush, the Karakoram, the Tien Shan and the Trans Alai.

It is as wild a region as can be found anywhere, and the fascination of it has drawn many famous travelers thither since Marco Polo crossed it on his way to the court of Kublai Khan. Here is to be found the great-horned mountain sheep, the *Ovis poli*, whose head is reckoned as one of the finest of sportsmen's trophies. And on these mountain slopes and in the valleys the Kirghiz hillmen pasture their flocks. For many years the Pamir has been occupied by Russia, and the present borders of Russia and Afghanistan were settled to run across the Roof of the World.

SOVIET REPUBLICS IN ASIA: FACTS AND FIGURES

AREA

The area is divided into five Soviet Socialist Republics:—Turkmenia, Uzbekistan, Tadzhikistan, Kazakhstan and Kirghizia. Total area, 1,537,607 sq. mi.; total population, about 23,000,-000.

TURKMENIA (TURKMEN S.S.R.)

Became a Soviet Republic in 1925. The area is 187,181 sq. mi. and the population, 1,400,000, is 60% Turkmenian, mostly Muslim, 20% Russian and 8.5% Uzbek. Agriculture is the main occupation of the people. Products include cotton, wool and astrakhan fur. The region is famous for its carpets and special breed of horses. There are rich mineral deposits. A railway, air line and motor communication serve the country. The chief towns are Ashkhabad (pop., 142,000), the capital, Mary, Krasnovodsk, Kerki and Tashauz.

UZBEKISTAN (UZBEK S.S.R.)

Became a Soviet Republic in 1925. The area is 156,640 sq. mi.; pop., 8,113,000, is ¾ Uzbek, largely Muslim. Agriculture, based on artificial irrigation, is the chief occupation, cotton the main product. There is a railway and air service. The chief towns are Tashkent, the capital (pop., 778,000), Samarkand, Bokhara, Khiva and Andijan.

TADZHIKISTAN (TADZHIK S.S.R.)

Became a Soviet Republic in 1929. The area is 54,826 sq. mi.; pop., 1,800,000, is ¾ Tadzhik. Capital, Stalinabad (pop., 191,000). Principal occupation is farming and cattle breeding, and there are rich mineral deposits.

KAZAKHSTAN (KAZAKH S.S.R.)

Became a Soviet Republic in 1936. The area is 1,062,242 sq. mi.; pop., 9,300,000, is 60% Kazakh, 35% Russian and Ukrainian. There are rich mineral deposits but the majority of the people farm and breed cattle. Capital, Alma-Ata (pop., 330,000).

KIRGHIZIA (KIRGHIZ S.S.R.)

Became a Soviet Republic in 1936. The area is 76,718 sq. mi.; pop., 1,900,000, is ⅔ Kirghiz. Capital, Frunze (pop., 190,000).

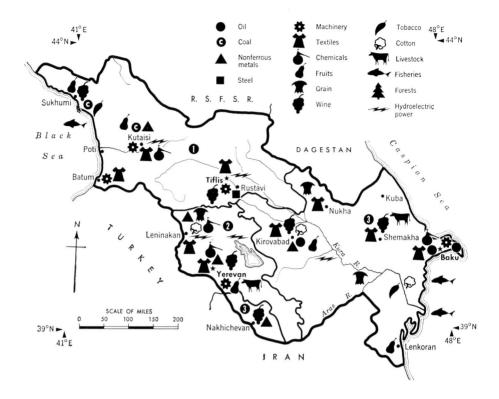

Caucasus Republics

... Armenia, Azerbaijan and Georgia

THE Caucasus is the richest as well as one of the most acutely sensitive areas in the whole Soviet Union. Its major wealth is petroleum, vital to the economy of the nation. It is also in the Caucasus that the U.S.S.R. is physically most exposed to the West. The southern border is shared with Iran and Turkey, and Turkey in particular is heavily armed besides being a member of NATO. Nor can it be forgotten in the Kremlin that the Caucasus was the last region to be pacified after the Russian Revolution. Civil war raged there until 1921.

Hardly any other part of the world of the same size contains such a bewildering variety of ethnic groups. Each has its own customs, and a multitude of languages is spoken. In Erivan, the capital of Russian Armenia, street signs give directions not only in five different languages but also in five different alphabets—Russian, Armenian, Georgian, Arabic and Roman. As these peoples were once so defiant, so also were they persecuted ruthlessly under Stalin. In the 1940's, during the war, whole groups were torn up, their members widely scattered through central Asia and their very names expunged from Soviet history.

Under Khrushchev, however, the policy seems to have been reversed. There were several announcements in the late 1950's that some deported minorities would be rehabilitated, and a few have been in fact. The official line now is that their exile was a "violation of the main principles of Leninist nationality policy." In addition the Government is somewhat encouraging ethnic cultures and languages, though in-

GEORGIA
ARMENIA
AZERBAIJAN

menian's tepid enthusiasm, naturally criticized, for government plans. It is true that practically all Armenian farmers belong to collectives, which benefit by the extensive system of irrigation. Otherwise the people seem to be as balky as they dare. For instance, Erivan has some 13,000 university students and yet not one volunteered for work in central Asia during Khrushchev's drive to lure young people to develop the land there. Numbers of industries have been established in Armenia but complaints are frequent of inefficiency and low output.

In contrast to the Armenians the Georgians were a nation of aristocrats. Before 1917 every seventh Georgian was a noble, and Georgian princes cut a dash in international society. Their resistance to the Bolsheviks was the most bitterly hostile of all. Even today they are lavish hosts, in the Oriental tradition. Their women are still relatively secluded. Within Georgia the nomadic Kurds form a minority group. Their homeland actually overlaps the U.S.S.R., Turkey and Iran. The boundaries of the Iranian "province" of Kurdistan are a delicate issue between Iran and the Soviet Union.

Before the Revolution, Georgia had no institutions of higher learning and about 85 per cent of the people were illiterate. All instruction had to be in Russian; and Georgian is an extremely complex tongue, quite different from Russian. There are nineteen colleges today and a claim of 100 per cent literacy is made, except among the very old.

As elsewhere in the Soviet Union, industry is being pushed. Among the most flourishing Georgian works are a motor plant, at Kutaisi, and a steel plant, at Rustavi. Automation is being introduced. The area's rich manganese ores are of great importance to the whole country.

Culturally, Georgia is the most interesting of the three republics. Every feast is enlivened with folk songs and dances. The well-run National Museum in Tiflis is a repository of some of the oldest and most exquisite icons ever fashioned. Among them is a jeweled silver masterpiece that dates from A.D. 886.

termarriage and the compulsory study of Russian would seem to be pulling in the opposite direction. Caucasus ancestry seems to be no bar to success in the U.S.S.R. Stalin was a Georgian, as was the late and unlamented head of the secret police, Beria. First Deputy Premier Mikoyan and the composer Kachaturian are both Armenians.

Armenia runs to extremes. Its people are largely of peasant stock and are very proud of their long history. Yet they are said to be among the best informed of Soviet peoples about the outside world. This doubtless has resulted from the immigration of 100,000 foreign Armenians, including several hundred from the United States, who settled in Armenia after World War II.

The foregoing helps to explain the Ar-

YEREVAN, AT THE FOOT OF MOUNT ARARAT

From Yerevan (or Erivan), capital of Armenia, you can look up to glacier-crowned Mount Ararat, the mountain that tradition makes the resting place of Noah's ark. Yerevan is an industrial city of 200,000 inhabitants, and the cultural center of Armenia. It has a university, an opera, a number of scientific institutes and a branch of the Academy of Sciences of the U.S.S.R.

182

Oil-rich Azerbaijan

Because of its petroleum, Azerbaijan is the wealthiest Caucasus republic. Oil production has been leaping ahead, though the center has moved from Baku to an oil-bearing area north of the Caspian Sea. This area is as large as Louisiana, Texas, Oklahoma and Kansas combined. Some 75 per cent of Russia's oil now comes from this vast pocket. From it, pipelines have been or are being built— to Poland and thence to Czechoslovakia, to East Germany, to the Black Sea, to Memel on the Baltic. Each can transport about 300,000 barrels a day. As there seem to be no plans to increase either automobile production or highway construction, and natural gas is now the preferred heating fuel, Russia may soon have more oil for export. Thus it might enter the world market, meeting competition by lowering the price. This could be a formidable weapon in the economic cold war.

Three fifths of the people of Azerbaijan are of Turkish stock, and Islam is the predominant faith. In Baku, however, Muslim customs have almost disappeared. Women go unveiled, Russian is the usual language and the people wear the Soviet version of Western dress. There is considerable interest in literature. In a recent year the State Publishing House issued 350 titles in Azerbaijanese alone and put 5,000,000 books into circulation. Twenty-five different research institutions work under the direction of the local Academy of Sciences.

Formation of the Republics

Arab invaders converted the people of Georgia and Azerbaijan to Islam in the seventh century. Armenia is generally regarded as the oldest Christian country. Intolerant of one another's religious beliefs, the two Muslim nations and Armenia were often at war with each other. In 1922, however, they were formed into a republic of Transcaucasia. Fourteen years later they were separated again and each became a republic in the Union of Soviet Socialist Republics.

A glance at the map shows us that the three republics occupy a bridge between Russia, Iran and Turkey. They are separated from Asia, on the east, by the Caspian Sea and from Europe, on the west, by the Black Sea. Forming a natural frontier on the north are the snow-topped Caucasus Mountains, the scenery of which rivals the Alps. Although the land is almost treeless and presents a bleak, rugged appearance, it has the charm of wildness. Highest of the mountain peaks are Mount Elbrus and Mount Kazbek. On the latter, according to mythology, Prometheus was chained as a punishment for giving fire to mankind.

Just over the border, in Turkey, isolated from the Caucasus range, is Mount Ararat, which rises from the surrounding plains to a height of 16,945 feet. On Mount Ararat, Noah is supposed to have landed after the Deluge.

Armenia's Complex History

Armenia, oldest of these countries historically, was once a great kingdom with territories to the south. Today it is divided between Turkey and the Soviet Union. It was first inhabited by tribes who are thought to have come from the east and settled around the foot of Mount Ararat. These nomadic peoples were conquered about the sixth century before Christ by the Medes and Persians. Then the territory was divided into two satrapies, or provinces, of the great Persian Empire. Eastern and Western Armenia, as they were known, became powerful in time and overthrew their overlord. This was accomplished mainly by Tigranes the Great who welded Armenia into one strong kingdom.

Conversion to Christianity

The Armenians were converted to Christianity early in the fourth century under Gregory the Illuminator and became most ardent in their faith. When Persia, their overlord, tried to make them adopt fire worship, they replied: "No one can move us from our belief, neither angels nor men, fire nor sword." So they have felt always even though it has meant massacre and the scattering of their people. Their faith

SOVFOTO

GRAPE-PICKING TIME IN ARMENIA

Irrigation has made nearly half a million acres of soil in Armenia suitable for agriculture. All but 2 per cent of the agricultural workers belong to collective farms that produce cotton (long-fibered variety), grapes and other fruit.

and again. Now and then they had a brief period of independence, as that which began in 571, under the leadership of Vartan, but which lasted only seven years. Since then Vartan has been a favored Christian name for Armenian boys and Vartan's Day is celebrated even now as a national holiday.

The Turkish conquest was completed about 1514, when Selim I set out toward the East on a campaign against Persia. Turkey was then at the zenith of her power but she was in time to be checked in the north by a nation whose strength in Europe had been greatly increasing. That was Russia. In the wars between them, during the nineteenth century, Russia advanced her Caucasus boundary well into Armenia, and since then Armenia, divided, has belonged partly to Russia and partly to Turkey.

Russia found her Armenian subjects intelligent and industrious, and able to help in the development of the country. She therefore encouraged emigration from Turkish Armenia into the provinces she owned. The Armenians on their part felt better protected in Russia. They accumulated property, became more progressive, and the land itself was noticeably better cultivated than on the other side of the line. Except for feuds with their Moslem neighbors the people were better off than they had been in centuries.

During the struggle between Russia and Turkey, there had been growing secretly a party called the Dashnacks, who sought to secure the independence of Armenia. Although it represented only the more

has withstood invasions of the Persians, Arabs, Seljuks, Mongols and Turks, but their territory has been conquered time

Sovfoto

MOUNTAIN CLIMBING AMONG THE PEAKS OF RUSSIAN ARMENIA

The ancient country of Armenia, divided today among Iran, Russia and Turkey, is on the southern edge of the breath-takingly beautiful Caucasus Mountains. They mark a land boundary between Europe and Asia. In the Russian part, there are many peaks above 10,000 feet; the highest, Alagöz, is 13,435 feet. These climbers are ascending the summits of the Aragats range.

radical element of the people, it brought about local warfare which served to arouse the Turks and as a result, during the years 1895 and 1896, thousands of the Christian inhabitants were exterminated in a series of massacres so atrocious that the story is almost unbelievable. Foreign nations were horrified and attempted to interfere, but as they could not agree to go to war with Turkey, their concern did little to help.

When World War I broke out the Turks again took occasion to rid themselves of their Christian subjects. Claiming that the Armenians were taking up arms against them, they slaughtered men, women and children with savage brutality and forced others toward Mesopotamia and the Syrian deserts to almost certain death. American and British missionaries helped to relieve the suffering by giving

MUSICIANS ENTERTAIN COLLECTIVE FARMERS AT HARVEST TIME

Armenia has undergone many changes since it became a Soviet Socialist Republic in 1920. A State Song and Dance Ensemble is the official musical group of the country. Some of its performers are shown here on a collective farm. Part of the Soviet program to encourage greater agricultural production is to supply on-the-spot entertainment for the workers at harvest time.

out food and first aid treatments, but in spite of their aid many thousands perished.

Russian Armenia quite naturally allied herself with Russia at the beginning of World War I, but the Russian Revolution three years later left her only partially able to protect herself. Caught between the advancing Turkish armies and the unorganized armies of the Bolsheviki who had control of Russia, she had a most difficult time. In addition the country became flooded with starving and disease-stricken refugees who had been able to escape from Turkey, and had trekked across Northwestern Persia to what seemed to be their only refuge. Unable to retain the independence which the Dashnacks had hastened to declare, Armenia finally decided to cast her lot with the Soviet Government which had succeeded the Bolshevists, and in 1920 became a republic of the Soviet Union under Russia. About 85 per cent of the people in the territory are Armenians.

The question of the Armenian people and Armenia was considered by the League of Nations. It was hoped that in time a national home could be es-

tablished in Armenia where those refugees who had reached other lands in safety might be repatriated. Armenians were especially interested in the plan as they had long desired a land of their own where they could live by themselves and could develop it into one of great prosperity.

Until the Soviet Government took the land over, it had been badly in need of development. In most of the region it was hard indeed for the peasant to make even a meager living. In the valley of the Araxes River, which girds Mount Ararat, there is rich and fertile soil, and tobacco, rice and cotton are grown as well as many varieties of fruits and vegetables. There are vineyards, but the vines must be buried during winter frosts. In the hilly districts, forestry is important and cattle are raised.

Agriculture is the main occupation of the people, and, as one might suspect, their methods have been quite primitive. Homemade wooden plows, drawn by oxen or water buffaloes, still serve some Armenian farmers. However, several large canals have been completed for irrigation purposes, and more than half the land is in large collective farms worked by modern machinery. Much of the irrigated land is devoted to the cultivation of cotton.

The houses of the peasants are usually built against the side of a hill or a mountain which saves the material necessary to make a back wall. Then, too, it gives protection from the wintry winds and thus saves fuel which is a very scarce article in this unforested region. The roofs are flat and are sometimes covered with earth, so that grass will grow and serve as pasture for the family cow or sheep. Inside the houses are almost bare of furniture—a few simple chairs and possibly a fireplace where the cooking is done. In the winter the cow and sheep are given a place in the house, for their body heat is needed to bring the temperature of the room a bit higher.

Accustomed to living in this mountainous region where the winters are long and severe, the Armenians are strong and energetic and not unused to hard work. They are usually dark and the women are noted for their beauty. Many Persians, Kurds and Turks have fallen under the spell of the beautiful black eyes of Armenian maidens, and have taken them back to their own countries as their wives. The women have won a reputation too for their beautiful handwork, which they do at home in order to help out the family income. Fine Armenian lace, lovely embroidery and Oriental rugs are made with painstaking effort, often at the cost of their eyesight

The Armenian farmer gets his real enjoyment out of a trip to market, for he likes to talk and argue, and the sale of a cow or sheep will give him a great opportunity. Like all buying and selling in Near Eastern countries, it will take hours, perhaps all day, to arrive at a price which each knew at first would have been perfectly satisfactory.

A birth or wedding also gives cause for a celebration. In the olden days a wedding in a prosperous Armenian home was a gala event. It would probably last all night and from start to finish, the tables would be piled with food and drink while the guests made speeches and danced, sometimes singly, sometimes together. The bride would be decked with jewelry—a headdress draped with coins, bracelets and necklaces, for, aside from their liking for decoration, the Armenians thought it safer to have their wealth in a form which would be easy to carry.

Suppose we had been invited to the home of a well-to-do Armenian and were pressed to stay to dinner. What interesting food we should have had! There would have been a meat dish consisting of tender bits of lamb combined with vegetables, in some appetizing way; there would have been pilaf, which is rice cooked in oil, and eggplant, probably, for the Armenians know many ways of preparing that vegetable—ways of which Western people have never heard. Then for dessert there would have been paklava, for that is, indeed, a delectable sweet—a light crusty pastry with nuts and honey. Of course, we should have wines to drink and small cups of sweet Turkish coffee, and we should all have agreed that we had had a delicious meal most bountifully served.

Armenians who have migrated to Europe or America have proved to be

SOVFOTO

A FISHERWOMAN of Azerbaijan brings her fine catch of sturgeon to a local fishery.

TECHNICAL SCHOOLS prepare future workers for Azerbaijan's expanding oil industry.   Here students listen to a lecture in the chemistry laboratory of an industrial institute.

valuable citizens. They are shrewd and energetic, qualities that make them successful in business.

Most of the cities of Armenia are small, in fact hardly more than towns. However, Yerevan (or Erivan), the capital and largest city, has a population of about 200,000. It was almost completely rebuilt during the 1920's and made quite modern in appearance. The city reflects the communist emphasis on education—though *what* is taught, of course, must follow the dictates of the state. The Armenian State University is here, as well as several colleges, a library and a Tropical Institute. There is also a branch of the Academy of Sciences of the U.S.S.R. Imposing buildings house the government offices and the state theater of opera and ballet. One of the most interesting old structures remaining is the Blue Mosque.

Yerevan is on the Zanga River. Since a hydroelectric station was built here in 1926, the city has developed numerous industries. Machinery, furniture, brick, leather goods, silk, glycerin, wine and brandy are among the many products.

A few miles west of Yerevan is the ancient monastery of Echmiadzin, the seat of the Armenian, or Gregorian, Church. The monastery is the residence of the Catholicus, or head of the church. Reports indicate that the Soviet Union has not attacked the church directly, knowing how deeply the Armenians are attached to it. Instead, it has been made an instrument of the state. Armenians outside of Russia consider the Catholicus a communist puppet.

At Leninakan (once called Aleksandropol), which is on a branch of the Araks River, is another hydroelectric station. The waters of Lake Sevan have also been harnessed. Altogether there are more than fifty hydroelectric stations in Soviet Armenia, for both power and irrigation purposes. Under the Soviets, the region has become an important industrial center. More than 80 per cent of its products are manufactured goods.

Mining has kept equal pace. Armenia has rich stores of copper, zinc, aluminum, molybdenum and other metals. These are

LIBRARY OF ARMENIAN LITERATURE

The monastery, Echmiadzin, includes the ancient and valuable library shown above. Though not beautiful architecturally, it contains a large collection of Armenian literature.

essential raw materials for heavy industry, which is one of the chief concerns of the communist planners. There is also a wealth of building materials.

Georgia is almost as old historically as Armenia and has suffered almost as many invasions. The Georgians, however, after their country had been devastated for nearly two centuries by the Arabs, finally succumbed to Mohammedanism and since then have not suffered persecution.

Tradition has it that the inhabitants of Georgia are descended from Japheth, son of Noah, but we cannot trace their history from that early time. We know of them first in the fourth century before Christ when Alexander the Great sent one of his generals to annex the territory then known as Iberia. The people were able to free themselves from the Macedonians after the death of Alexander and then enjoyed independence for over a hundred years. However, Georgia was not to be left alone. The great Persian Empire, always eager for more territory, was to the East what the Turks and the Byzantine Greeks later were to the West. Georgia had some friendly connection with the Byzantine Empire, for Constantine, the first Byzantine emperor, had sent Christian missionaries who had converted the Georgians. Therefore, when Persia's strength had somewhat weakened, Georgia took the opportunity to appeal to the Byzantine

A SABER DANCE performed by the state ballet company in Erivan (or Yerevan), the capital of the Armenian Soviet republic. Classic ballet developed to a high peak in tsarist Russia, and ballet has remained extremely popular in the Soviet Union. Like the saber dance—once probably performed by cavalry men—some ballet patterns stem from folk dances. Operagoers are familiar with the wild Polovtsian Dances from *Prince Igor*.

Empire for a king. She was granted a viceroy, and the Bagratid dynasty which was then founded ruled from 571 to 1803.

In the seventh century came the Arabs and for 180 years the country was overrun until the people finally accepted Islam. Georgia then enjoyed a period of relief during which the boundaries were extended from the Black to the Caspian Sea and at one time included part of Armenia. She had successfully repulsed the Seljuks and the Persians, but was not able to withstand the Mongol hordes who came west led by Genghis Khan. Again the land was overrun by the Mongols under Tamerlane who set fire to the entire country. Wars between the Persians and the Turks during the seventeenth century caused Georgia to seek the help of Russia and in 1801 she became a Russian province

Since then Georgia has been independent for two short periods—from 1904 to 1906, when Russia was at war with Japan, and from 1918 to 1921. The latter period of freedom came immediately following the Russian Revolution, when Georgia felt she had an opportunity to break off, but she was finally forced to join the Soviets and to become a republic.

Like Armenia, Georgia is an agricultural country, but it is much more fertile owing to the fact that the melting snow from its many mountains and an irrigation system provide water in plenty for those who live in the valleys. However, those living in the mountains are wretchedly poor and have a hard time making a living from the barren soil. Rye bread and mutton are their principal foods, and a traveler sometimes finds that the village inn or rest house cannot provide any kind of meal at all.

In the valleys, one may see fruit of many varieties, both tropical and subtropical: corn, grown for food by nearly every valley peasant, wheat, barley, cotton, tobacco, tea and rice. A great variety indeed! Mulberry trees are seen, too, for silkworm culture is one of the oldest occupations of the people. Grapes grow in great luxuriance, sometimes wild, and so the making of wine has become the industry for which Georgia is most noted.

In a few areas, the workers still use a primitive press for squeezing the grapes, and when the wine is ready it is put into tarred buffalo skins and then piled on wooden carts which joggle along the rough mountain roads until they reach the city. In 1930, the Soviet Union made plans for a great expansion of the industry. One of the most important points in the plan was for the development of champagne!

Because of the mountains, Georgia has rich mineral deposits, chief of which is a fine quality of manganese, but there is also copper and iron and there are numerous mineral springs, both hot and cold, containing sulphur, iron and radium.

So much for Georgia's products. Let us now see what the people are like. The majority are Georgians, although there are a goodly number of Armenians, Tatars and Russians. The Georgians speak a language that is supposed to have been connected with the Sumerian-Babylonian and so difficult has it proved that very little has been translated into other languages.

The Georgians are fine looking people and very intelligent and they delight in colorful costumes. The women, even though poorly dressed, usually seem gay with many colors. The well-to-do women wear a long coatlike garment of silk covering loose trousers which are caught at the ankles. On their heads they wear scarlet velvet caps decorated with pearls. The men usually wear a tall cap made of astrakhan which is called a papahk, and a shaggy wool coat. Part of the male costume is a dagger or sword for Daghestan.

Near East Relief

ANCIENT CHRISTIAN CHURCH OF ECHMIADZIN

The monastery of Echmiadzin, west of Erivan, was the seat of the Catholicus or primate of the Armenian church. Among the buildings is an ancient Christian church which is thought to have been founded by St. Gregory the Illuminator in 302, and is said to be the oldest Christian church. The Church of the Nativity in Bethlehem also claims this distinction.

A SHEPHERD AND HIS FLOCKS IN THE GRASSLANDS OF GEORGIA
A shepherd watches over his sheep as they graze on the rolling Shiraki Steppe of southern Georgia. In the summer the flocks trek more than a hundred miles to mountain pasture.

that province of Georgia which borders on the Caspian, is famous for its fine artistry in silver and steel.

In the mountainous districts, the houses are built on terraces, but in the more prosperous places they are made of rough stone or baked mud and often have large wooden balconies around the first floor, and roofs of undulating red tiles. The houses of the rich are often very beautiful, especially those which are decorated with colored glazed tiles, indicating the Persian influence.

Now and then there is a neat, orderly village inhabited by German people. Early in the tenth century, the founders of these villages started toward the Holy Land because they thought the end of the world was near. They made their way slowly until agents sent in advance returned to report that all was not as they believed in Jerusalem and so they stayed where they were. They farmed as they had done in Germany, built villages on the German

plan and retained their German language until recently. Since World War II, German place names have been changed to Russian, and the people speak Russian.

One may see also villages where the Molokans reside. These people belong to a sect of the Russian Church comparable to our Quakers. They derive their name from the custom of living on milk (*moloko,* in Russian) on fast days. The Molokans have no organized priesthood.

Tbilisi (Tiflis, in Russian) is the capital. It is the largest and one of the oldest cities in Georgia. The old section has an Asiatic air. A tangle of narrow, crooked alleys and primitive architecture, it is in the center of the city. To the north and to the south extend modern industrial and residential areas where the buildings are European in style. Tbilisi has many scientific and technical institutions, among them the Georgian Academy of Science.

The people of Azerbaijan are mostly

192

A DANGEROUS CURVE ON A MOUNTAIN HIGHWAY IN GEORGIA

A gigantic cliff leans menacingly over the road from the right, and on the left is the deep Kheva
Gorge.   The narrow highway through the mountains is a masterpiece of engineering skill.

Tatars, or Tartars, a people related to both the Turks and the Mongols. The Tatars (also called Azerbaijanians) follow the Mohammedan faith, but just how this religion has fared under the Soviet Government is hard to determine.

A Divided Land

Since 1920 the ancient country of Azerbaijan has been divided between Russia and Iran, with Russia holding the smaller but richer part to the north. In 1936, this was organized into the Azerbaidzhan Soviet Socialist Republic (A.S.S.R.). The republic also includes two other sections—with jawbreaking names—the Nakhichevan Autonomous Soviet Socialist Republic and the Nagorno-Karabakh Autonomous Region. Nakhichevan is a high plateau, on the Iranian border, separated from the rest of the A.S.S.R. by a narrow strip of Soviet Armenia. The forest-clad mountains of Nagorno-Karabakh, also on the Iranian border, form a continuous part of the A.S.S.R.

Only about three-fifths of the population of Soviet Azerbaijan is now of Tatar stock. The balance is made up of Armenians, Georgians and Russians. Too, national groups such as the Tatars have been disappearing. In 1949 a mass deportation, probably to somewhere deep in the interior of the Soviet Union, was carried out, mainly against people of the Caucasus border. At the time, Soviet officials said that this was necessary to guard against "enemy agents, diversionists, spies, saboteurs and all doubtful and suspicious people." All of which would seem to indicate that the Tatars, among other minority groups in the Caucasus, have never been completely reconciled to communist rule.

The central part of the A.S.S.R. is a plain, naturally arid, through which the Kura River and its tributaries flow to the Caspian and empty into that vast inland sea south of Baku. North of the plain are the moist, cool slopes of the eastern end of the Caucasus Mountains, and to the south are the eastern peaks of the mountains of Armenia.

In former years, Azerbaijan was a pastoral country, remote from the world's bustle, where the Tatars wandered with their flocks of sheep. Like many other people who live in mountainous lands, they were proud and independent. They could also be fierce fighters on occasion. Indeed, to English-speaking people the name of "Tartar" calls up a fellow with a violent temper—whether or not the Tatars really deserved this reputation. Hospitable to a fault, they would kill a sheep in a stranger's honor. After it was cooked whole in a huge pot, the host would fish out delectable morsels and pop them, willy-nilly, into his guest's mouth. The mutton would be washed down with kumiss—fermented mare's or camel's milk—poured into a bowl from which all drank.

Where the shepherds once roved there now are vast state farms with irrigated fields and numbers of drab little workers' settlements. The greatest change of all is represented by the oil derricks that bristle the land along the coast of the Caspian Sea. Here is one of the world's largest petroleum fields, which supplies the Soviet Union with about 75 per cent of its oil. Baku—center of the industry, seaport and capital of the A.S.S.R.—commands a bay on the south shore of the Apsheron Peninsula, which juts out on the southwest coast of the Caspian. There are oil wells on the peninsula, on off-shore islands and even in the bed of the sea itself, near the shore.

Baku, the Petroleum City

Baku is one of the largest cities in the Soviet Union, with a population of around 800,000. The old part of the city, to the west, dates back to at least the ninth century A.D. Here the streets are narrow and crooked, with a decidedly Oriental atmosphere. In their midst a medieval mosque still stands. Most of Baku, however, which has grown with the oil industry, is modern, with tall buildings and boulevards. It has a university and technical schools. Baku is connected with the Black Sea by two railroads; and it handles more tonnage—mostly oil, as one would expect —than any other port in the Soviet Union. Much of the crude oil is treated on the spot, and there are large refineries. The

SOVFOTO

A FOUR-HUNDRED-ACRE TEA PLANTATION, PART OF A COLLECTIVE

In Georgia, on the subtropical coast of the Black Sea, tea is one of the most important crops of the collective farms. The worker is removing the ripest leaves from the shrubs.

city also has chemical plants for processing fertilizer and rubber. This rubber is made from kok-sagyz—the Russian dandelion—which is being cultivated extensively in southern Russia.

From very ancient times it was known that the area around Baku was rich in oil, but it was not until 1871 that the first scientifically drilled wells were sunk. In 1901, Baku supplied half the world output of oil, although, of course, the total was quite small in comparison with production today. Development of this tremendous resource leaped forward after the U.S.S.R. came into existence. Some of the wells have now been drilled to a depth of more than 8,500 feet.

Pipe Lines and Tankers

Nevertheless, the Baku field is only part of a great petroleum area that spreads north beyond the boundary of Azerbaijan. Grozny, to the northwest, is second only to Baku in Russian oil production; and the Maikop field, still farther west, is almost equally important. From Baku to Batum, on the Black Sea just north of the Turkish border, there is a double pipe line, one pipe for crude oil and one for refined. However, much of the Baku oil is shipped by Caspian tankers to the Volga River—which empties into the Caspian some distance north of Baku—and thence distributed throughout the Soviet Union. Other pipe lines carry the "black gold" from the Grozny and Maikop fields to Tuapse, also on the Black Sea, or to Trudovanya, in the eastern Ukraine. All of the oil fields are electrified and connected with Baku. Altogether they yield at least 175,000,000 barrels of petroleum a year.

As we indicated earlier, Azerbaijan has also been transformed by means of irrigation, large-scale machine-farming methods and hydroelectric power. Three huge pumping stations alone on the Kura River, powered by hydroelectric installations, are said to irrigate about 75,000 acres. In fact, the A.S.S.R. has become a center of subtropical agriculture. Excellent Egyptian and Sea-Island cottons (long-fibered) are being grown in the one-time semi-desert of the central plain. Too, at various seasons of the year, the irrigated tracts may be golden with ripe wheat, grayish green with alfalfa or show the pale jade of rice seedlings.

In the mountain valleys, in addition to walnut orchards and vineyards, silk culture has become important. It is claimed that Soviet scientists have bred a new kind of silkworm, one which gives twice as much silk as the older Bagdad variety. For the silkworms, mulberries are raised in the north.

On the Caspian coast, where malaria used to be rife, the marshlands are being drained, and there are thriving tea and tobacco plantations and groves of tangerines, pomegranates and figs.

Few travelers from the West have ever visited this Caucasian region, even before it was organized into three Soviet republics. Until the days of the airplane, Caucasia was a long journey from Western centers of civilization, although those who made the difficult trip were rewarded by some of the most magnificent rugged mountain scenery to be found anywhere.

Today, the Caucasian republics are of critical importance to the Soviet Union. They contribute a large share to the state's wealth. Soviet economy and industry—not to speak of Russia's fighting forces—are at least partly dependent on the petroleum of this region.

Caucasia—Question Mark

Even more important, perhaps, is the fact that this is a border region where the Soviet Union has no buffer satellite countries to take the brunt in the event of war. Across the mountains lie a strong Turkey, closely allied with the Western community of nations, and an unpredictable Iran. The oil wells of Baku are only a brief flying distance from either of these countries. From another point of view, it is through Caucasia that Russia could reach the fabulous petroleum wealth of all the Middle East and the long-coveted water route of the Persian Gulf. One may be certain that all these possibilities have entered into the calculations of the councils both of the Western powers and of the Soviet Politburo.

RICH OIL FIELD IN BAKU

In the seventies of the last century, Baku, on the Caspian Sea, was a sleepy village of some 1,500 inhabitants. Today it has a population of more than 809,000. The increase has been due to the discovery of rich oil deposits in the neighborhood. The forest of derricks photographed here from offshore is in the Ilyich oil field. Baku is in the Azerbaidzhan Republic.

TRANSCAUCASIA: FACTS AND FIGURES

THE COUNTRY

Region south of the Caucasus Mountains and north of Iran and Turkey between the Black and Caspian seas; was known as the Transcaucasian Federation. Armenia, Azerbaijan and Georgia, the members of the federation, have, since 1936, been administered as separate republics within the Union of Soviet Socialist Republics.

ARMENIA

In southern Transcaucasia: area, 11,500 square miles, and population, 1,600,000. Soil is fertile and major industry is agriculture. Chief crops are grain, cotton, tobacco, sugar beets, grapes and other fruits. Irrigation and hydro-electric works and projects have been built. Livestock, 1,600,000 head. Mining of copper, zinc, aluminum and molybdenum is important. Other industries include production of synthetic rubber, fertilizers, building materials and textiles. There are 1,193 elementary and secondary schools, 51 technical schools, 14 institutions of higher education and the Armenian branch of the Soviet Academy of Sciences. Populations of chief cities: Yerevan (or Erivan), 200,000; Leninakan, 67,800.

AZERBAIJAN

In eastern Transcaucasia, it includes Nakhichevan Autonomous Republic, an enclave within Armenia, and Nagorno-Karabakh Autonomous Region, within Azerbaijanian borders. Total area, 33,000 square miles, and population, 3,400,000. Oil production, centered on the Caspian coast around Baku, and agriculture are the leading industries. Chief farm products are grain, cotton, rice, fruits, vegetables, tobacco and silk. Other products include copper, chemicals, building materials, food, timber, salt, textiles and fish. There are 3,600 primary and secondary schools, 91 technical colleges, 20 institutions of higher education, 1 university at Baku and a branch of the Soviet Academy of Sciences. Chief cities: Baku, 901,000; Kirovabad, 98,000.

GEORGIA

In northwest Transcaucasia, it includes Abkhazian and Adzhar autonomous republics and South Ossetian Autonomous Region. Total area, 29,000 square miles; population, 4,000,000. Chief crops are tea; citrus fruits; tung, eucalyptus and bamboo trees; tobacco, and grapes. Livestock, 4,100,000 head. Mountain streams afford immense electrical power. Chief minerals are manganese and coal. There are large iron and steel works and auto plants. Batumi is the terminus of an oil pipeline from Baku. There are 4,777 primary and secondary schools, 22 schools of higher education, also technical schools and colleges, a branch of the Soviet Academy of Sciences and 80 research institutes. Population of chief cities: Tbilisi, 519,200; Kutaisi, 81,500; Batumi, 70,800.

197

OIL PIPELINES snake the hills near Agha Jari, an oil town in the southwest. The pipes link it with Abadan, the oil-refining center and port at the head of the Persian Gulf.

Iran ... *land of the Persians*

UNDER the leadership of Mohammed Reza Pahlevi, the Shah, Iran is trying to catch up with the twentieth century in a hurry. It has several outstanding assets. A basic one is that money is available for development projects. Besides, Iran has the foreign exchange necessary to buy the machinery and critical materials essential to economic development. In a recent year the revenues from its nationalized oil industry amounted to $250,000,000. Iran lies in the midst of one of the world's richest oil basins. Another fundamental asset is that for all their internal differences the Persians, or Iranians, are unified by pride. The pride rests on their Aryan (Iranian), non-Arab descent and a continuous history that goes back almost three thousand years. A common faith, the Shiite branch of Islam, binds them still closer. Further, Iran is almost unique in having no overpopulation problem; and its people are hard-working and vigorous.

The upheaval that followed on the nationalization of the oil industry in 1951 is discussed farther on in this chapter.

It brought Iran to the brink of ruin and very nearly dethroned the Shah and brought the Communists to power. Since then the Shah has taken firmer control, no doubt guided by the example of his forceful father, Reza Pahlevi, who became Shah after a successful revolt in the early 1920's. Reza Shah was determined to Westernize Persia as Kemal Atatürk had transformed Turkey. Reza's methods were ruthless, even brutal, but he pushed through much-needed improvements in the country's government, industry, transportation and educational system. By 1941, when Reza Shah was forced to abdicate in favor of his son, Iran was by and large government-run. Middle-class businessmen have been playing a large role since.

Mohammed Reza Shah was educated in Switzerland and intellectually and emotionally he leans toward the West. His main goal also is reform. Persians call his plans the White Revolution. In 1956 a seven-year plan was launched, which is financed by oil revenues. Irrigation and power dams, electric lighting, roads,

LADEN CAMELS plod past an abandoned fort on the road to Yezd. In this central area of Iran the barren land bakes under a merciless sun.

street paving are among the many projects. Teheran and Shiraz already have piped water systems, replacing the old unsanitary *jubes*—curbside streams. One of the most ambitious projects is being constructed in Khuzistan, a province of 58,000 square miles on the southwest. It is best described as "Iran's Tennessee Valley Authority." Certainly it will transform the region.

In an effort to bring about a fairer distribution of land the Shah himself has given away about 10 per cent of the vast estates he inherited. An effort is being made to wipe out graft and corruption, rife in Persia since the days of foreign domination. But formidable obstacles stand in the way. There are the "Thousand Families," aristocratic, absentee landlords of 70 per cent of the land. They have notably failed to follow the Shah's example in yielding any part of their domains.

Corruption has been taken for granted so long that most Iranians view the effort to uproot it cynically. Not long ago a Teheran official declared that all beggars would be taken from the city's streets by a certain date "notwithstanding all pressures and recommendations." This led a newspaper to comment: "The implication is that even begging is a racket that can bring pressure to bear on the municipality. Presumably there are beggars who can pull a few strings to start a flow of friendly notes and telephone calls to take the 'heat' off the beggars."

With rising prosperity, a middle class is emerging in Iran. Its members, though far from blameless themselves, and the intellectuals seem to be at one in dislike of imperialism and resentment of inefficiency and corruption. They have yet to form any organized opposition to the Government. Yet it is significant that 60 per cent of the Iranian students educated abroad never come home because opportunities are slim unless a young man has important connections. Most of the country's intellectuals consider corruption a more basic menace than communism. If corruption continues unchecked, a communist revolution might well result.

199

The foregoing has an indirect bearing on Iran's international relations. The Shah and his Government are firmly in the Western camp. Iran is a keystone in the Central Treaty Organization, formerly the Baghdad Pact, whose main purpose is to strengthen the "northern tier," the defense line between the U.S.S.R. and the seething Arab states. Even in czarist days, Russia, almost landlocked, cast covetous glances at the Persian Gulf. Nor do the Persians forget that they were pawns in the struggle for influence in central Asia between Britain and Russia in the 1800's, or how hard it was to get the Soviet forces to leave after World War II. Iran's armed forces have been built up with American help though they would still be no real match for Soviet military might. Nevertheless, Iran exhibits little fear. When a Soviet diplo-

mat complained that Iranian-American treaty talks threatened the U.S.S.R., Manouchehr Eghbal, the Iranian prime minister, replied: "It is for the Iranian Government to decide whether this treaty is directed against the Soviets. Other governments have no say in the matter. I want you also to realize that the old tactics of intimidation are out of date. No empty threats can frighten us . . ."

Iran, or Persia, consists mainly of a vast plateau between Afghanistan and Pakistan on the east and Iraq on the west. To the north lies the Caspian Sea and on each side of this stretch of water the Persian frontier adjoins that of Russia; to the south lies the torrid Persian Gulf, which has one of the most ghastly climates in the world.

The beginning of Persia is legendary, but it is thought that nomadic tribes

wandered from parts farther east and, attracted by the Caspian Sea, settled near its shores. In about 550 B.C. Cyrus the Great made himself known to history. He conquered all the neighboring tribes and formed the Persian Empire. His successors extended the boundaries from the Punjab in India to beyond the desert in Egypt and sought to conquer Greece. They were defeated by Alexander the Great, who in 331 B.C. practically made Persia a Greek province.

The next great period began about six hundred years later under Sassanian rulers, who again brought to Persia the glory and splendor of her earlier period. This empire endured until it was overrun by the Arabs in the seventh century A.D.

Up to the time of the Arab invasion, the Persians were followers of Zoroaster and worshiped the sun and fire. After the Arab conquest they were converted to Islam.

Invasions from the East

Arab rule, however, fell before the warring Mongols under Genghis Khan, who in turn gave way to Tamerlane the Tatar and his hordes who swept over the country on their way westward. In the sixteenth century, a strong leader, Ismail I, came to power and founded the Safavid Dynasty. Under the first Safavid rulers, the boundaries were extended and Persian art, especially miniature painting and hand-woven carpets, reached a height of perfection that has never been surpassed.

Weak rulers followed, and the next centuries saw the territory reduced to its present boundaries. In the twentieth century, the country fell into a sad state of political corruption under the Kajars. It is they who were ousted by Reza Pahlevi.

The climate of Persia is one of extremes. While frost is common enough in winter the heat in the summer months is intense, especially in the low-lying provinces bordering on the Persian Gulf. As a rule the heat is dry and the climate on the plateau is delightful, but the storms are horrifying.

The present population of Persia is about 21,000,000. As the area of the country is about three times that of France, it is widely scattered. Owing to the scanty rainfall, there is a lack of water except in the Caspian provinces. Great uninhabitable areas exist. The country is largely a desert with its cities and towns lying where water is available.

The Elburz Mountains run across the north of Persia, south of the Caspian Sea, from which the superb cone of Demavend rises to a height of 18,600 feet—the loftiest mountain of Asia west of the spurs of the Himalayas.

Elsewhere in Persia the ranges generally run from southeast to northwest, a fact that has made transportation, except by air today, difficult. The chief cities, such as Teheran (or Tehran), Meshed, the sacred city of Persia, and Tabriz, a trade center, are close to the mountains. The country relies for its water on the snow on the mountains which melts in the spring and fills the irrigation channels.

The most important feature of Persia, which has impressed itself forcibly on the life and character of the people, is the Dasht-i-Kavir desert. It occupies the center of the country.

Little Rain and Few Rivers

Because of the meager rainfall and the high ranges surrounding the plateau, there is no great river in the many hundreds of miles of coast that lie between the mouths of the Indus and the Shatt al Arab (recently in dispute with Iraq). It is the Ab-i-Diz River, farther north, that is being dammed for power and irrigation.

The Persian Gulf, which washes the southwest and south coasts of Iran, is an almost completely landlocked body of water 700 miles long and about 120 miles wide. It is shallow and receives the waters of the Tigris and Euphrates, which are united in the broad stream of the Shatt al Arab.

People of southwestern United States can well imagine a country so dry that

WANDERING TRIBESMEN OF LURISTAN

About a fifth of the inhabitants of Iran are nomads, wandering tribesmen who drive their flocks and herds from place to place seeking fresh pasture. They set up rough, temporary shelters as they go. On crude looms the women weave tent cloth, blankets and other textiles. The tribesmen in this picture are Luris, of Luristan, in the west-central part of Iran.

BATHHOUSES, NOT IGLOOS

In the towns of northern Iran, the village bathhouses are the cleanest structures in the section. Their mortar surfaces are painstakingly scrubbed to a dazzling perfection. Elsewhere cleanliness is less evident. Bad sewage, inadequate medical facilities and the lack of pure water are responsible for the prevalence of diseases that thrive in unsanitary surroundings.

trees and crops can be grown only where the land is well irrigated. The vegetation consists of bushes, generally of a thorny nature and only two or three feet high, with a little grass which shows green for a month in the spring and then disappears.

Where there is water, crops of wheat and barley (which is the staple horse food), millet, cotton, opium, lucerne (known here as alfalfa), clover and tobacco are grown. Rice and corn flourish in the moist Caspian provinces. Persia is rich in fruits, which grow well in spite of the lack of scientific cultivation. Pears, apples, quinces, apricots, black and yellow

plums, peaches, nectarines and cherries are produced in great abundance. Figs, pomegranates and the famous almonds and pistachio nuts grow best in the warmer districts, and the date-palm, orange and lime are confined to the low-lying "Hot Country." The grapes and melons of Persia are famous. We owe to Persia the peach, the pistachio nut, spinach, the narcissus and lilac, all of which have retained their Persian names.

Persia has long been famous also for her carpets and rugs, and a trip to the rug dealer's shop is a very interesting experience for the proprietor will probably

203

serve coffee and cigarettes while lengthy discussion takes place. Bargaining is quite the order of the day, and one must never seem in haste for then the dealer will surely get the better of it. Among the Persians themselves, it sometimes takes days to conclude a transaction satisfactorily.

Persia's Industries

With the exception of rug-weaving and the manufacture of silk and cotton textiles, pottery and some leather goods, Persia has few industries. Most of the manufactured goods used by the Persians must be imported.

Persia's chief wealth is in her oil fields, which cover about five-sixths of the country. The richest single oil field in the world is in the southern region. At Abadan, a town near the head of the Persian Gulf, is the world's largest oil refinery.

Oil and the British

For many years the fields were operated by a British company. Persia could not run them herself, at least partly because there were few Persians with the necessary technical training. This arrangement began in 1901, when Persia granted a monopoly in the exploitation of the oil fields to an Englishman, William Knox D'Arcy. His venture eventually became the Anglo-Iranian Oil Company—53 per cent British-owned. Then in 1919 Persia agreed to a convention by which British advisers were placed in various departments of the Persian Government, military as well as civil. This made Persia practically a British protectorate.

As the years went by, resentment against British domination grew more open and bitter in Iran (Persia changed its name to Iran in 1935). After World War II, the unrest came to a boil, particularly over the oil situation. It was heated still further by a growing spirit of nationalism—Iran for the Iranians—the same spirit that has been emerging in so many other parts of Asia since the war.

The climax came in the spring of 1951. Under the leadership of Mohammed Mossadegh, who was Prime Minister of Iran at the time, Iran suddenly nationalized the oil industry. This meant the end of British control. It also brought the industry, Iran's chief source of income, to a standstill. The British technicians departed and there were few trained Iranians to take their places. Regardless of Iranian feelings, it was obvious that the industry could not be operated without outside help of some kind.

An International Problem

The Western world was alarmed. Here was one of its chief sources of oil idle. What is more, there was a threat that communism might gain headway in Iran just as it has thrived on turmoil elsewhere. The specific dispute between Britain and Iran was carried all the way to the UN Security Council, but that body failed to settle it.

When the oil industry came to a halt, its Iranian labor force of about 65,000 was thrown out of work. These men received unemployment compensation, a drain on the Iranian treasury. On the whole, however, the stoppage affected the great mass of the Iranians much less than one might expect. Actually, very little of the wealth from the oil fields had ever trickled down to them. Their standard of living had always been low.

Oil Begins to Flow Again

In 1953 popular backing of the Shah led to an uprising and overthrow of Premier Mossadegh. The new premier, Fazlollah Zahedi, reopened the oil issue. In the following year an agreement was reached with eight British, United States, Dutch and French companies to get Iran's frozen oil industry humming again. Under a twenty-five year plan, the companies began to extract, refine and market the products of Iranian oil fields.

With the resumption of earnings from the petroleum industry, plus borrowed money, Iran embarked on an ambitious five-year development program to increase agricultural and mineral production, to improve transportation and communication facilities, and to develop a huge hydroelectric project in Karaj.

In ancient times, the Iranians obtained valuable pearls from the Persian Gulf and even now pearl fishing is carried on to some extent. The principal export is oil, followed by rugs, dried fruits and some medicinal plants. The exports are brought overland or down the Tigris River to the ports on the gulf and the Caspian Sea.

For centuries, the only means of land communication were the caravan routes. In the last few decades, however, under an ambitious government program, new roads have been constructed and old ones improved. Many hundreds of miles of railways have been opened with more under way. Telegraph, telephone and radio systems have been installed. Airplanes fly regularly from the capital, Teheran, and Kermanshah to Bagdad, where there are scheduled flights to Western countries.

Iran has awakened to her need for improvements, but many obstacles stand in the way. The greatest, perhaps, is the mutual distrust that exists among the different groups within the country. The lawmakers fear one another and are all jealous of the Shah. Whatever money is made is not reinvested in Iran, but banked outside the country.

The peasant is the backbone of the nation. His village is sometimes enclosed within a high mud wall, in which case the houses are small and dark. The open space in the center of the village, where the cattle are driven at night, is usually dirty. When the houses are scattered about, each occupies a good deal of space, having one courtyard around which the living rooms are grouped and a second courtyard for the cattle. Adjoining many of the houses are orchards, surrounded by mud walls. The peasants are still prac-

EWING GALLOWAY

SHAH ABBAS I built the Ali Kapu in the early seventeenth century. It is a gateway structure in Isfahan.

tically serfs under a real feudal system and they are the people who are most eager for improvements to be made. The land is sparsely settled and labor is scarce. The most primitive methods of agriculture are still in use. A few model farming communities exist, but they have been built with outside aid. The ruling classes may be divided into the landowners, who have a great deal of wealth, and the prosperous merchants of the towns and cities who own their own shops or cafés. The peasant has little voice in the Government.

Besides these, Iran has many nomadic tribes, who live in tents of goats' hair and

A BAS-RELIEF FROM THE DAYS OF THE SASSANIAN KINGS

At Taq-i-Bustan, near Kermanshah, there are arched recesses cut into the rocks containing bas-reliefs. In this one King Ardashir II appears to be presenting a trophy to the victor of a battle. The sculptures date from the Sassanidae, a dynasty of Persian kings who ruled from the third century A.D. and were finally overthrown by the Arabs in the seventh century.

TRIBUTE-BEARERS ON THEIR WAY TO A PERSIAN CONQUEROR

The sculpture is from a building wall still standing among the ruins of Persepolis, the dazzling capital founded by Darius the Great around 500 B.C. Under Darius and his successor, Xerxes, the Persian Empire was at the height of its power. The story of its vanished glory may still be read from the sculptures at Persepolis, though the city has long been dust.

CHILD WORKERS IN IRAN

Children are shown weaving carpets in Hamadan, a district where famed Persian rugs are produced. Rug-making ranks among the top native industries in Iran, and in normal times about $3,000,000 worth of carpets are exported to the United States alone. The law of 1943 calling for the gradual establishment of compulsory education has lagged in enforcement.

207

PEACE WITHIN THE SHELTERED GARDEN OF A MOSQUE IN TEHERAN

Students reflect on the Koran by a serene pool, where their eyes may rest on exquisite mosaic tile. The teeming, noisy city just outside their retreat seems far away.

STREAMLINED MODERN ARCHITECTURE FOR THE SHAH OF IRAN

The Shah's palace in Teheran is in vivid contrast to the delicate design of the guarded gateway. The appearance of Iran's capital has been undergoing rapid changes in recent years.

A YOUNG IRANIAN PRACTICES AN OLD ART WITH A SKILLED HAND

The boy is painting a graceful design on the kind of pottery for which Qum is well known. The shelf above is stacked with bowls, and there are lids in the hole behind him.

move about with their flocks and herds in search of fresh grazing-grounds. They spend the summer months in the mountains and move down to the plains at the approach of winter. They follow the same route year after year. Physically, they are splendid people, but they are very fond of raiding villages and of plundering caravans. When they are on the march the old men, the women and children look after the sheep, goats, cattle, camels and donkeys, while the fighting men act as scouts and try to rob any villages that may be in the vicinity.

In Persia the position of the men is far better than that of the women. When a boy is born the father receives congratulations, whereas the birth of a girl passes almost without notice. The baby will have amulets to avert the evil eye hung around its neck; no glass may be brought into the room lest its rays might cause the child to squint and indeed the very word glass may

not be mentioned. Moreover, no one wearing black clothes is permitted to enter.

The baby is swaddled tightly and, when taken out for an airing, is dressed in coarse clothes—this again being to avert the evil eye. Friends may admire the child without causing him ill-luck provided they exclaim "Mashallah!" (that which Allah wished).

In former times, upon reaching the age of eight, the boy was placed in charge of a manservant, and a mullah, or priest, undertook his education, which consisted mainly of learning to read and write. The textbook was the Koran (the Moslem scriptures) and the unfortunate pupil was forced to learn sentence after sentence in the original Arabic with its meaning in Persian. He repeated it exactly as a parrot so he learned neither Arabic nor Persian. Little else was studied under private instruction or in the numerous religious schools.

WOMEN THRESHING GRAIN BY A CENTURIES-OLD METHOD

When the sieve is shaken vigorously, the grain falls through to the rug spread to catch it and the chaff is left behind. It is a tedious method that yields little in proportion to the effort.

211

COURTHOUSE OF BANDAR SHAH VIEWED ACROSS A PUBLIC GARDEN

The attractive building is one of many modern structures in the port on the southeast coast of the Caspian Sea. Bandar Shah is the northern terminus of the Trans-Iranian Railway.

THE SIMPLEST OF SCALES SUFFICES THIS MERCHANT

The stones in one pan determine the weight as the scales are held aloft and filled with raisins or nuts. The technique is old, but no one questions its accuracy.

MASJED-I-SHAH (SHAH'S MOSQUE) ON THE ROYAL COURT IN ISFAHAN

Covered with glazed tiles and ornamented with gold and silver, the Masjed-i-Shah is a dazzling sight. The court—the Maidan-i-Shah—is an enormous rectangle 1,680 feet by 522 feet.

If a boy was idle, his feet were tied to a pole and beaten by canes. This punishment of the bastinado is known as "eating the sticks." All exhibitions of high spirits were discouraged and it was impressed on the young pupil that it was undignified to run or to jump.

The result was that a boy soon became a miniature man. He wore a long coat much kilted at the waist and the same kind of "kulla" or astrakhan headdress as his father. His manners, too, tended to become artificial and when greeted by a friend, he would reply, "May your nose be fat," "May your shadow never grow less," and other similar compliments that formed an important part of Persian etiquette.

When a boy reached the age of sixteen, his mother arranged a marriage with a cousin, whom, perhaps, the boy had not seen since he was a child, for women were kept strictly secluded and were always veiled in public.

The bride and bridegroom then met and gazed intently at one another's faces which were reflected in a mirror at which they both looked together. Finally the bride was taken, with rejoicings, to her future home, where the young couple par-

took of bread, cheese and salt that had been brought by the bride, and were left by their relatives to settle down.

This plan of selecting a wife and the marriage customs are still practiced in some parts of Persia, but as girls are now admitted to the public schools, this, as well as other old customs, is dying out in the face of rapid Westernization.

Great progress has been made in education. Modern schools have been established, which, in the lower grades, are attended by boys and girls together. Hundreds of students have been sent abroad to study so that they may return to teach in the schools or become leaders. A university in Teheran gives higher education in all branches of sciences and arts.

We have said that the position of women is lower than that of men. This is true in any Mohammedan country. The Koran, by which the followers of Mohammed model their lives, makes no provision for the education of women and puts many restrictions on them. Nevertheless, the number of both women and men who cannot read or write is decreasing, and women without veils are seen more and more. In wealthy families, women are given

213

A BRASS BOWL TAKES SHAPE BETWEEN ANVIL AND HAMMER

The clang of the worker in brass is an ever present sound in cities and villages. Almost every kind of household utensil is made of the bright metal. Articles may be polished smooth or they may be left with the marks of the hammer showing—beaten brass. A great advantage of brass, especially in warm countries, is that it will not rust, as iron utensils would.

special quarters, called in Persia the anderun, in which no man except a relative may enter. Turkey was the first to throw off these customs and Persia is following slowly. To-day, Persian women may attend the theater and movies unveiled and are encouraged by the government to adopt the dress and the manners of Western women.

The new order which is gradually taking the place of the old in Persia is due to a large extent to the efforts of Riza Khan, who was Shah from 1925 to 1941. His story is a fascinating one. A man of humble birth, he began his career as a trooper in the Persian Cossack Brigade. He gradually rose in rank through sheer energy and ability and at last assumed command of the brigade. In February, 1921, being then in command of more than 2,000 Cossacks, he overthrew the Persian Cabinet. He became Minister of War in the new cabinet formed by the Shah.

In this Middle East land of Omar Khayyam the Allies had a land bridge. In Iran's capital, Tehran, was held the historic conference of November, 1943, at which the leaders of the United States, Great Britain and the Union of Soviet Socialist Republics, among other statements of policy, pledged the independence of Iran.

Iran presents a medley of East and West, ancient ways and modern magic of the machine age. The single-track Trans-Iranian Railway streaks by baked-mud villages whose outlines were old a thousand years ago. On its way it ducks into more than 200 tunnels, crosses thousands of bridges, and in some places winds so sharply it can be seen at three different levels. Yet Iran still holds the flavor of the old East, from the lonely shepherd on the mountainside to the crowded, covered bazaars where bearded merchants bargain over products of Oriental handicraft. As planes fly over, a nomad with a hawk on his wrist looks up respectfully. Strange to us are many Iranian customs—the still sheltered lives of women, the Moslem taboo against drinks and dogs; their particular rituals of prayer and fasting.

IRAN (PERSIA): FACTS AND FIGURES

THE COUNTRY

An independent kingdom which occupies the western and larger half of the Iranian plateau. It is bounded on the north by Transcaucasia, the Caspian Sea and Turkestan, on the east by Afghanistan and the Dominion of Pakistan, on the south by the Arabian Sea and the Persian Gulf, and on the west by Iraq and Turkey. The total area is about 629,343 square miles, and the population is about 21,037,000, of whom about 3,000,000 are nomads.

GOVERNMENT

Legislative government consists of a lower house, or Majlis, of 136 deputies elected every two years. Since 1950, there has been a Senate of 60 members, of whom 30 are appointed by the shah. The shah appoints the prime minister, who selects a cabinet approved by the Majlis.

COMMERCE AND INDUSTRIES

Food products include wheat, barley, rice and fruits. The production of gums, tobacco, cotton, silk, wool and opium is important. Sheep-raising is carried on to some extent. The minerals, though numerous, are, except in the case of oil, undeveloped. They include deposits of iron ore, coal, copper, lead and manganese; there are turquoise mines in Khorasan worked by primitive methods. Weaving of rugs and carpets is by far the most important industry. Chief exports include petroleum, carpets, raw cotton, and wool, and the imports are cotton piece goods, sugar, tea, machinery and automobiles. Monetary unit, the rial.

COMMUNICATIONS

About 1181 miles of railway. Much of the country's commerce is carried on over the great trade routes. There are over 11,436 miles of telegraph line. There is a regular air service.

RELIGION AND EDUCATION

Bulk of population belong to the Shiite sect of Islam, and there is a large minority of adherents to the Sunni persuasion. Besides these Muslims, there are small minorities of Nestorian, Gregorian, Roman Catholic and Protestant Christians. Education is free and compulsory between the ages of 7 and 13. There are over 5,000 primary schools, 400 high schools, religious and technical schools, 21 teacher-training colleges and 1 university.

CHIEF TOWNS

Teheran, capital, has a population of 1,010,-000; Tabriz, 272,000; Abadan and Khorramshahr, 201,000; Isfahan, 192,000; Meshed, 191,-000; Shiraz, 129,000; Hamadan, 122,000; Rasht, 120,000; Kermanshah, 106,000.

Iraq ...*by the*
Euphrates and
Tigris rivers

IRAQ is a land that has been swept by the violent winds of change in recent years. A swift, spectacular revolt in June 1958, ending in the death of King Faisal II, changed the country from a constitutional monarchy into a republic. The rebels promised a "new look" in foreign policy—no more toadying to the West. It promised stepped-up public works and land reform.

Actually, the Faisal regime had had a constructive program. Friendly ties with the West had produced soaring oil revenues for the oil-rich country, most of which were diverted into public works.

216

Large sums were invested in flood control, for example. But a group of nationalistic army officers grew restive. They not only opposed Faisal's allegiance to the pro-Western Baghdad Pact and his federal alliance with Jordan. They claimed that Faisal's Government was honeycombed with corruption. Finally they rose up under a brigade commander, Abdul Karim el-Kassem, to establish the republic.

At first the West feared that Kassem would join forces with the United Arab Republic, then making overtures to the Soviet Union. Kassem's first moves hardly helped quiet these fears. He repudiated the Baghdad Pact. He withdrew from the union with Jordan. Soon, however, a good many Iraqis began to speak out against close ties with Nasser's U.A.R. The anti-Nasserites in Iraq feared that he would dominate any such alliance. These Iraqis wished to maintain business dealings with the West, at the very least, in order that oil revenue might continue to flow. They believed that on this basis they could maintain political

ENTHUSIASM IN BAGHDAD.
Supporters of Premier Kassem joyfully greet his appearance in a car.

independence. Without such funds, Iraq would be forced, as it feared the U.A.R. had been, to trade freedom of action for aid from one of the great powers.

Political Tightrope

Kassem soon began to act as if he agreed with this reasoning, much to the temporary relief of the West and to the dismay of Nasser. He condemned what he called "narrow tendencies." He avowed neutrality in the cold war. He made at least some moves toward curbing communist power and "government by street mobs" by banning political activity. He declared that Iraq would respect Western investments. On the other hand, he welcomed Russian investment and know-how. Also he has continued to enjoy and accept communist support. The question remains, how far can he go in accepting this support and yet prevent Iraq from being drawn completely into the communist camp? Kassem's followers are primarily what might be called "international Communists." (The Arab nationalists in Iraq are anticommunist and in most respects anti-Kassem.) He must therefore avoid any alliance, particularly with the "imperialist" West, that might impair the sovereignty of his state. If he does not, he risks strong opposition within his own ranks.

Iraq's precious oil industry is largely in the hands of the Iraq Petroleum Company. This is a combine made up of several foreign independent firms, mainly American, British, Dutch and French. The company provides the equipment and trained personnel, Iraq the oil, and the two parties split the profits. It is the sort of arrangement that prevailed in neighboring Iran until 1951. Iran nationalized the industry and attempted to run it herself. She was crippled by a lack of technicians and by a world-wide British boycott on her oil. As a result, revenue dipped badly. It may be that Iran's example weighed heavily in Kassem's decision to shun nationalization, at least during the early years.

Iraqi agriculture, by contrast, is hardly a going concern, but its future possibilities are good. Iraq is blessed with five rivers, two (the Tigris and Euphrates) quite sizable. The land between these two rivers is fertile and productive. The Iraqis hope to extend such fertile belts by means of modern irrigation methods. In central Iraq, the rivers are deeply entrenched. In summertime the water must be lifted ten to twenty feet in order to bring it to the level of the surrounding land. Add to this Iraq's sparse, unpredictable rainfall and you have all the makings for an agricultural industry tightly strapped to fortune's wheel. The wheat and barley crops, for example, fail on the average every five years, due to light rainfall. Toward the south, Iraq is mottled with extensive marshes, unsuitable for any crop except rice, which is planted around the margins. The banks of the Shatt, between Qurna and Tao, however, support extensive date gardens. Oranges, apricots, grapes and a wide variety of other semitropical fruits are also grown there.

Irrigation and Flood Control

Proper irrigation might well make Iraq agriculturally self-sustaining. With three times as much tillable soil as Egypt, Iraq has to feed only 5,000,000 people, compared to Egypt's 22,000,000. Strides are being made in this direction. One of Iraq's irrigation projects, begun under Faisal II, involves watering 741,000,000 acres. Gigantic flood-control projects were also begun under Faisal. The largest completed were the twin dams on the Tigris, at Samarra, and on the Euphrates, at Ramad. These, along with several other dams, will at last spare central Iraq from severe flooding. The republican Government has similar plans in mind, including a stepped-up program of land reform. For many centuries, Iraq's farmland has been owned by absentee landlords who take almost 90 per cent of the produce for themselves. Now the great estates are being trimmed, and the excess sold to the men who work them. If the Government can accompany this changeover with widespread irrigation (and also introduce modern farming

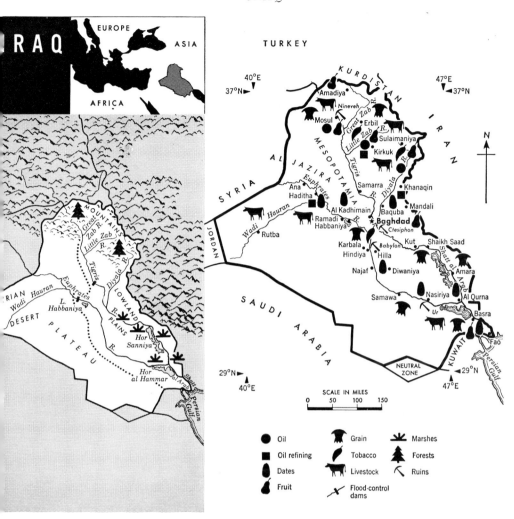

methods), Iraq may prove the 1957 boast of its development minister. "Almighty God," he cried, "has given us a wealth very seldom bestowed on countries with such a small population."

Once known as Mesopotamia, the site of Iraq is often referred to as "the cradle of civilization," not only because the human race is thought to have begun there, but because the ruins of mighty empires lie under its soil. Tradition also says that the Garden of Eden lay somewhere in this land. Modern excavation has shown that there once existed here what is believed to be one of the oldest civilizations on earth—the Sumerian.

The Sumerians, whose intellectual achievements included the arts of writing and astronomy, were eventually conquered by a Semitic people related to the Arabs and Jews.

From this fusion of Sumerians and Semites rose the Babylonians and Assyrians. The first Babylonian Empire was founded about 2100 B.C. Its chief city was the Biblical Babylon. Centuries later the Assyrian nation arose in the north and there was a long struggle for supremacy between the two kindred nations. Babylon and Lower Egypt, for a time, fell under the sway of the bold Assyrian conquerors, and then Nineveh, its capital

THE GATE OF ISHTAR, THE BABYLONIAN GODDESS OF LOVE

Bulls and goats molded from glazed bricks decorate the Ishtar Gate in Babylon. Nearby is E-Sagila, the great temple of the god Marduk and the site of the Biblical Tower of Babel.

—the ruins of which are found on the bank of the Tigris opposite Mosul—was the premier city of the world. With the destruction of Nineveh in the seventh century B.C., Babylon again rose to power. Nebuchadnezzar rebuilt the city, enclosing it with mighty walls which, with the "hanging gardens," formed one of the Seven Wonders of the World. The ruins of Babylon lie to the south of Bagdad (Baghdad)..

But Babylon, as recorded in the Bible, was taken by Cyrus, king of the Medes and Persians. The Persians in turn fell before the Greeks under Alexander the Great. The Greeks were followed by Parthians, Romans and then Persians again. After the death of Mohammed in 632 A.D. his Arab followers overran the Persian Empire. At Ctesiphon, the Parthian and Persian capital, they found great treasure and the materials of its wonderful buildings were used for the construction of Bagdad in 762. Under the famous Harun-al-Rashid, Bagdad became the centre of the wit, learning and art of Islam. Then in 1516 A.D. the country finally passed to the Turks, under whose misrule it remained for about four hundred years.

KEYSTONE

A WINGED GUARD OF KHORSABAD

A minister to a sacred winged bull flanks a gate to the palace of King Sargon II of Assyria.

And so, during the centuries, the greatness of Babylon and Assyria passed away. Their magnificent cities were used to supply the bricks for succeeding towns and villages, and such ruins as the barbarians left fell into decay until they became shapeless mounds whose very names were forgotten. The peoples of these cities had used a curious writing called "cuneiform," which they had developed from the script of their Sumerian ancestors. They scratched figures with a triangular pointed instrument on soft tablets of clay which they afterward baked. The knowledge of this writing also passed away.

That old phrase "the changeless East" is obsolete. Change is resistless. Following the expulsion of the Turks, Mesopotamia was left under British control. In 1921 Emir Feisal was crowned King of Iraq under a British Mandate. Then Iraq became independent in 1932. Governmental shifts, plus oil, speeded up far-reaching changes.

The "Mosul question," involving rich oil areas, caused international rivalry and dispute. Mosul, city of northern Iraq,

OPEN-AIR FERRY ON THE TIGRIS

The glorified raft, or kelek, as it is called, is made of alternating layers of planks and logs supported on the inflated skins of sheep or goats. This one is ready to float its load of passengers comfortably down the Tigris from Diarbekr, Turkey, to Mosul, Iraq. Keleks are as familiar on the Tigris as ferryboats are on the Hudson River and the St. Lawrence.

ROOFS OF REED BY THE EUPHRATES

An old-time Arab village by the Euphrates, of a type rarely seen nowadays. The houses, or huts, are made of reeds and are roofed with reed matting. The Tigris and Euphrates once emptied into the Persian Gulf through separate mouths. Now they meet, on land which they themselves have laid down bit by bit through long centuries, and flow into the gulf as one.

OUTSIDE THE WALLS OF OLD BAGDAD—THE TOMB OF ZOBEIDE

Herdsmen lead their flocks near the base of the strange building outside Bagdad where Zobeide, wife of Harun-al-Rashid, is buried. He was the great caliph who ruled over Bagdad at the height of the city's power, when it dominated most of the Arabian world. The roof of the tomb, a pyramid of small overlapping domes, surmounts a bold octagonal base.

MOSUL, the chief town in an oil-bearing province, stands on the Tigris River opposite Nineveh, the ruined capital of ancient Assyria. A treeless city, Mosul's skyline is relieved by towers, domes and minarets. The Great Mosque, formerly dedicated to St. Paul, has leaning minarets. Here the Tigris is crossed by a floating bridge, a span that rests on boats placed side by side and is similar to a pontoon bridge. Mosul was once known for its fine cotton goods, which fact has given us the word "muslin" for a kind of sheer cotton fabric, though muslin may also be heavy.

RODD

THE ARCH OF CTESIPHON was once a part of the royal palace in Ctesiphon, the capital of the great Persian Empire when it extended over Mesopotamia, or Iraq as it is called at present. It became an important city and in 550 A. D., Chosroes I built this magnificent palace there. Beneath the arch, which was the roof of the audience chamber, there was once a blue ceiling set with gold stars to imitate the sky. The ruins are very important from an architectural standpoint for they are among the few existing examples of construction in the Sassanid or Persian period.

THE ROUND BARGES OF THE TIGRIS, LADEN WITH WATERMELONS

On the Tigris at Bagdad, Iraqi boatmen guard their striped, delicious cargo. For perhaps as long as man has been transporting goods on the waterways of Mesopotamia, the unwieldy, almost unsinkable gufa has been bounding its useful way from farm to market. The gufa is made of reeds, covered with hides and plastered inside and out with pitch for waterproofing.

is on the west bank of the Tigris. Each large house is built round an open courtyard. The houses are of burnt brick faced with slabs of a kind of gray marble, quarried nearby. The same marble serves for paving and for wall panels in the interiors. There is a fine mosque, the cupolas and minarets of which are of turquoise blue tiles. The summers are very hot, and for three or four months the inhabitants are glad to sleep on the flat roofs. The winters are rainy, and frost is sometimes experienced.

Although there is a railway line, considerable trade on the upper Tigris is by means of native craft. As some parts of the river are very shallow, use is made of rafts of saplings lashed together and packed underneath with inflated goatskins. These are floated and paddled down the river, but the return journey has to be made by road for at Bagdad the raft is pulled to pieces and sold.

Iraq is not a well wooded country. Much of the north is undulating pasture land, but wheat, barley, linseed and flax are grown and, if the rainfall be sufficient,

yield good crops. A little distance to the north of Bagdad we find an alluvial plain formed of the mud which the two rivers have deposited. This was once the most fertile and thickly populated spot on earth. Here we meet the first palm trees in the narrow strips of cultivated land beside the rivers. Wherever the land is irrigated it responds readily to cultivation. The growing of wheat is increasing and the cotton crop shows a yearly gain. But the land under cultivation is only a small proportion of the entire country, and that is the reason why Iraq is so sparsely settled.

The clay of the plain, mixed with chopped reeds and grass, can be baked into a hard substance by the sun alone, and of this the single-storied dwellings of the villages are built. We find also huts made of reeds, which in some of the swamps grow to a height of 20 feet. The larger canes, placed side by side, are bent over in a half loop for the framework and are then covered with mats made of rushes. The end walls are of reed straw bound together, and the entrance is covered with a hanging mat. These huts can be put up in a day and can be taken down and moved elsewhere whenever the owner wishes.

The nomadic tribes who wander about with their flocks and herds use tents made of goat hair. The houses in the towns are mainly strong, two-story buildings. In order to lessen the terrific summer heat, screens made either of camel thorn or of licorice twigs, are hung before the windows and kept moist by having water thrown over them.

The Tigris is navigable by steamers as far as Bagdad, and though the passage of "the Narrows," just beyond Ezra's Tomb,

is difficult for large craft, the river is crowded with boats of all descriptions, carrying passengers and merchandise. The famous round basket which is known as the "gufa" was in use in the days of Nineveh's glory. Below Sheikh Saad the gufa gives place to the canoe-shaped "bellum."

The Euphrates, which is navigated by native craft only, is much better wooded than the Tigris. In its lower reaches it passes through marsh land which by draining is becoming rich and fertile. At Kurna the rivers unite and form the Shatt-al-Arab, and the cultivated land near this

SAWDERS FROM CUSHING

LINES OF DRYING WOOL ON FLAT ROOFTOPS

The nomadic tribes of the Middle East depend upon their flocks for their living. They wander with their herds of sheep and goats looking for suitable pasturage. Shearing time is a big event in their lives, for cropping the wool means that they will soon have money. Then the nomads halt to cut and dry the wool, often using rooftops as a drying place.

RODD

KERBELA is a very holy city to the Shiah Mohammedans, or Shiites, since here is the tomb of Hussein, grandson of the prophet Mohammed. Hussein was killed at Kerbela, and is regarded as a martyr. Thousands of pilgrims visit his tomb every year, and seem so grief-stricken by Hussein's death that it would be easy to imagine that he had died recently and not years ago.

RODD

THE PORT OF BASRA is Iraq's chief outlet for world trade. Situated on the Shatt-al-Arab, seventy-five miles upstream from the Persian Gulf, the port is open to ocean-going vessels. Basra is also connected by rail with Bagdad, Iran and Kuwait. There is a busy commerce in various cereals, and the city is also an important livestock market.

IRAQI FARMERS AND THEIR CRUDE HORSE-DRAWN THRESHING SLED

The sled-like contraption separates the grain from the stalks. It is by no means the crudest of implements in a land where tractors and other farm machines are seldom seen. In fact, the design of the contraption, rough as it is, shows a considerable amount of ingenuity.

estuary is one of the largest date-producing centers of the world. Nearly 200 varieties of dates are grown, and they are a staple article of food and a big item of export.

In the midst of this fertile strip, and 70 miles from the Persian Gulf, stands Basra, the principal port of the country. During World War II, Basra's trade and importance greatly increased. The modern city has up-to-date shipping facilities and is a road, rail and air terminal. Basra has been called the Venice of the East for all through and about the city are numberless waterways and creeks.

The majority of the population of Iraq is Arab. There are Arabs of all types and ranks with a large admixture of Persians. These people are Mohammedans and are divided mainly into the Shiah and Sunni sects. In this country are some of the most famous places of pilgrimage in the Moslem world.

The holy city of Nejef, which lies to the west of the Euphrates, stands on a cliff overlooking the desert. The golden dome of the mosque which covers the tomb of Ali, the murdered saint, makes a most conspicuous landmark. The city is walled, and consists of very narrow streets where tall houses shut out most of the light and air. Some of these houses stand on as many as three, four or even five floors of cellars hewn out of the rock, which form a cool retreat from the stifling heat of the crowded city above. A broad bazaar, a quarter of a mile long, leads up to the mosque. This small city of devout citizens during certain feasts has as many as 120,000 pilgrims pass through its gates.

Everything required in the city has to be brought from without and water has to be carried in skins a distance of three-quarters of a mile.

The Jews, who today number only a few thousand—we remember the captivity of their race in Babylon and the fact that Abraham their founder came from Ur of the Chaldees, which was near the junction of the canal Shat-el-Hai with the

232

BUYING POLISHED COPPERWARE AT A SIDEWALK SHOP IN BAGDAD

The robes might have been worn in Harun-al-Rashid's day, but the merchandise comes from modern factories in the capital. Present-day Bagdad is a manufacturing and trading city.

COOLING OFF IN THE WATERS OF THE TIGRIS RIVER, NEAR MOSUL

There is very little rainfall in Iraq, and river water is doubly precious. Iraqis wash and bathe in the Tigris, finding surcease from the heat when the sun is high.

Euphrates—have also their holy places of pilgrimage here. The Jews are chiefly men of the towns, traders, shopkeepers and sometimes bankers.

The Christians, who are more in number than the Jews, are found around Mosul and are mainly Assyrians. Being better educated than the rest of the natives they form for the most part the professional class. In addition to these people there are wild Kurds from the north, nominally Mohammedans, and representatives of many other nationalities and religions. Among the latter are two communities that call for notice, the Sabæans and the Yezidis.

The Sabæans, or Subbis, get their name of Star-Worshipers from the fact that they turn to the polar star when praying, under the belief that the supreme deity has his residence beyond that star. Sunday is their holy day, they practice baptism once a week and they have a ceremony in which bread and wine are used. They are not Christians, but they have great veneration for John the Baptist. They are a very handsome people. Living among the marshlands in the south, their chief industry was the making of canoes until the war made their wonderful inlaid silver work known to the British troops. When the latter captured Amara the Sabæans migrated thither, and their silver work has brought them increasing prosperity.

The Yezidis are often called Devil-Worshipers. Although they believe in God the

Creator, they hold that the devil is very powerful and treat him with deference.

The characteristic headgear of Iraq is the khaffiya. This is a piece of material, usually cotton, that is draped over the head and held in place by a thick cord of wool. The poorest Iraqi man may wear only a long shirt and a khaffiya. In the cities, however, Western clothes are the rule.

Most Iraqi rise early, and rest during the afternoon heat. They sip coffee many times a day, and much of the men's leisure time is spent in coffee shops. Most of the women still lead rather secluded lives, as elsewhere in many Muslim countries, though educated, younger women are breaking away from the old customs.

In spite of all the vestiges of the past, twentieth-century currents are beating hard against Iraq. Back in 1950 the Government established a Development Board to divert 70 per cent of the country's enormous income from oil into such major projects as road building, irrigation dams, and cement, textile and power plants. The scheme has moved by fits and starts, blocked in part by the lack of trained technicians. At the same time, Iraq, unlike some other Arab nations, seemed to be a firm friend of the West. In 1955 it entered into the Baghdad Pact with the United Kingdom, Turkey, Pakistan and Iran. (Early in 1958 the United States joined the pact, somewhat informally.) In February 1958, Iraq and Jordan (following the creation of the United Arab Republic) formed the Arab Union.

In July 1958 the Baghdad Pact received what appeared to be a death blow and the Arab Union was dissolved when the Iraqi monarchy was overthrown in a military *coup d'état*. During the uprising, King Faisal II, the prime minister and other members of the royalist regime were slain. The rebellion's chief leader was Abdul Karim el-Kassem, a professional soldier. Iraq was declared a republic and Kassem became the premier. Without Iraq, the other members of the Baghdad Pact revitalized it in 1959 under the name of the Central Treaty Organization (CENTO).

Basically the revolt seemed to be the result of two overlapping things: resentment, accumulated over years, against feudal conditions; and the nationalism rife throughout the Middle East. Moreover, the Communists, who always try to profit by such situations, seemed to be gaining great influence in Iraq. There was also considerable rivalry with Nasser's U.A.R. for leadership of the Arab world.

IRAQ: FACTS AND FIGURES

THE COUNTRY

Consists of the former Turkish vilayets of Baghdad, Basra and Mosul, which are bounded on the north by Turkey, on the east by Iran, on the south by the Persian Gulf and Kuweit, on the southwest by Arabia and on the west by Jordan and Syria. The total area is 171,599 square miles, and the population is more than 6,540,000.

GOVERNMENT

A republic (monarchy overthrown July 14, 1958) under a temporary constitution. Titular head is a 3-man Council of Sovereignty. Lawmaking and executive powers are in hands of cabinet headed by a prime minister.

COMMERCE AND INDUSTRIES

Chief product is oil. The rich soil is now being developed by irrigation. Cotton, wheat, barley, oats, linseed and flax are produced though mostly in the experimental stage. Dates are grown. Principal exports are oil, barley, wheat, wool and dates; imports are textiles, sugar, carpets, tea. The monetary unit of Iraq is the dinar.

COMMUNICATIONS

Railway length is 1,100 miles; roads, about 10,000 miles; 37,800 motor vehicles. There are over 42,000 telephones. One domestic and several foreign airlines. Radio and TV broadcasting.

RELIGION AND EDUCATION

The bulk of the population is Muslim. There are primary and secondary schools. In Baghdad, a university is being organized.

CHIEF TOWNS

Baghdad, the capital, has a population, with suburbs, of about 1,086,000; Mosul, 180,000; Basra, 165,000; Kirkuk, 90,000.

Baghdad

BAGHDAD is one of the world's oldest cities. It has occupied the present site under its present name for some four thousand years. When the Arabs took it over in the latter half of the eighth century A.D., Baghdad was therefore already an old town. The Arabs raised it to an eminence few cities have known. Caliph al-Mansur made it the new capital for the vast Islamic empire then straddling Asia and Africa. He chose the site because of its military importance. "Besides," he said, "here is the Tigris to put us in touch with lands as far as China and bring us all that Syria, al-Raqqah and adjacent lands have to offer."

Al-Mansur's hopes were fulfilled. The old town was planted between and fed by the waters of the Tigris and Euphrates. It was also the crossroads of the caravan routes through southwest Asia. Baghdad served Al-Mansur well. What the old town couldn't provide, furthermore, Al-Mansur would. Some 100,000 architects, craftsmen and laborers, drawn from all over the empire, rebuilt the town in four years. The result was circular in form with double brick walls. A deep moat and a third, innermost wall, rising ninety feet, surrounded the central area. The walls had four equidistant gates from which four highways, starting from the center of the circle, radiated like the spokes of a wheel to the four corners of the empire. The whole formed concentric circles around the caliphal palace, called the Golden Gate because of its gilded entrance.

It is hard for us today, living in such different times, to imagine the lush opulence in which the all-powerful caliphs lived. An Arab historian, Abulfeda, described tenth-century Baghdad as decked out for a state visit: "The caliph's whole army, both horse and foot, was under

NEW RESIDENTIAL UNITS blend modern and traditional. Walled roofs remain, for family use; small windows guard against glare.

...the city of the Arabian Nights

arms, which together made a body of 160,-000 men. His state officers and favorite slaves stood near him in splendid apparel, their belts glittering with gold and gems. Near them were 7,000 eunuchs, 4,000 of them white, the remainder black. The porters, or doorkeepers, were in number 700. Barges and boats with the most superb decorations were seen swimming upon the Tigris. Nor was the palace itself less splendid, in which were hung up 38,000 pieces of tapestry, 12,500 of which were of silk embroidered with gold. The carpets on the floor were 22,000. A hundred lions were brought out, with a keeper to each lion. Among the other spectacles of rare and stupendous luxury was a tree of gold and silver spreading into eighteen large branches, on which, and on the lesser boughs, sat a variety of birds made of the same precious metals, as well as the leaves of the tree. While the machinery affected spontaneous motions, the several birds warbled their natural harmony. Through this scene of magnificence the Greek ambassador was led by the vizir to the foot of the caliph's throne."

In the midst of all this extravagance and waste, genius, as it was later to do during the European Renaissance, flourished. The Arab mind, played upon by ideas drawn from ancient Greece, from India, from China, brought together and preserved this precious heritage. The energy of the Arabs was inexhaustible. Within seventy-five years of Baghdad's rebuilding, they had translated into Arabic the chief philosophical works of Aristotle and the Neoplatonists (a group of thinkers of the early Christian Era), most of the writings of Galen (the Greek physician) and many Persian and Indian scientific works. The importance of such activity to the development of Western culture is hard to exaggerate. The Arabs preserved Greek literature for us. They preserved the teachings of Indian medicine and added discoveries of their own. The Arabs established the first apothecary shops, founded the first school of pharmacy and produced the first pharmacopoeia. The whole body of this wisdom formed the chief guide to medical science in the West from the twelfth to the seventeenth centuries. From the Chinese the Arabs learned how to use the decimal system and how to manufacture writing paper. These arts, too, they refined and passed on to us. The great palaces have crumbled but not these gifts, which we are still using.

It was probably sometime during this period that the tales we know as the Arabian Nights gained wide circulation. Though many of the stories came from India they are associated with Baghdad.

Baghdad reached the apex of its power during the reigns of Harun al-Rashid (786–809) and his son, al-Mamun (813–833). In the middle of that century the Arab leaders shifted the capital to Samarra, seventy miles to the northwest. Despite recurring periods of greatness, Baghdad never scaled the heights again. The real downfall came in 1258 when Hulagu the Mongol and his hordes overran Mesopotamia (modern Iraq). The damage they inflicted is still felt today. The foundation of the Arab empire had been the agricultural wealth of Mesopotamia. The caliphs, to that end, maintained enormous drainage and irrigation projects, some of the canals dating back to Babylonian days. The Mongols deliberately broke down the irrigation system, thus converting a green oasis into a wasteland where only pastoral nomads could eke a living. It is not surprising, therefore, that the modern restoration of

Baghdad should be coupled with a massive plan to undo the Mongols' work and once again water the fields surrounding the city.

That restoration has come only after long years of neglect and foreign domination. From 1258 until the twentieth century, Baghdad was never independent save for the briefest periods. At the beginning of the fifteenth century, it fell under Turkoman domination. In the next century it became part of the Persian kingdom. A traveler described Baghdad in 1538 as "a towne not very greate but very populous and of greate trafficke of strangers for that is the way to Persia, Turkie and Arabia, and frome thence doe goe Caravans for those and other places."

Present-day Baghdad

To see Baghdad as it is today, we might sail up the Tigris River. We pass under several new bridges, the shining spans in striking contrast to the occasional encampments of Bedouins on the banks. Within a few miles of Baghdad, river traffic thickens. The chugging steamer that has brought us from the Persian Gulf threads its way through a maze of craft of all descriptions, and berths at one of the rough wooden jetties. We are in the center of the land of the caliphs, of Sindbad the Sailor, and the peris and genii of which we have read in the Thousand and One Nights.

The site of modern Baghdad is not the one of the caliphs. Their city was on the west bank and now almost all that remains of its glory are some of the royal tombs and the shrine of Zobeidah, the favorite wife of Harun al-Rashid.

Several bridges connect the old city with the present city which is situated on the east bank of the Tigris. Here the buildings straggle along about two miles of the shore and each end is marked by the North and South Gates which were used formerly when the city was protected by a wall. Bright-colored domes and minarets greet our eyes, for Baghdad is still one of the centers of the Shiite sect of Muslims and the faithful come

from afar to worship in these old mosques.

Connecting North and South Gates, a distance of about three miles, is a broad thoroughfare called New Street, today New Republic Street. Begun during World War I it has been extended northward. Many wide avenues now crisscross Baghdad though the most important thoroughfare in the city is still Rashid Street, the center of Baghdad life. The road-building program was begun under the monarchy, and to make way for it many squalid old blocks of buildings were demolished.

Plans for the Future

The Iraqis are determined to turn Baghdad into the show- and marketplace of their state. Much cleaning and rebuilding is being done, in addition to the road program. Some of it began under Faisal II and is being completed by the new republican government under Premier Kassem. Some of it is brand-new. Mud-brick slums have been pushed aside. Clean, sparkling residential areas have sprung up. Drainage schemes have been undertaken, so that the city may spread farther back from the river. Among the new buildings planned and being completed are a railway station, a royal guardhouse, a museum, a new university designed by the American architect Walter Gropius, a library and a tourist hotel. Total cost: at least $6,000,-000. The price is high, to be sure, but at last Baghdad's nearly 1,000,000 residents (at its height, the city held 2,000,-000) can look forward to the future with pride.

Baghdad hopes to become once again a communications center for northern Africa and southwest Asia. It is the junction between the standard-gauge rail line from Syria and Turkey and the meter-gauge lines to Basra and Kirkuk. Thus the city is the center from which roads radiate eastward to Iran, westward across the desert to Syria, Jordan and Israel, northward via Mosul to Turkey and southeastward to Basra. It is also a major air and water port.

Baghdad is now the capital of Iraq, which

TENDING THE VALUABLE SKINS OF KARAKUL LAMBS NEAR BAGDAD

The karakul is a hardy breed of broadtail sheep that thrives in dry regions. Newborn lambs have a tightly curled, glossy fur, sometimes called astrakhan, that is widely used in clothing.

HOW COTTON IS SPUN IN THE LAND OF DATE PALMS AND TURBANS

The climate of Bagdad is so dry that some kinds of factories may be rigged up out-of-doors in a shady spot. Cotton is an important crop in Iraq, and its production employs many people.

239

THE BAGDAD RAILWAY, the most important route of overland transportation between Europe and the Middle East, has been made famous by adventure stories of international intrigue.

BARGES ARE LOADED at Bagdad with goods for export. The small boats will steam down the Tigris River to Basra where their cargoes will be transferred to ocean-going vessels.

was formerly under British mandate. In 1932 the mandate ended and Iraq became independent. Iraq took an active part in founding the Arab League and has been a member of the United Nations since the signing of the UN Charter in 1945. British influence in Iraq, as in most Middle East countries, declined after World War II, though British and American firms still held large interests in Iraqi oil.

From Tomb to Park

Cutting the boulevards begun in the 1950's presented odd problems. Some of the routes ran across what devout Muslims considered sacred ground. In one case the tomb of a Muslim holy man stood in the way. So the progressive mayor at that time decided on a scheme straight out of the Arabian Nights. Under cover of darkness he had a small army of workmen demolish the tomb and then plant trees and turf on the spot. Next morning the citizens of Baghdad found such a lovely park to enhance the new street that not even the most pious Muslims raised a protest.

A large number of the population is Arab but as we go wandering about we shall see also Syrians, Armenians, Indians, Persians, Turks—members of all the tribes and races of the Near and Middle East. The languages used mostly are Arabic and Turkish, and the principal religion is, of course, Islam.

Let us take a walk through the bazaars, where we shall see the life of Baghdad. On market days they are crowded with town and country-folk who come in from the surrounding districts laden with the produce of the field and looms and with various articles made at their homes. All classes are represented, from the rich merchant to the beggar who clamors for alms amid the din of bargainings.

Importance of the Letter-writer

Here and there in the narrow streets, we may see a fortune-teller who for a small sum promises life-long prosperity to his patrons; and the professional letter-writer is also a common sight. He sits cross-legged with paper spread out upon his lap. Clients gather round him and recite documents and letters and the scribe writes it all down. Education is not so universal as in the West, so the professional letter-writer is kept very busy on market day, when the terms of the bargains have to be recorded and deeds of sale drawn up.

The development program launched in the 1950's includes many other projects for Baghdad besides avenues and parks. One building that will probably never be finished is an air-conditioned palace. It was there that King Faisal II was killed early in the morning of July 14, 1958, during the revolt.

Late in the 1950's, Baghdad had five bridges across the Tigris, with two more to follow. Though there was always danger of floods, Baghdad long clung to the riverside because it had poor water-supply and sewer systems. Today there are flood-control dams. At the same time, water mains and sewers are being extended so that eventually, it is hoped, the city will spread back from the river.

A number of place names in the city have been changed since the 1958 revolution: King's Bridge is now Republic Bridge; Ghazi Street, Struggle Street.

Houses Built for Extremes of Climate

The houses in Baghdad are interesting because they are built to meet extremes of climate. From the end of April until the beginning of October the heat is excessive, so the houses are constructed partly underground with windows high enough to admit light and air. The occupants sleep on the roof in summer, retiring to the cellar at sunrise for soon after that time the temperature will rise to as much as 110° Fahrenheit in the shade. During the winter the weather is cold and there are often ice and snow.

Primary and secondary education is free and compulsory, but facilities are extremely inadequate. There are less than two thousand elementary schools. There are fourteen institutions of higher learning, all incorporated in the University of Baghdad, besides some vocational, technical and teacher-training schools.

REPUBLIC BRIDGE, ACROSS THE TIGRIS RIVER

Until July 1958 the graceful span was named for Faisal I, modern Iraq's first monarch. For many years there were only two bridges, of the pontoon type, over the Tigris at Baghdad. Today there are five, three of them modern steel structures, and two more are likely to be built in coming years. Meanwhile the old city is beginning to expand away from the riverbanks.

A MODERN SQUARE IN THE HEART OF THE CITY

The view is taken from a department-store roof. The buildings under construction and the office of the state-owned Iraqi Airways are examples among many of how twentieth-century communication, transportation and technology are changing such ancient cities as Baghdad. For all its age the city has few historic monuments. It was ruthlessly sacked many times.

242

THE ICE-CREAM VENDOR IS A POPULAR FELLOW, EAST AND WEST

Arab children in a street in Bagdad gather eagerly to clamor for a portion of the cooling sweet. Hundreds of years ago ice cream was such a rare delicacy that only kings and emperors could enjoy it, but today it is for everyone. These youngsters would probably enjoy it in cones. Instead, they are eating it from little flat dishes, and the hot sun says, "Hurry."

The schools tend to be nationalistic, that is, they teach the rich history of Iraq's past and try to stimulate the pupils to think about the future of their country. In the campaign against illiteracy nearly 150 tribal schools have been opened and free books are distributed to those students who cannot afford to buy texts.

Many children do not attend the more progressive government schools, but are taught by comparatively ignorant teachers in badly organized, primitive classes. The pupils in such poor schools must sit on the ground at desks made of rough-hewn logs. Some sing their lessons aloud, in an ancient Oriental belief that the mind

243

A PAUSE AND A POSE ON THE WAY TO MARKET IN BAGDAD

With airy nonchalance, the farmers appear quite willing to have their picture taken, while their laden donkey waits patiently. Harun al-Rashid may have walked this byway long ago.

244

A FEAST to celebrate the end of Ramadan, the Muslim month of fasting. Crisp cucumbers, peppers, tomatoes balance the rich dishes swimming in cream or olive oil.

absorbs knowledge through the ears rather than by the eyes.

There is one thing that we do not meet with in Baghdad. This is caste—the distinction between classes that is such a handicap to the people of India. Here any means of livelihood may be adopted, and no one will sneer at a man because of his trade.

Market day reveals typical Middle Eastern dress. The undergarment is usually a long shirt, over which is a close-fitting coat of colored cloth drawn together at the waist by a cord. Above this, if it is cool, there may be a cloak of camel's hair, often with black-and-white stripes. Men in from the hot desert may wear a scarf arranged over the head so that the long ends hang from the shoulders and protect the neck against the rays of the sun. No desert people ever forget the power of the sun.

The food of the people consists of wheat, barley, corn and mutton, and the date is also an important article of diet. It is, in fact, the staff of life of the Arab. The Prophet Mohammed directed all his followers to honor it as they would their parents. Coffee is another thing of which the people are very fond, and the first thing an Arab does in the morning, after he has said the early prayers ordered by his religion, is to take a cup. It is said that coffee was first discovered by an Arab near Baghdad, who one day lighted a fire beneath a wild shrub. A most uncommon and pleasing smell resulted which led to the discovery of the famous beverage. At first it was considered an intoxicant and was forbidden by Islam. However, it quickly became so popular that prohibition failed.

Coffeehouses, usually extending out onto the sidewalk, are found almost everywhere in Baghdad. There the gossips congregate to discuss the news of the day and a great deal of business is accomplished over the cups. As the Baghdadis are strict Muslims they observe the fast of Ramadan, the foremost religious observance of Islam, when a devout Muslim does not even sip water between dawn and sunset. It is at evening then that the coffeeshops are most crowded.

Ramadan is a period of fasting because Muslims believe that the Koran was revealed to Mohammed during this month. Besides the ban on food and drink, no form of material pleasure is allowed. The fast is considered broken even by the fragrance of perfume.

During the hours of complete darkness, eating is permitted, and so the coffeeshops remain open all night. They are gay with lights and other attractions until the coming of dawn, when the fast begins again. While the idle may lessen the severity of the ordeal by turning night into day, its hardships fall heavily upon workers, who must continue their daily labors.

All through Baghdad we shall find evidence of the historic past. Today, however, it is gradually being developed into a prosperous city again.

245

Turkey ... *Anadolu and Trakya*

AN ancient tombstone in an Ankara cemetery bears the epitaph "He died without fighting the Russians." It is a regrettable distinction to the Turks, for their hatred of the Russians, based on centuries of economic and political rivalry, is fierce. During the winter of 1914–15, thirty thousand Russians and Turks slew each other in one of the most terrible battles of World War I. Though it is not the only motive, bitter enmity lends strength to Turkey's alignment with the West in the cold war.

At the same time, Moscow is haunted by the fact that Turkey controls the Dardanelles and the Bosporus, the U.S.S.R.'s only outlet (from the Black Sea) to the major sea lanes. By the Montreux Convention of 1936, Turkey may close the straits if it is at war or threatened with invasion. Otherwise, in peace or war, unarmed merchant ships that are not helping any warring nations have free passage. That these provisions are somewhat contradictory disturbs the Turks not at all; and they blithely ignore all hints from the Soviet Union that it would like to be a partner in guarding the straits.

Three per cent of Turkey's total area lies in Europe—Eastern Thrace or, to the Turks, Trakya. Most of the country, of course, occupies Anatolia or, in Turkish, Anadolu—the historic peninsula of Asia Minor.

Turkey is not overly interested in ties with other Middle Eastern countries. It is far more advanced than most of its neighbors and though Muslim is non-Arabic. The Turks consider the Arabs unstable and politically immature. Moreover, Turkey casts suspicious eyes on Russian aid to such countries as the United Arab Republic.

Kemal Atatürk Westernized Turkey not with a whimper but a bang. It was set well on the road to becoming a modern nation during his presidency, 1923–38. The Government, by and large, has continued his efforts. While the major class division, between peasants and non-peasants, still exists, the line becomes dimmer yearly. A large part of this is

246

THE TWO FACES of Turkey —new and old—show themselves on a street in Ankara.

report, Turkey could both double production and meet future-investment needs in fifteen years. The proposal involves adding 5,583,000 acres to the land under irrigation (to avoid dependence on the scanty rainfall), reducing the acreage devoted to grain by 20 per cent (to prevent further erosion of unsuitable land) and expanding grazing lands by 20 per cent (to conserve the land and provide more meat).

Meanwhile Turkey is pushing ahead on various other projects. Several dams are either completed or under construction that will yield almost 550,000,000 kw-hr of electric power a year. (Between 1948 and 1957 power had already risen from 700,000,000 kw-hr to 3,000,000,000.) A 956-mile pipeline is being built from the Qum field (in Iran) to Iskenderun, and a refinery is going up. New harbors have also been built.

Already, electricity and piped water are reaching many villages. Radios are common even in the most remote areas. Most noticeable change of all, camels are vanishing, replaced by tractors. At a village wedding a rich peasant may provide a whole fleet of tractors for the bride, groom and guests. The greatest impact of American aid on the countryside has been the construction and maintenance of motor highways.

All in all, Turkey seemed to be one of the most stable countries in the Middle East. Offsetting this in the late 1950's was the growing authoritarianism of the Government, in spite of a highly vocal opposition, led by journalists and university students. Nevertheless it was a shock when the Government was overthrown in May 1960. Then a six-man military junta took provisional command, under General Cemel Gursel.

Before it began to crumble late in the seventeenth century, the Ottoman Empire, with Turkey at its heart, was a great power. Under its conqueror-sultans it reached out to embrace all of North Africa, the Balkans east of Vienna, Arabia and other parts of Asia.

The ancestors of the Ottoman Turks, a handful of nomads from central Asia,

due to the spread of education. As the children of peasants learn to read and write, the more intelligent and ambitious move to cities and towns. There a capitalist middle class is emerging. However, the peasants of farms and villages cling rather obstinately to old ways. This is an obstacle to improvement of farm methods. On the other hand it makes the villagers deaf to communist siren songs. Turkey is the only Middle East country that has escaped trouble with local Communists.

Turkey's agriculture is ailing, and this, in turn, affects the country's industrial aims. A 1959 survey by the UN Food and Agricultural Organization proposed a revolution in farming as the basis for one in industry. Its report stated, "A truly heroic program of land use adjustment is required." In most years Turkey must buy vast quantities of food abroad. Even so, masses of the people get barely enough to eat. The usual diet includes only an ounce and a half of meat a day. Yet, according to the

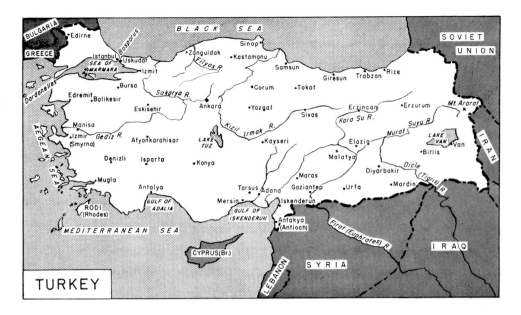

TURKEY

Map labels: BULGARIA, GREECE, BLACK SEA, SOVIET UNION, Edirne, Bosporus, Sinop, Istanbul, Zonguldak, Kastamonu, Uskudar, SEA OF MARMARA, Filyos R., Samsun, Giresun, Trabzon, Rize, Izmit, Bursa, Corum, Tokat, Sakarya R., Dardanelles, Edremit, Balikesir, Eskisehir, Ankara, Yozgat, Erzincan, Erzurum, Mt. Ararat, Sivas, Kara Su R., Suyu R., Manisa, Izmir (Smyrna), Gediz R., Afyonkarahisar, LAKE TUZ, Kizil Irmak R., Kayseri, Elazig, Murat, LAKE VAN, Van, Bitlis, Denizli, Isparta, Konya, Malatya, Dicle (Tigris) R., IRAN, Mugla, Antalya, Maras, Diyarbakir, Mardin, AEGEAN SEA, Tarsus, Adana, Gaziantep, Urfa, Mersin, Iskenderun, RODI (Rhodes), GULF OF ADALIA, GULF OF ISKENDERUN, MEDITERRANEAN SEA, Antakya (Antioch), Firat (Euphrates) R., IRAQ, CYPRUS(Br.), LEBANON, SYRIA

entered Anatolia in the thirteenth century and settled there under their chief, Ertogrul Bey. Anatolia was then in the hands of the Byzantine Greeks and the Seljuk Turks, who had overrun Asia Minor in the eleventh century. By the time Ertogrul and his tribesmen appeared, the once-mighty Byzantine, or Eastern Roman, Empire had shrunk in size and power and was at the mercy of the Seljuks. Its capital, Constantinople, was threatened by Slavs pressing across Thrace. Also by this time the Seljuk Empire had broken up into many jealous factions which were constantly at war with one another or with the fading Byzantine Empire. Ertogrul's nomads made their home between these two fast-decaying powers. Since they were a hardy, energetic people, unspoiled by the wealth and luxury that had weakened their neighbors, they at once began to forge ahead.

Ertogrul's son Osman expanded his holdings and was proclaimed the first sultan of the newly arrived Turks. It is from him that the Turks derived their name of Osmanli or Ottoman Turks, which distinguished them from their Seljuk cousins.

Many of the Seljuk princes rallied under Osman, and soon a small new nation took root in the soil of Anatolia. After Osman's death his son Orkhan, banking on the growing strength of his country, led his warriors across the peninsula of Gallipoli. There they gained a foothold in Europe, which proved to be a fateful event.

The Turkish soldiers who helped to extend the boundaries of the Ottoman Empire were called janizaries. At that time they constituted the best-disciplined fighting force in the world. At first they were recruited by force from among the young sons of Christian subjects. These youths were taught Islam and, in fact, became Turks. Later, children of well-to-do Turkish families were enrolled, for it was an honor to be admitted to the *Ojak* (hearthstone) of the janizaries. With these fearless troops the Ottoman sultans overran the Balkans. Finally, in 1453, Sultan Mohammed (Mehemet) II, called Fatih (the Conqueror), captured Constantinople, thus crushing Byzantium and erasing the old Eastern Roman Empire forever.

Thus, in less than two centuries after they had settled in Anatolia, the Ottoman Turks not only crushed the Eastern Roman Empire but built an empire of their own. As for the Seljuks, they had long ago been absorbed by the Ottomans. Only one power remained in Asia Minor —the Ottoman Empire, with its new capital Constantinople, or Istanbul as the Turks called it.

Successive sultans pushed the empire's frontiers westward and eastward. Under Suleiman the Magnificent, whom the Turks called the Lawgiver, the Ottoman Empire reached the height of its power. It included Hungary, Transylvania and other areas in the Balkans, the Caucasus, Azerbaijan, Mesopotamia and the Arab peninsula. The Sudan and Egypt were also under Turkish dominion, and the Turkish banner had been carried into Ethiopia and Libya. Suleiman's janizaries marched to the gates of Vienna and threatened the city. But Vienna did not fall, and from that time the Turkish tide began to recede.

After the reign of Suleiman the Mag-

nificent, the rising might of Russia and the Austrian Empire threatened the power of the Ottomans. Jealousy and corruption began to undermine the Turkish government. The janizaries became so unruly that Mahmud the Second, in the nineteenth century, had to crush them and disband the corps. The Moslem clergy opposed all reforms that might have saved the empire and sided with the ignorant to keep Turkish lands backward. This happened at a time when the Western world was taking enormous strides in political and social reforms and in the sciences.

Several attempts were made at Westernization, but they could not check the downfall of the Ottoman Empire. The most important period of reform was in the middle of the nineteenth century.

BLACK STAR

DRY AND WARM in his embroidered felt cape, a Turkish shepherd takes his sheep up from the Mediterranean plains to the plateau of the Taurus Mountains for spring pasturage.

HOUSES OF PUMICE are dug from the lava plateau of Cappadocia. The cone in the back-ground is one of many left by erosion of deposits of an extinct volcano in central Turkey.

250

Then a constitutional government was established under a liberal sultan. But when the tyrant Abdul Hamid came to the throne in 1876, there began one of the most despotic periods in the empire's history. For a short while, Abdul Hamid allowed a constitutional government, but tyranny soon returned and lasted until 1908, when the parliamentary constitution was restored. From then until its collapse, the empire was under a form of constitutional monarchy.

The Ottoman Empire allied itself with Germany in World War I and was defeated. In 1918 the Allied armies of occupation moved into Turkish territory to enforce the terms of the armistice. Two years later the victorious powers imposed on the Ottoman Empire the Treaty of Sèvres. It took from the Turks not only the territories they had possessed as an empire but also lands that were purely Turkish in population. These areas were to be divided among Great Britain, France, Italy and Greece. Under the leadership of Mustafa Kemal, the Turks unfurled the banner of independence and, after a grim struggle, ousted the foreign troops of occupation.

Like the people of the United States, the Turks call their struggle for freedom the War of Independence. It began in 1920 and officially ended on July 24, 1923, when the Treaty of Lausanne was signed and the world recognized the new Turkish state. When, on October 29, 1923, Turkey became a republic, Kemal was elected its first president.

As a first step toward Westernizing his country, Kemal accomplished the seemingly impossible—the separation of church and state in a Moslem country. The sultanate and the caliphate were abolished, and so were the veil and the traditional

BLACK STAR

YOUNG GIRLS in some sections of southern Turkey wear an elaborate braided hair-do and take pride in the length of their tresses. After marriage, a scarf covers the braids.

POURING OUT YOGHURT, prepared from ewe's milk. Yoghurt may be thick or thin and is something like cottage cheese. It is delicious served, say, with fruit or sliced cucumbers.

headgear, the fez. The schools were taken out of the hands of the religious authorities, and a program of free, compulsory education was set up. The Turkish language was partially purged of Persian and Arabic words. The Latin alphabet was adopted instead of Arabic script, and adult Turks were taught to read and write the new letters. International calendar, clock and metric systems were also introduced; and various European civil, penal and commercial codes replaced the old Moslem law. Women were freed, given the right to vote and permitted election to the Grand National Assembly. Everyone acquired a family name. Kemal's was Atatürk, which means "father of the Turks." The Constitution of the Turkish Republic summarizes the change from the feudal estate: "Every Turk is born free and free he lives."

Atatürk realized that, in order to enjoy equal standing with European nations, Turkey must become an industrial country. He initiated a program of economic and technological development which attempted to rush through centuries of Western evolution within a few decades. Turkey, straddling East and West, definitely stepped into the Western world.

Turkey in Europe and Asia

Turkey is divided into two parts by the small Sea of Marmara and the narrow straits of the Bosporus and the Dardanelles. The smaller European part is bounded by Greece and Bulgaria. The larger part occupies the Anatolian Peninsula in Asia. It is bordered by the Black Sea on the north, the Soviet Union and Iran on the east, the Mediterranean Sea, Syria and Iraq on the south, and the Aegean Sea on the west. Turkey is about 1,000 miles long and 350 miles wide and covers 296,185 square miles—an area larger than the state of Texas.

Turkey lies in about the same latitude as Spain. Along the Black Sea, the Pontic Mountains rise steeply to heights of 7,000 feet in the west and 12,000 feet in the east. On the south, the Taurus and Anti-Taurus ranges are just about as high. Between the mountains lies the interior plateau, parts of which are desert. For the inhabitants of this plateau, life is a ceaseless struggle against the forces of nature. The land yields good hard grain and provides pasture for the goats that produce the soft Ankara wool (Angora mohair), which derives its name from Ankara Province. But long, cold winters, with snow lingering into May, and dry summers, with frequent droughts, are a constant menace to man and beast as well as to the land and its yield.

Ancient City with a Modern Air

Ankara, the capital of Turkey since 1923, is about two hundred miles southeast of Istanbul on the interior plateau. Although it is a very ancient city, its appearance today is that of a modern metropolis, with broad boulevards, fine new buildings and spacious parks.

It is only near the coastline of the peninsula that the land and climate of Turkey become more kindly. The mountains that fringe the central plateau are, in turn, fringed by a narrow strip of green and fertile plain, where there is a variety of climates and products. On the Black Sea coast, there is rain and dense vegetation through all the four seasons. Istanbul, which sits astride the cross currents of the Black Sea in the north and the Mediterranean in the south, often becomes as cold in winter as Toronto or New York, but in summer it enjoys dry and breezy days.

Mild Climate, Fertile Soil

South of Istanbul, on the Aegean Sea coast, is the part of Turkey that faces Greece, and the climate is much like that of Italy and Spain. The winters are mild and the summers hot and dry. It is a fertile land of olive trees, figs and grapes. Here are the remains of ancient cities, such as Pergamum and Ephesus. This is one of the country's main export regions, in the midst of which stands modern Izmir—ancient Smyrna—the second largest city of Turkey and one of the important cities of both contemporary Mediterranean civilization and the early world.

Farther south, in the region of Adana, around the town of Tarsus where St. Paul

TURKISH TOBACCO, collected in great baskets, begins its journey to world markets.

was reared, the coastal strip broadens into the Plains of Cilicia, an area of large-scale agriculture. Here, in a subtropical climate, cotton, sugar cane, oranges and bananas flourish.

The vast majority of Turks are producers of food and other agricultural products. The agricultural resources of Tur-

key are varied and rich in quality rather than quantity. Despite its rough climate, the central plateau throughout the course of history has been renowned for its wheat. Nine out of ten cultivated acres in Turkey are devoted to cereals, and wheat forms about half of the total grain production. It is an important item in Turkish domestic economy because wheat bread is the most important staple food of both the village and town folk. Barley, rye and oats are other cereals grown in the central plateau. All of these play a large part in the domestic economy, but in Turkey's foreign trade other products are more important.

Crops Raised for Export

In the regions around Izmir on the Aegean coast and in the Samsun and Trebizond areas on the Black Sea, one finds the crops that, from the standpoint of quality, enjoy the highest reputation in the markets of the world.

Tobacco ranks first among these choice products. The United States, the largest cigarette producer in the world, is also the greatest purchaser of Turkish tobacco, which is the country's leading export. This tobacco is used for blending purposes to lighten the color, to add flavor and aroma, and to increase the burning qualities of cigarettes. Almost all cigarettes made in the United States contain from 4 to 8 per cent Turkish tobacco.

Raisins and figs—particularly dried figs—are the next most important of Turkey's high quality agricultural products for export. Opium-poppy seed, olives, olive oil, flax, hemp, sesame, spices and attar of roses are also valuable export items.

With over 40 per cent of the land available for grazing, livestock raising is an important aspect of Turkish rural life. Some 60,000,000 sheep, mohair-producing goats, cattle, horses and donkeys are raised; sheep account for about half that number.

The principal minerals are coal, lignite, chrome, iron, salt and copper. Other minerals being mined include manganese, mercury, antimony, asbestos, sulfur and

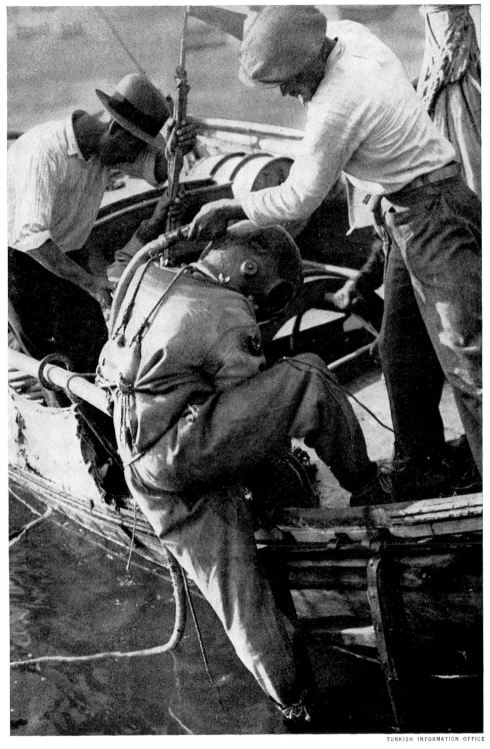

HIGH-QUALITY SPONGES are found in Turkish waters, where they are gathered from May until about October. Many Mediterranean sponge divers today use modern equipment.

SLENDER MINARETS of mosques lift their white spires above Bursa (or Brusa), near the Sea of Marmara. The garden city was the residence of many Turkish sultans.

emery. Turkey has a virtual monopoly on meerschaum, the white or cream-colored mineral used in making fine tobacco pipes. Oil fields in the southeastern part of the country are considered promising and are being developed by domestic and foreign private capital.

In consumer goods, textiles, sugar, paper, leather, shoes, food processing and alcoholic beverages rank highest. Major heavy industries include iron and steel, metalwork, cement, building materials and chemicals. Practically all of these industries have been established within the last two decades.

Education in Turkey is compulsory and free in the government-operated schools between the ages of seven and sixteen. The average citizen of today is interested in learning. In 1923, when the Republic was founded, only one out of every ten people knew how to read and write. Today five out of every ten are literate. There are many primary schools as well as universities in Istanbul and in the capital city of Ankara. Students from poor families are given scholarships which enable them to attend both high schools and colleges. Hundreds of foreign students attend Turkish universities, and many Turkish students are enrolled in North American educational institutions. Technical and vocational schools are well attended. A great many students in Turkey's universities are women, and throughout modern Turkey one finds an increasing number of women doctors, lawyers and judges.

A person who has never been within Turkish boundaries probably pictures the Turks as wearing baggy trousers and red fezzes. To him, Turkish women may still

THE BEST SMYRNA FIGS are grown about sixty miles inland from Turkey's Aegean coast. The figs, ripened and partially dried on the tree, are gathered after they have fallen.

KUTAHYA in western Turkey is noted for its decorative ceramics and tiles. These vessels are being made by hand on a potter's wheel. Notice the beautifully fluted rims.

be hiding themselves behind a mysterious veil. But the minute he steps on Turkish soil, he learns that the picturesque costumes and customs he expected to find disappeared with the Ottoman Empire. The fez and the veil are no more. He will find blondes and brunettes and even freckled redheads. Turkey has not been the bridge between East and West for thousands of years without showing it. People of all races, creeds and cultures have intermingled there, but the dark-haired, swarthy Mediterranean type is predominant.

The same person who expected to see costumes of an earlier day may be surprised to learn that Turkey has adopted such Western sports as football and base-

BLACK STAR

AN OLD COVERED WAGON serves for a holiday ride into the countryside near Istanbul. There are many picturesque spots along both shores of the Bosporus north to the Black Sea.

AN EARLIER DAY'S GRANDEUR. Among the older structures remaining in Ankara is a former palace, set among formal gardens. The building now houses a government department.

ball. Horse racing has long been one of the national pastimes. Every year a field day is held in which Turkish youths participate in various sports and exercises.

Turkey's main aim in her foreign policy is to preserve her independence and territorial integrity. Since the foundation of the Republic, she has constantly cultivated the friendship of all countries touching her borders. With the majority of them, such as Greece, Iraq and Iran, she has succeeded in basing her relations on sound principles of co-operation and understanding.

Since the fall of 1939, following the outbreak of World War II, Turkey has had a treaty of mutual friendship with Great Britain and France. The war also cemented friendly ties with the United States, and in 1947 the Truman Doctrine of military aid to nations threatened by the spread of communism resulted in a great strengthening of Turkish defenses. Relations have been developed with Italy during the postwar period; in 1950 Tur-

key and Italy signed a treaty of friendship. Turkey is taking active part in the military planning of the North Atlantic Treaty Organization for the defense of the Mediterranean. She signed the defensive alliance with Greece and Yugoslavia in 1953.

Turkey is a member of the United Nations and of all its auxiliary organizations, such as the World Health Organization, the International Labor Organization and the Food and Agricultural Organization. In July 1950, she responded to the United Nations' appeal for troops to resist aggression in Korea. In the Korean conflict, the Turkish brigade quickly won the respect and admiration of its allies.

Ties with the Western World

Geographically, historically, politically, economically and culturally, Turkey today is a European country. Her geographical status in Europe is determined not so much by her European territory as by the fact that the Turkish Peninsula has turned its back on the Asian continent. The mountains that rise on the eastern borders of the country increasingly open up toward the Mediterranean and southeastern Europe as they fan out into fertile western valleys. Historically Turkey has been a part of Europe since the conquest of Istanbul in 1453. It would be very hard to name any event in the last five hundred years of European history that has not influenced Turkey or that has not been directly influenced by

her. Since the founding of the Republic in 1923, Turkish political thought and institutions have been based on Western European political philosophy. Turkey's place in the Organization for European Economic Cooperation shows that her trade and commerce are part and parcel of European economy. Her social reforms since the 1920's have united Turkish everyday life with that of Western Europe.

By SENIHA TASKIRANEL

TURKEY: FACTS AND FIGURES

THE COUNTRY

In the eastern Mediterranean, between Europe and Asia, it occupies the greater portion of Asia Minor and a small part of the Balkan Peninsula. It is bounded on the northwest by Greece and Bulgaria, on the north by the Black Sea, and on the northeast by the U.S.S.R.; on the east by Iran; on the south by Iraq, Syria and the Mediterranean; on the west by the Aegean Sea. Area, 296,185 sq. mi.; population, 25,000,000.

GOVERNMENT

In 1921 the Grand National Assembly at Ankara drew up a constitution which declared that all sovereignty belonged to the people and that the legislative and executive power was vested in the hands of this Assembly representing the people. The term "Ottoman Empire" was abolished and the country officially designated Turkey. A republic was proclaimed in 1923, and Mustafa Kemal became first president. In 1924 a new constitution provided for election of the Assembly every four years. All citizens over 22, including women, may vote. Executive power has been exercised since May 1960 by a six-man military junta, headed by General Cemel Gursel.

COMMERCE AND INDUSTRIES

Agriculture is the main occupation of the people. A land reform bill, passed in 1945, distributed large tracts of agricultural land among peasants who had none. Despite the fact that two thirds of the population is rural, only about 20 per cent of the fertile land is cultivated and irrigation is underdeveloped. The rich mineral

deposits also need further development. Main products are cotton, wheat and other grains, tobacco, figs and raisins, mohair, filbert nuts, olives and olive oil, coal, copper, iron and chrome. Principal exports include tobacco, grains, chrome ore, copper, dried fruits, nuts, opium and skins. Imports chiefly machinery, textiles, vehicles, iron and steel products, mineral oils and chemicals. Monetary unit, the Turkish lira.

RELIGION AND EDUCATION

Most of the people are Muslims, though Islam is not a state religion. Primary education is compulsory. State schools, which include primary, secondary and preparatory schools, are free. Total school enrollment in a recent year, 2,900,000. There are 6 state universities: Istanbul, Ankara, Istanbul Technical, Aegean (in Izmir), Middle East Technical and (opened 1958 in Erzurum) Atatürk.

COMMUNICATIONS

Roads, 21,700 mi. all-weather; railroads, state-owned and operated, 4,800 mi.; 76,000 motor vehicles; in a recent year, Turkish State Airways, Inc., flew 80,800,000 passenger-miles; merchant marine, 668,000 tons; 4 radio stations, government-run; 1,097,965 radio sets; 173,730 telephones, about 87% automatic; 356 daily newspapers in Turkish (50 in Istanbul, 16 in Ankara); 237 motion-picture houses.

CHIEF CITIES

Ankara, capital, 460,000; Istanbul, 1,215,000; Izmir, 290,000; Adana, 175,000; Bursa, 132,000; Eskisehir, 125,000.

RUSH-HOUR TRAFFIC at the Galata end of the Galata Bridge. Across the Golden Horn the minarets of the Süleymaniye Mosque mark Istanbul's old quarter.

Istanbul

...city of two continents

THE oldest part of Istanbul lies on a triangular peninsula, washed on the south by the waters of the Sea of Marmara, on the east by the strait of the Bosporus and on the north by the Golden Horn, an inlet of the Bosporus.

This storied city, so long known to the Western world as Constantinople, is today a bustling metropolis. And like every other large modern center, it has a vexing traffic problem. This spurred the Turkish Government to launch a drastic development plan in the late 1950's. The old-fashioned streetcars are gone and hundreds of buildings have been torn down. In their place, buses rumble along wide boulevards and new highways skirting the Bosporus. More than 100,000 trees have been planted. At the same time, the city's priceless historic buildings are being carefully preserved. A number of modern hotels, some luxurious indeed, have also been erected. The most enticing face the city's fringe of wide, sandy beaches on the Sea of Marmara and the Black Sea. All of this is making Istanbul one of the most popular tourists' centers in the Mediterranean.

But, alas, if a visitor asks for the famous "Turkish coffee," his waiter is likely to answer with a tired smile, "Kahve yok." (No coffee.) Coffee has never thrived in Turkish soil but was imported, in large quantities, for centuries. Around 1955, however, when foreign exchange ran low, the Turkish Government stopped the import of what had become the national beverage. Today, most Turks sip *chay* (tea), which grows on the hillsides along the Black Sea. Efforts are being made, nonetheless, to find a kind of coffee shrub that *will* grow in Turkey.

In 1958, two of Istanbul's best-known institutions of learning merged—Robert College and the American College for Girls. Robert College was established in 1863, the work of the Reverend Cyrus Hamlin, an American Protestant clergyman. The college was named for Christopher Robert, of New York, its chief supporter. It was never a missionary institution and from the beginning its doors have been open to Muslim and Christian young men alike. The girls' college was founded in 1871. The two beautiful campuses are only three miles apart and overlook the Bosporus.

Because of its peculiar situation, Istanbul's climate in several respects recalls not only that of the Mediterranean but also that of central Europe and of the Black Sea. There are marked changes of temperature according to the season and the year. The prevailing winds of this zone are from the north. When

262

they blow from the northwest in winter, they bring frigid weather and snow. Winter is a short season, however, and spring comes in abruptly. In spring and autumn the wind usually blows from the south and is often followed by rain. In summer the sky is clear and the climate mild owing to northeasterly breezes. From every point of view, the best season in Istanbul is the autumn, which is long and beautiful.

The Golden Horn is a narrow fiord that cuts European Istanbul in two—Galata and Pera on the north and old Istanbul on the south. From Saray Point, at the entrance to the Bosporus, the inlet is about five miles long. The broadest part is between the districts of Kasimpasa and Cibali, where it is 770 yards wide. It is said to owe its ancient name, Chrysokeras, meaning "golden horn," to the resemblance of its outline to a bull's horn. But others hold that it owes its name to its great wealth in fish. It is a unique natural harbor, almost made to order for shipping. The waterway is unaffected by tides and can take vessels of deep draft.

Pouring through the Bosporus, which is seventeen miles long, the waters of the Black Sea divide the great continents of Asia and Europe from each other. These waters also divide the whole of Istanbul in another way. Like a river, they flow between the European and Asiatic parts of modern Istanbul. About halfway along the rushing Bosporus there is a mile and a quarter stretch of water called the Kanal. At either side of the narrowest part of the Kanal, 605 yards, where Europe and Asia come closest, there are medieval fortifications: Rumeli Hisari (Castle of Europe) and Anadolu Hisari (Castle of Anatolia).

For the Byzantines, the Bosporus had only military importance and was neglected. But under Turkish rule the natural beauty of both shores was more appreciated. Villas, gardens and castles were laid out along the sparkling waters of the strait. Among the most picturesque of the old structures still remaining are the palace of Beylerbey on the Anatolian shore and the fortresses of Rumeli and Anadolu mentioned earlier.

A ride of only ten minutes on a ferryboat across the Bosporus takes you from old Istanbul to the Anatolian coast and its lovely summer resorts. Here, also, is the Istanbul district of Uskudar (Scutari). Once it, too, was a summer resort, and its aging houses and cobbled streets still have much of their old charm. The section is rich in Turkish monuments, and the Karaca Ahmet cemetery with its cypress trees is a lovely spot.

263

Within a short distance of Istanbul, scattered like jewels on the Sea of Marmara are the Adalar (the Islands, or the Princes Islands). There are nine islands in all; the most important are Kinali (Proti), Burgaz (Antigoni), Heybeli (Khalki) and Buyuk (Prinkipo). The last one is especially lovely, with its dreamlike villas nestling mid pine groves, and its elaborate gardens.

No one knows exactly when Istanbul was founded. The Roman historian Pliny, however, wrote that in the ninth century B.C. a small settlement named Lygos existed on what is now Sarayburnu.

Advice from the Delphic Oracle

A more certain date is 658 B.C. That year the Megarians (Greeks of the city of Megara), wishing to found a colony, followed the advice of the Delphic oracle and built a city on Sarayburnu. They called it Byzantium, supposedly from the name of their leader, Byzas. The city flourished and expanded, and became the object of numerous attacks and invasions at the same time.

In 513 B.C., the Persian King Darius I crossed the strait and occupied Byzantium, as part of his campaign against the Scythians. Persian domination ended in 478 B.C., when the Spartans under Pausanias colonized the city. Later Athens and Sparta disputed possession of Byzantium. Philip of Macedon besieged the city in 340 B.C. It fell into the hands of Alexander the Great, Philip's son. On Alexander's death, the small states founded by his generals, Byzantium among them, fought among themselves. At length it became a self-governing city under Roman rule.

Because the city had taken sides against him, the Emperor Septimius Severus razed it to the ground in A.D. 193–95 but rebuilt it shortly afterward.

There were now many conflicts within the Roman Empire, partly in regard to religion. The city of Rome was still largely pagan. This is one reason why the Emperor Constantine I, after he was converted to Christianity, made Byzantium his capital, on May 11, 330. Under him the city was enlarged and renamed Constantinople (City of Constantine). In 395 the Empire was permanently divided into Eastern and Western parts; and Constantinople became the capital of the Eastern, or Byzantine, Empire.

For several centuries thereafter, it was besieged in turn by Huns, Goths, Ostrogoths, Bulgarians, Slavs and, in the seventh and eighth centuries, by Muslim Arabs. However, the rapidly expanding city was strongly fortified by Theodosius II (408–450); and in 507–12 the Emperor Anastasius I built the Long Walls extending from Silivri (about forty miles from the city) to the Black Sea Coast. Justinian I (483–565) built further fortifications in Thrace to safeguard the city.

Ebu Eyyib Halid Ibn-i Zeyd, at whose house the prophet Mohammed stayed following his flight from Mecca to Medina, took part in one of the Arab sieges and was killed before the walls of the city in 668. For centuries his grave was venerated by the Byzantine people and became famous as a place where they went to pray for rain. After the capture of Constantinople by the Turks, in 1453, a big tomb was built over the grave—a tomb that today is the heart of the locality known as Eyup.

Early in the thirteenth century, Constantinople was in the hands of the Crusaders, who set up various Latin kingdoms on Byzantine soil. At the same time there was large-scale destruction of the city and many landmarks vanished.

The Historic Siege of 1453

Meanwhile, a new Greek empire formed at nearby Iznik developed with great speed. After prolonged and fierce battles, its ruler succeeded, on July 15, 1261, in capturing Constantinople. The city failed, however, to regain its former magnificence. It now became subject to pressure from the Ottoman Turks. Finally, on May 29, 1453, after a siege that lasted fifty-three days, Sultan Fatih Mehmet (Fatih means Conqueror)—or Mohammed II—captured Constantinople.

ISTANBUL UNIVERSITY is on the edge of Beyazit Meydan. This inviting square, with its fountains, is in the Latin Quarter, a part of the most ancient section of the city.

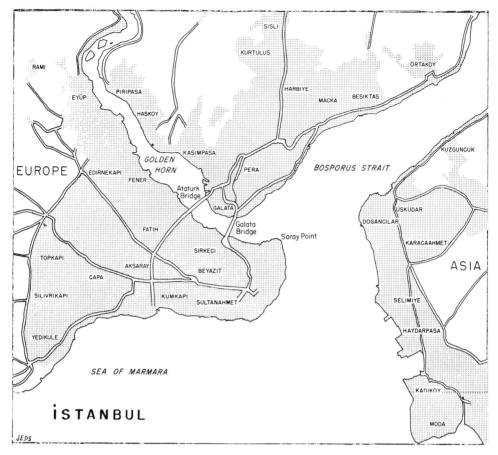

Thus it became the capital of the Ottoman Empire. Sultan Fatih Mehmet's conquest was an amazing feat. He hauled seventy-two ships of his fleet from the Bosporus overland down to Kasimpasa on the Golden Horn, thus outflanking the chains that had been strung across the narrow Bosporus to keep the Turkish vessels out. When the news of this feat came, despair fell upon the people of the doomed city, yet they resisted stubbornly for four more weeks. But after the general assault of May 29, the city was forced to yield.

The capture of Constantinople (now to be known by its Turkish name of Istanbul) by the Ottoman Turks is generally regarded as a climax in history. With it the Renaissance, or rebirth of learning, that had slowly been developing now took on a swifter pace. When Constantinople fell, scholarly Greeks fled, with many tokens of a bygone culture, to Italy. Besides this, the situation of the city had

made it a key point on the old trade routes between the Orient and the Occident. Consequently, the Italian states, since their trade was now in danger, supported those seeking other routes to the Far East and thus opened the way to the discovery of America.

As the Turkish capital, a new life opened for Istanbul. The culture of Islam, including the beautiful works of Muslim craftsmen, began to appear. Libraries were established. Scholars and artists of all races were encouraged. Even at this early date, there was concern for the needy, and free kitchens were opened for them.

After the Egyptian campaign of Sultan Selim in 1517, the already great importance of Istanbul was enhanced by the fact that it became the seat of the Caliphate. Also, as the Ottoman Empire rose, so did Istanbul grow and prosper, becoming the greatest center of learning and the arts

266

and commerce in the Islamic world. Graced with numerous masterpieces of Turkish architecture, such as monuments, palaces, mosques, public baths, madrasahs (theological colleges), villas and so on, Istanbul expanded far beyond the boundaries of the old Byzantine city. However, Byzantine monuments and works of art were preserved with meticulous care.

After the first World War, the Turkish people won freedom for themselves and complete independence of any foreign power, under the leadership of Atatürk. When the Turkish Republic was proclaimed in 1923, Ankara (in Anatolia) became the capital. But Istanbul was in no way neglected by the republican government.

Istanbul, which for 467 years was the center of the Ottoman Empire, is today a vilayet (province) of the Turkish Republic. However, its historic riches, its culture, trade, taxable value, attraction for foreign visitors, its industries—all remain of great importance.

In regard to architecture and archaeology, Istanbul is unique. For 1,600 years it was in turn the capital of Roman, Byzantine and Ottoman empires, so almost everywhere there are historic structures. Exhibits that display the old civilizations as well as the magnificence of the Ottoman Empire are to be seen in the Istanbul museums. Their collections are priceless.

Although life in modern Istanbul is quite different from what it was in the past, the city is still evocative of the

PIX

HOTELS, STORES and other buildings in the modern part of Istanbul are often built with pillared arcades at street level. The thoroughfare is nonetheless quite Western-looking.

THE BLUE MOSQUE is the only one in the world with six minarets. It was built in the seventeenth century, and the interior is adorned with exquisite tiles in soft shades of blue.

HAGIA SOPHIA, architectural gem erected under Byzantine emperors. The name means "holy wisdom." Originally a church, today it is a museum, filled with priceless treasures.

CHARLES D'EMERY, MANUGIAN STUDIOS

EARLY MORNING HAUL. The waters that flow past Istanbul teem with finny creatures. This is particularly true of the Golden Horn, perhaps so named because of its wealth in fish.

legendary East. At every step, one is confronted by history. Yet old and new stand side by side in delightful and harmonious contrast.

Hagia Sophia, the glory of Byzantine art, was first a Christian church, then a mosque and in recent times has become a museum. (Hagia Sophia means "holy wisdom"; to the Turks it is Aya Sophia.)

It is one of the noblest buildings inspired by religious faith in the world. As architecture, it is on a par with St. Peter's, in Rome, or St. Paul's, in London.

Originally built by Constantine, in the year 347, Hagia Sophia was destroyed by fire in 404. Justinian the Great had the present structure built on the old site between 532 and 552.

AN ANCIENT FIRE TOWER overlooks the courtyard of Bayezit Mosque, in the heart of old Istanbul. There are several such towers; fire must have been a threat from very early times.

THE GORGEOUS INTERIOR of the Blue, or Sultan Ahmet, Mosque. As one looks up toward
the great dome, the eye is enthralled by the intricate, flowing designs worked out in blue tiles.

271

THE MEDIEVAL TOWERS of Rumeli Hisari (Castle of Europe) are on the European side of the narrowest part of the Bosporus. In the historic siege of 1453, the city's defenders strung

chains across the racing waters from this castle to Anadolu Hisari (Castle of Anatolia) on the Asiatic shore. The Turks, however, outflanked the chains by dragging ships overland,

FRESH FRUIT AND VEGETABLES for sale along a cobbled alleyway. The produce is an enticing blend of colors and fragrances—figs and dates, oranges, lemons and succulent greens.

The magnificent pile of Hagia Sophia covers an area of about 75,000 square feet. Within it gives the impression of being one vast domed space, though the details are actually intricate. At ground level there are 40 great columns and on the raised gallery section 67 more. Some of these columns are of dark green marble, and others are of dark red porphyry. The massive central dome, which seems to float without visible support, is 180 feet above the ground. The buttresses that keep the structures erect today were built by the Turkish architect Sinan the Great. Among the building's priceless treasures are the exquisite mosaics, dating from the fourth to the fourteenth centuries, on the floor, vaults and domes. Since 1935, when Hagia Sophia became a museum, extensive work has been done to uncover and restore its masterpieces of Byzantine art to their original beauty.

Rumeli Hisari, the famous fortifications on the European shore of the Bosporus, was constructed in 1452 in the amazingly short time of three months, by order of Sultan Mehmet the Conqueror. He was then getting ready to lay siege to Constaninople. It was from Rumeli Hisari that the chain meant to thwart him was stretched across the strait to Asia. From far back in the mists of time, the place where Europe and Asia almost touch has been called the most beautiful on earth. As the light is caught in the sparkling waters of the Bosporus, there is an ever changing interplay of color.

Istanbul is famous for its ancient cisterns, or reservoirs, for the supply of water. They are enormous underground structures, their roofs upheld by countless columns. The Sunken Cistern is also known as the Yerebatan Sarayi, or Sunken Palace, or the Basilica Cistern. It was constructed by that great builder, the Emperor Justinian, in the sixth century. One of the largest of the Byzantine cisterns, it is 154 yards long by 77 yards wide. It has 336 columns, each about 26.5 feet high. It is the only one of the old Byzantine cisterns that still contains water, which is brought from reservoirs in the forest of Belgrade to the northwest. Electric lights have been installed in this cistern, and it is possible to ride through in a rowboat.

The Cistern of a Thousand and One Columns is said to have been constructed by a great Roman dignitary named Philoxenus, one of the senators who followed Constantine to his new capital, though some historians give Justinian the credit. This is the biggest cistern of all, designed to contain more than 7,000,000,-000 gallons of water. Inside, it is 220 feet long and 184 feet wide. Actually there are not a thousand and one columns, but only 224—2 feet in diameter, arranged in 15 rows, and all identical. Light is admitted to this cistern through 11 air holes. There is a small entrance.

Though the ancient Hippodrome has vanished, it was once one of the city's most impressive structures. It was first laid out by the Emperor Septimius Severus in 196. Here the people wit-

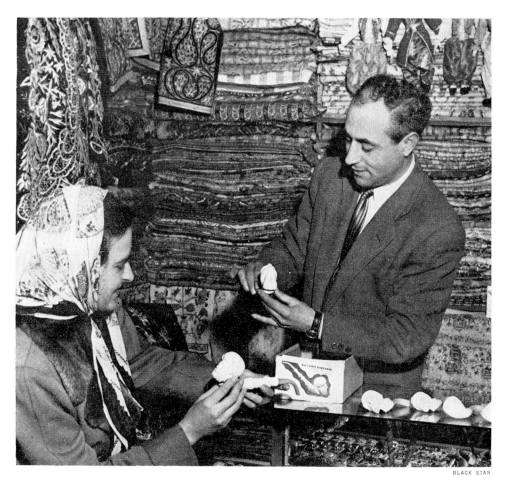

BLACK STAR

MEERSCHAUM PIPES, brocades, tapestries—all at a single shop in the Covered Bazaar. Most of the world's meerschaum—a fine claylike mineral—is mined in Turkey, near Eskisehir.

ANCIENT GRAVES are scattered all over Istanbul. Long ago, noted men were buried beside the institutions they had founded. Today such graves may be in the midst of busy markets.

THE GOLDEN HORN, looking toward the north shore. An arm of the Bosporus, the Horn cuts through the European part of Istanbul. Right center is the fifth-century Galata Tower. The area around it had foreign colonies at an early date and is still the city's most cosmopolitan section.

THE GALATA BRIDGE sweeps across the Golden Horn just above its entrance into the Bosporus. Connecting the ancient and modern areas of the city, the span carries heavy traffic.

EXHIBITION HALL, built to display the great variety of Turkish products and to attract foreign trade. Since World War II, Turkey's commerce with Western Europe has increased.

ON THE FERRY across the Bosporus between European and Asiatic Istanbul. The ride takes only twenty minutes. Turkish newspapers are printed in Roman rather than Arabic letters.

MILES OF SHORE along the Golden Horn and the Bosporus provide delightful settings for homes. In some places the houses are built right at the water's edge with only a narrow footpath in front. Dwellings atop the cliffs offer the added charm of long views.

nessed games, including the chariot races that were their favorite pastime. The noble Hippodrome, with all the astonishing wealth of decoration lavished upon it, saw its best days in the reigns of Constantine the Great and Theodosius II. On the site today are the German Fountain (the gift of Kaiser Wilhelm II, in 1895), the Mosque of Sultan Ahmet, the Cadastral Office and the School of Economics and Commerce.

The Serene Blue Mosque

The Sultan Ahmet Mosque, a seventeenth-century masterpiece of Turkish religious architecture, is also known as the Blue Mosque. Its serene, lovely interior is adorned with azure tilework. It was completed in 1617, after eight years of work under architect Sedefkâr Mehmet Agha. The Blue Mosque is near the site of the ancient Hippodrome, facing Hagia Sophia, from which it is separated by a landscaped square. The mosque covers an area 208 by 235 feet. Surmounting it is a central dome 110 feet in diameter, 8 feet more than the diameter of the great dome of Hagia Sophia. The outline of this fine mosque, with its 6 slim minarets —it is the only mosque in the world that has 6—is a specially wonderful sight from the sea. Attached to the mosque are a madrasah (theological school), imaret (free kitchen) and other social and cultural institutions which were founded by Sultan Ahmet.

Towering over the third of the seven hills on which Istanbul is built, the Süleymaniye Mosque is one of the most magnificent works of Sinan, greatest of all Turkish architects. It is considered one of the five noblest religious edifices in the world. The mosque was completed in 1557, and its great central dome stands at a height of 174 feet and has a diameter of 105 feet. There is a series of smaller domes, each of which is 75 feet in diameter, at a height of 131 feet above the ground. The interior (207 by 226 feet) is illuminated by 138 windows. Matchless marble paves the courtyard of the Süleymaniye, which is circled by 24 pink-and-white marble columns. Con-

sidered the most glorious of any building in Istanbul, Süleymaniye has a symmetrical beauty on the outside as well as within. When it was finished the Sultan handed a golden key to Sinan so that the architect himself might open the mosque, a gracious tribute to the genius of the architect.

The Yeni (New) Mosque is a masterpiece of Turkish architecture of the seventeenth century. Situated on the old Istanbul side of the Galata Bridge, which spans the Golden Horn, its tier upon rising tier of domes dominates the skyline. These domes are supported by long galleries of marble columns. The interior is a treasure house of priceless tilework in every imaginable shade of green and blue. Seen in the soft light that sifts through the picturesque windows, the soothing colors help to create an atmosphere of unequalled peace and serenity.

The Mosque of Bayezit, in the middle of the square of the same name, is the oldest and least changed of any Istanbul mosque since its construction. It was completed in 1506 by the architect Hayrettin Aga, and the work took five years. In this mosque the great dome is supported by four stout columns and has four great arches, each of which supports two half-domes. Two of the arches are filled in with sculptured walls.

Into the Covered Bazaar

The Covered Bazaar is one of Istanbul's most extraordinary landmarks, and its like can hardly be seen today even in any other Oriental city. Actually the bazaar itself is a vast roofed city, divided into districts. One such is the old Cloth Market, which was built by Mehmet the Conqueror in 1461. It was enlarged in the reign of Süleyman the Lawgiver, when much timberwork was added. Visitors enter the maze of twisting streets by way of thirteen enormous wrought-iron gates, which are locked at night. Even on the hottest day, the passageways are cooled by breezes and drafts. Unhappily, this fact adds to the danger of fire. In the sixteenth and seventeenth centuries, the bazaar was severely damaged by fires and earthquakes. On July

HAMMERED COPPERWARE for the bazaars, where such utensils are sold by the hundreds. There are skilled Turkish artisans in many fields. Some have a special gift for work in metal.

282

10, 1894, it was completely burned down after a violent earthquake. Four years later, however, it was rebuilt. One of the worst fires in the twentieth century (November 24, 1954) destroyed four thousand shops. In a little more than a year, however, they were restored.

The Topkapu (or Seraglio) Palace, the residence of the Ottoman Turkish sultans from 1472 to 1853, is today a museum. "Seraglio" refers to its former women's quarters. The treasures it holds cover nearly five centuries of Turkish culture. In its four vast wings there are oil portraits of the Ottoman Sultans, a fabulous collection of jewels, beautiful fabrics and hand embroideries from the sixteenth to the eighteenth century, Turkish tiles, the most remarkable collection of Chinese porcelains in the world (six thousand items dating from the ninth to the thirteenth century), Japanese porcelains, Turkish miniatures from the thirteenth to the eighteenth century, wall texts in exquisite Arabic script, antique Turkish and European watches and clocks, musical instruments, royal and state coaches and saddles ornamented with trappings in cloth of gold and silver, ancient royal kitchen utensils and silver table furnish-

BLACK STAR

CLAMBERING UP A HILL from the Golden Horn. The European part of Istanbul is built on seven hills. Climbing the steep streets is worth the effort for the views from the top.

ings—a dazzling repast for the eyes.

Standing like sentinels around the palace are four charming but widely different structures called kiosks—open pavilions. Taken in turn, they are the Tile Kiosk of the fifteenth century, built only nineteen years after the conquest of Istanbul in 1453; the Baghdat in 1638, erected by Sultan Murad the Fourth; the Mustapha Pasha Kiosk of the eighteenth century, which represents Turkish rococo (an ornate architectural style) at its best; and, finally, the so-called New Kiosk of the nineteenth century.

In the Military Museum is a unique collection of ancient weapons used by Saracens and Crusaders, including the sword of Mehmet the Conqueror. There is in the museum an armlet worn by Tamerlane, the Mogul conqueror. The gallery houses wax figures dressed in the colorful costumes worn by Turkish soldiers, starting with the famous Janizaries, who constituted the first regular army to be organized anywhere in the world. In the courtyard are tombs of Byzantine emperors.

As the name would suggest, the Museum of Antiquities houses superb examples of Hittite, Greek, Roman and Byzantine art and archaeology. There are also Egyptian, Sumerian, Babylonian

PIX

SOCCER, BASEBALL, whatever the game, the spectators in Istanbul's stadium are finding it thrilling. The Turks are a vigorous people and are keenly interested in all kinds of sports.

A PALATIAL HOTEL that caters to luxury-loving globe-trotters. From the roof garden one looks out over the old city, with its domes and minarets, to miles of sparkling blue water.

and Assyrian relics. In addition to sculptures, terra-cotta work, jewelry, pottery, coins and medals, there are some magnificent tombs. Prize of them all is the sarcophagus of Alexander the Great, in delicate pink marble.

The four main galleries of the "Evkaf" Museum of Turkish and Islamic Art contain ancient Turkish rugs and carpets dating from the thirteenth century, rich brocades, fifteenth-century illuminated manuscripts, costumes worn by sultans and princes of the Ottoman Empire, embroidered dresses, and mother-of-pearl caskets studded with precious stones.

In the midst of all this ancient grandeur, life goes on much as it does in any other large cosmopolitan city. There are excellent restaurants, and Turkish food can hold its own with the best anywhere. Theaters and fine shops line Beyoglu Caddesi (Avenue), and for night life there is Taksim Meydan. From the nearby city park of Taksim there is a superb view of the Bosporus. For, above all, it is the surrounding waters that give Istanbul its greatest charm.

By SENIHA TASKIRANEL

285

A STREET PHOTOGRAPHER in Damascus. Pictures of human beings are becoming common though the Koran forbids depiction of any living creatures.

Syria

*...United Arab
Republic region*

THE Syrians are a people deeply devoted to the cause of Arab unity. For the Syrians, their golden age was the Ommiad Caliphate, which spanned the end of the seventh and beginning of the eighth centuries A.D. The followers of Islam then commanded an empire greater than Rome at its zenith. It stretched from the Bay of Biscay to the Indus and the confines of China, and from the Aral Sea to the cataracts of the Nile. Its capital, like that of present-day Syria, was Damascus, famed for rich brocades and metalwork. Mohammed, so the story goes, was so impressed by the city's glory that he refused to visit it because he wished to enter paradise but once. Modern Syrians have no illusions about recreating such an empire. But they are strongly in favor of closer co-operation among Arabs, under a single flag if possible.

Pan-Arabism began to gather impetus toward the end of the nineteenth century, and Syrian intellectuals were at the very core of the movement. Both Syria and Lebanon were then yoked to the Ottoman Empire. It was only natural, therefore, that Syrians and Lebanese then studying at the American University in Beirut should seize eagerly upon the past glories of Arab civilization. The study of Arabic language, history and literature was raised to a new level of prestige. The Syrians were also predominant at the Arab Congress in Paris in 1913. Effective Arab co-operation had to wait on several decades of foreign domination, however. Although Turkey's power in the Middle East declined after World War I, that of Great Britain and France rose. On mandate from the League of Nations, they took over most of Turkey's old possessions. Syria did not win independence from France until World War II, for example.

The foreign policy of the new Syria was dominated by its adherence to the Arab League (1945) and the Arab Collective Security Pact (1950). Despite the outward show of unity, however, continual feuding marred relations between the Arab states. In all of these feuds, Syria took the side of Egypt. Finally, in 1958, the natural bond between these two countries was implemented and the cause of Pan-Arabism strengthened by the federal union of Syria and Egypt. Thus, on February 1 of that year, the United Arab Republic was created. Nasser of Egypt became president, and the cabinet and

VILLAGERS LISTEN intently to the radio in a local shop. Syria has a modern broadcasting system which brings the most remote areas news of current events.

other officers of the new state included some Syrians as well as Egyptians.

Union with Egypt had solid popular support, bolstered by widespread fear of a communist takeover, but it has meant that Syria is no longer a sovereign, independent nation. It is a "region" ruled from Cairo, not Damascus. Under the old government the Syrians elected their legislature. Now Nasser appoints their Legislative and Executive Councils. He too, has initiated land reforms, taxes and import controls, which may be resented.

One of the few bright spots in the Syrian economy is agriculture. The subtropical fringe fronting the Mediterranean coast boasts a wide variety of crops. This is why some Syrians are opposed to land reform. They fear that productivity will decrease when the farms are split into smaller units. The U.A.R. hopes to combat small-farm inefficiency by setting up co-operatives. These will buy machinery, market crops and advise the new landowners.

Agriculture and sheep raising long dominated the economy. It was not until World War II that Syria's industrial potential was explored. Cut off from foreign goods the country had to rely upon

itself for manufactured materials. A thriving local market developed. Among the new industries were sugar and alcohol, glucose and starch extraction; refrigeration; extraction of vegetable oils; glass and soap making; new tanning processes; chemical dye works; manufacture of perfumes; and diamond polishing. These, added to the old standbys—cotton ginning, the extraction of oil from seeds and the manufacture of yarn and textiles—gave Syrian industry some much-needed diversification.

Syria's main industrial drawback, though, seems insoluble: a lack of natural resources. Along with Egypt, it is one of the few Arab lands that does not command sizable oil deposits. When drought hits the land and crops are poor the Syrian economy is in drastic straits. If relations with Lebanon are strained, as they were in the early days of the U.A.R., the Syrian economy suffers again. For Lebanon is Syria's best customer, and Beirut is a far better trading outlet than Syria's still growing port of Latakia. The Lebanese, tied closely to the West by reasons of trade and culture, have been disturbed by Syria's militantly pro-Russian elements. Before the union with

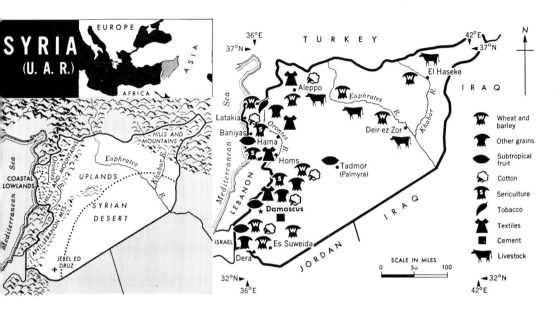

Egypt, the Syrian Army was beginning to turn communist and it still possesses communist arms. Furthermore, the Lebanese have complained about Syrian attempts to infiltrate Lebanon. Syria's economic future depends not only on the U.A.R.'s ability to open up new markets in the Soviet bloc but to maintain good relations with the traditional ones.

Syria's boundaries once embraced not only the area it contains today but also Lebanon, most of Israel and Jordan and parts of Saudi Arabia. Modern Syria stretches from Turkey on the north to Jordan on the south. It is bordered on the west by the Mediterranean Sea, Lebanon and northern Israel. To the east and southeast lies Iraq.

In northwestern Syria, an extension of the Lebanon mountain chain parallels the country's short Mediterranean coast line. Its western slope dips gently to the sea. The eastern slope falls away sharply for some three thousand feet to the marshy, malaria-infested Ghab Valley and the rich valley of the Orontes River. Farther to the east the land rises to a plateau. The well-watered and relatively productive valley of the Euphrates River lies in northeastern Syria and forms part of the Fertile Crescent. This extends inland from the Mediterranean, along the mountains of southern Turkey and then

down the Tigris-Euphrates basin to the Persian Gulf.

Along the Lebanese border are the main peaks of the Anti-Lebanon Mountains, which are arid and largely uninhabited. The chain is continued southward in the equally inhospitable and uninhabited Hermon range and reaches its high point of more than nine thousand feet at Mount Hermon.

Southern Syria, below Damascus, is a plateau region of long-extinct volcanoes. Some of the cones reach a height of three thousand feet. The lava-enriched soil of the Plain of Hauran in the southwest has long been cultivated. In ancient times this section was a main source of grain for the Roman Empire, but its modern output is on a much smaller scale. The volcanic plateau reaches its highest level in the Jebel Druse region of the southwest, where one cone rises almost five thousand feet above sea level.

The country's climate ranges from the cold winters and very hot summers of the desert to the mild Mediterranean climate of the western coast. Sufficient rain falls in the western mountains, but droughts are frequent in steppe and desert regions. Strong winds, some of great force and violence, blow the hot, dust-filled air from the deserts across the face of the country, leaving a parched path.

288

Rival City-States

Because of the land's varied geography the ancient Syrians, who were of Semitic stock, never developed a single, strong and politically united civilization such as those existing on the great river plains of Egypt and Mesopotamia. Instead, a group of small city-states sprang up, each one jealous of the others. As the early civilizations of Egypt and Mesopotamia grew and spread, their merchants established trading routes across Syria, and the city-states came to depend on the rich commerce of the larger empires.

The first known invaders came down from the north and included the Hyksos, or Shepherd Kings, the Kassites, the Mitanni and the Hittites, all vigorous and ingenious peoples. They brought with them the horse and the chariot; and the Hittites introduced their discovery of iron, which was later to replace the bronze then in common use. Invaders also moved in from the southern desert regions and settled around some well-watered areas. In this way a number of communities grew up and gained in power and cultural influence. Prominent among them were communities of the Philistines, Canaanites, Israelites and Phoenicians.

Part of Syria's history in this period is told in the Old Testament. It was in Syria also that the Phoenician civilization flowered after about 1250 B.C. A trading and seafaring people, the Phoenicians planted colonies all around the shores of the Mediterranean Sea and ventured all the way to the British Isles (probably Cornwall) to secure tin.

Syria fell in turn under the rule of the Egyptians, Assyrians, Babylonians, Persians and Macedonians. The Persians, in their attempt to unite all the Middle East under a single ruler, spread a common language (Aramaic) throughout Syria and introduced the Semitic culture of the west to the great Indo-Aryan culture of the east. The Macedonians found that they could exercise their power in Syria more readily through the townspeople than through the farmers. Therefore they established a number of new cities, and

Syria became a center of Greek life, with Antioch (now Antayka in Turkey) as its capital.

Roman Rule

The legions of Rome conquered Syria in 64 B.C., and Roman engineers built a chain of fortifications along the old trade route across Syria to the East. The bases reached from the Hauran and Jebel Druse in the southwest, through Damascus, and then across the desert by way of Palmyra to the mountains near Nisibini in the extreme northeast. A Roman fleet occupied the country's coastal harbors.

Under Roman rule, Syria reached heights of prosperity probably not equalled since. The land was intensively cultivated for grain to supply the growing needs of the Roman homeland. New industries flourished, notably textile production, glass blowing, and metalworking. Antioch was the center of Rome's rule and was said to have had a population of three quarters of a million people.

Syria Falls to the Muslims

When the Roman Empire was divided into two parts, East and West, Syria came under the domain of the Eastern, or Byzantine, Empire. In 636 the Arabs wrested the country from the weakened empire, and ever since Syria has remained an important part of the Muslim world. In the eleventh century the Seljuk Turks overran the land.

For about a century, beginning in 1096, Crusaders from Europe established strongholds in Syria and tried to take the holy places from infidel hands. They were eventually driven out of the country by the brilliant Muslim warrior Saladin and his Saracen armies. It was about this time that savage Mongol hordes from the wilds of central Asia began to terrorize the Middle East. They ravaged the countryside and destroyed cities, massacring the inhabitants. Tamerlane (Timur), a Mongol leader, pushed on into Syria where his armies looted and burned the cities of Aleppo, Homs and Damascus.

The barbaric Mongols were finally checked by the Ottoman Turks who rose

ALL THAT REMAINS OF THE BIBLICAL "CITY OF PALMS"

The Bible refers to this site as Tadmor, meaning the "city of palms." It is supposed that it was built by Solomon. The present-day village near these ruins is called Palmyra.

HITTITE SCULPTURES CARVED PERHAPS 3,500 YEARS AGO

Though the sculpture of the Hittites was crude, it had force and imagination. The Hittites were vigorous fighters, and these carvings represent archers and warriors armed with shields.

to power rapidly after they had captured Constantinople in 1453. These fanatical Moslems ruled all Syria by 1516. Their control was maintained through a highly trained military police force known as Janissaries. It was during the period of Turkish rule that Syria began to decline economically and politically.

The discovery in 1498 of a new overseas trade route around the Cape of Good Hope to the markets of the Orient spelled out doom for the affairs of Syria. The difficult overland trade route across the country fell into neglect and Syria's decline was rapid. From the sixteenth century until trade began to flow through the newly opened Suez Canal in 1869, Syria and other countries of the region held an unimportant place in world affairs.

The Era of French Control

The weakened Ottoman Empire controlled Syria until World War I. In 1920 the country was placed under French protection by a mandate from the League of Nations. A French-controlled government was set up, but internal unrest plagued Syria and several times disturbances had to be subdued by armed force.

With the outbreak of World War II, Syria was still a part of the French colonial empire. After France surrendered to Germany, the pro-Vichy government collaborated with the Germans in Syria. Consequently British and Free French forces, after some fighting, occupied the country in 1941. By the end of 1946 occupying troops were withdrawn, the French mandate was formally ended, and Syria was declared a sovereign republic.

The Government of independent Syria was extremely shaky. Upheavals were frequent, many of them led by military groups. Side by side with internal unrest, the Syrians were strongly infected with the idea of Pan-Arabism—union of the Arab world. Playing on this old dream, President Nasser of Egypt at last prevailed on Syria to join Egypt in the United Arab Republic. The union was proclaimed on February 1, 1958. Syria is now a "region" in the new republic, whose capital is Cairo.

BLACK STAR

ORCHARDS ON WALLED TERRACES

Apricots, figs, almonds and pomegranates grow on the narrow plots to the top of the hill.

291

A SYRIAN FARMER GLOWS WITH PRIDE OVER HIS NEW TRACTOR

Though few Syrians who work the land have such up-to-date equipment as this, modern agricultural methods are slowly making headway. There is good soil, which could give greater yields.

PRECARIOUS WORK—SPLITTING A LONG LOG LENGTHWISE

The saw is rigged to move up and down, and as the man wields it he must also keep his balance as he steps backward. This ancient way of cutting logs seems awkward in the extreme.

FROWNING LANDMARK IN ALEPPO—THE ANCIENT CITADEL

Built in the late fourth century B.C., the Citadel has witnessed the rise and fall of empires. Aleppo is on a plateau in northwest Syria, and the Citadel is on a still higher hill.

TROLLEY TRACKS GUIDE A COUNTRY FAMILY THROUGH THE CITY

Riding donkeys, this family has come from a remote district and it is probably their first sight of a city. All their worldly goods are stowed on the backs of the patient animals.

WHO'LL BUY MY COFFEE—HOT, SWEET AND THICK?

Most people of the Middle East love coffee, and vendors are a common sight on city streets. The beverage is usually made in the Turkish way, so sweet and thick it is almost a sirup.

"THE STREET WHICH IS CALLED STRAIGHT" IN DAMASCUS

The famous byway, mentioned in the New Testament in connection with Paul's conversion, is really crooked. It runs from the eastern to the western gate, flanked by bazaars.

The people of Syria are mostly of Arab origin. Arabic is the principal language although some Armenian, Turkish, Kurdish and Syriac is spoken. The large majority of the people are Moslems and most of them follow the Sunni branch of Islam. The rest of the population is divided between Christians and Jews.

Around the volcanic plateau of Hauran in the southwest live the Druses, a proud people famed for their fierce fighting qualities. More is told about them and their customs in the chapter on Lebanon.

Many tribes inhabit Syria, particularly the Bedouins of the desert region. In northwestern Syria dwells a group known as the Ismaili, or Assassins. They are the remainder of a once-powerful secret order of religious fanatics who flourished during the eleventh and twelfth centuries. From his stronghold in the wild Syrian mountains, Sheik el Jebel (the Old Man of the Mountain), leader of the sect, dispatched young men to assassinate enemies of the order. So that the killers would be unafraid, they were first drugged with hashish. Because of this practice, these religious murderers became known as *hashashin,* from which comes the English word "assassin." Today the production of hashish is a concession of the Syrian Government and is an important source of revenue.

Another group of the northwest is the Alawi who live in the Jebel Ansariyeh, a part of the Lebanon mountain range. Though they are considered Moslems, they have taken over the celebration of Christmas from the Christians and also practice certain ceremonies of pagan origin.

The Yezidi, a small group, live in northeast Syria. The largest body of them is in neighboring Iraq. These people still possess a strange pagan religion and believe that evil powers dominate the world. Their rites to ward off the evil spirits have led outsiders to call them devil-worshipers.

The life of the nomadic Bedouins has

THE MODERN FACE OF PERHAPS THE WORLD'S OLDEST CITY
Twentieth-century shops and apartment houses line a street in a section rebuilt within the old walls of Damascus. Most other parts of the city, however, have an Oriental atmosphere.

297

A MODEL OF ISTANBUL'S HAGIA SOPHIA HIGH ON A PEDESTAL

The attractive square, laid out with formal flower beds, is in the center of Damascus. Its most curious feature is the replica of the celebrated Byzantine structure in Istanbul.

PIX

PICNICKING ALONG THE BANKS OF A RIVER IN DAMASCUS

In the cool of the evening families come to enjoy a meal beneath the trees. Two rivers flow
through the city—the Barada and the A'waj—called the "waters of Damascus" in the Bible.

299

A CUP, A BOWL, A COFFEE URN—BRASS DAZZLING IN THE SUN

The Syrians have always excelled in metal work. In the days of chivalry a blade of Damascus steel was prized above all others. That craft has vanished but not the skill with metals.

A MARKET SQUARE—OPEN-AIR DEPARTMENT STORE AND GROCERY
Whatever a Syrian needs for his house or his person he is likely to find in the market square.
Bargaining is the order of the day, a game of wits that both buyer and seller relish.

changed but little down through the centuries. Their life and customs are described in detail in the chapter entitled The Desert Rangers. It has been said that if Abraham were to return today to a Bedouin encampment in the Syrian desert, he would feel quite at home, noting few changes since his time.

Bedouin tribes rarely combine with one another. If some strong leader does accomplish a union of a number of tribes, it proves to be a temporary arrangement that falls apart at his death. There is an almost perpetual state of warfare and feuding between tribes. Warfare is conducted according to strict rules. It is through warfare that a young Bedouin proves himself a worthy member of the tribe. Tribal territorial limits are carefully drawn. Some tribes remain in a relatively small area; others travel great distances in their search for pasture for their livestock.

Despite the numerical importance of the Bedouin and the farmer, or Hadhar, the dominant element of Syria's life centers about the cities. Here live the great landowners or feudal lords, owners of most of the nation's arable land. The landowners and traders or bazaar merchants guide the political career of the country. In recent years, however, as we have seen, the better-educated military class has begun to wield considerable political power.

The principal cities are all in the western part of the country and near the foothills of the mountains where there is an ample water supply. Damascus and Aleppo are the two main cities, followed by Homs, Hama and Latakia.

Damascus, the capital, is sometimes called the Pearl of the Desert because of the beauty of its surroundings. It is said to be the world's most ancient city, and it appears to have been a notable place as early as 1913 B.C. At one time Damascus was a thriving center for the trade between Europe and the Orient and its bazaars and markets overflowed with goods from the Eastern and Western worlds.

301

A PURCHASE OF FRUIT CALLS FOR SERIOUS CONSIDERATION

The vendor of the fruit appears indifferent to the outcome and ready for a nap alfresco. Meanwhile his unhurried customers examine the fruit and discuss its possible merits.

A HAWKER CRIES HIS WARES—HEAPS OF LUSCIOUS FRUIT

What passer-by would not be tempted by the fragrance and colors of downy apricots, pomegranates bursting with red pulp or ripe, purplish figs with the morning dew still on them?

The plain on which the capital is situated is watered by the Barada River and is rich with orchards of figs, apricots, almonds, pomegranates, lemons, oranges, plums, pears and apples.

The modern city has preserved its Oriental character. The Muslim section is considered the best and wealthiest quarter of Damascus and has wider streets, better houses and a more abundant water supply than other parts of the city. Elsewhere the streets are narrow and crooked and often extremely dirty. The house fronts are generally prisonlike in appearance, with a few small grated windows piercing their mud walls. Sometimes, however, a drab and forbidding front conceals a luxurious interior.

The trade and commercial life of a Middle Eastern city centers about the bazaar section, an area where the merchants buy and sell almost everything under the sun. In Damascus the bazaars and khans (inns housing men and pack animals) are very large affairs. To the noisy, bustling bazaars come the Bedouins to exchange wool, leather and other products for cereals and the few manufactured things they need. The varied products of field and orchard are brought there, and cargoes from overseas find their way to the bazaars. Although the city no longer makes and sells the famous Damascus steel, fine handmade metalwork can be bought in the bazaars. There are tea merchants, sellers of beautiful textiles, dealers in fine leatherwork and furniture, jewelers and merchants who handle imports from other countries. If you should wish to buy a radio or a typewriter, they, too can be found in the colorful bazaars of Damascus.

Damascus is linked by railway with Amman, the capital of Jordan, and with Aleppo in the north. There is a connecting railway with Beirut and Cairo, too, and several international airlines service the airport there. An excellent road connects Beirut and Damascus.

Syrian education, long under par, is improving. Schools sprout everywhere and the illiteracy rate is down to 35 per cent. Much work remains to be done, though, in this as in every area of Syrian life.

By E. S. FERGUSON

SYRIA: FACTS AND FIGURES

THE COUNTRY

Under French mandate 1920–41; then independent republic until 1958, when it joined the United Arab Republic. Bounded on the west by the Mediterranean and Lebanon, on the south by Israel and Jordan, on the east by Iraq, and on the north by Turkey, Syria has nine administrative districts: Aleppo, Damascus, Euphrates, Hama, Hauran, Homs, Jebel de Druz, Jezire and Latakia. Area, 72,000 sq. mi.; population, about 4,280,000 including some 250,000 nomads.

GOVERNMENT AND CONSTITUTION

The provisional constitution of the United Arab Republic provides for a president, a 34-member cabinet (12 from the Syrian and 22 from the Egyptian region) including 4 vice-presidents (2 Egyptian, 2 Syrian) and 2 ministers of state. Each region has an executive council which administers local government. The republic has a common legislature, a unified army, and one flag.

COMMERCE AND INDUSTRIES

Agriculture and cattle raising are the leading occupations. But only 12% of the land that is fit for cultivation is tilled. Chief crops: wheat, barley, oats, maize, sesame, hemp, sugar cane, lentils and chickpeas. Fruit trees: banana, orange, lemon, olive and the mulberry for feeding silkworms. Cotton cultivation has increased and it is exported together with its products, raw wool and silk. Cereals and manufactured goods are the biggest imports. The mineral deposits, though largely undeveloped, include iron, lignite, gypsum, marble and building stone. Currency: the Syrian pound.

COMMUNICATIONS

Railway mileage, 600; roads, 4,500 mi. Several international airlines use Syria's only airport, at Damascus. There are 37,000 telephones. Steamer service is regular.

RELIGION AND EDUCATION

About 75% of the inhabitants of Syria are Muslims, chiefly of the Sunni sect. The Christian element constitutes about 12% of the population. There are 2,636 primary schools, 244 secondary schools, 13 technical schools, 6 teacher-training schools, 1 university and an Arab academy.

CHIEF TOWNS

Damascus, regional capital, has a population of 400,000; Aleppo, 450,000; Homs, 294,000; Hama, 173,000; Latakia, 105,000.

Lebanon

...old land
and young nation

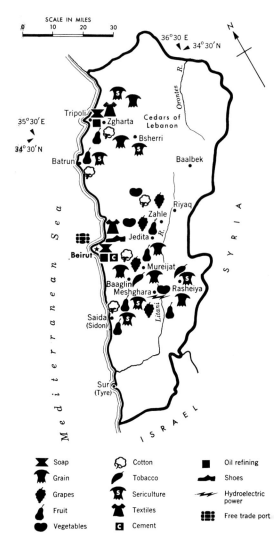

Soap
Grain
Grapes
Fruit
Vegetables
Cotton
Tobacco
Sericulture
Textiles
Cement
Oil refining
Shoes
Hydroelectric power
Free trade port

A FEW miles north of Beirut, the capital of this little republic, the road passes a famous group of inscriptions carved into the base of a hillside. Nineteen inscriptions in eight languages are carved into the face of the rock. They were left there over a period of some three thousand years by foreign invaders to commemorate their victories. The first of these was Ramses II, pharaoh of Egypt, who made his mark in the early thirteenth century before Christ. His successors were an imposing lot: Esarhaddon of Nineveh, Nebuchadrezzar of Babylon and "the invincible Emperor Marcus Aurelius Antoninus," among others. British soldiers, in 1919 and 1930, and French soldiers, in 1920, carried the custom into this century. The last inscription is the most important of all to modern Lebanon, however: "On December 31, 1946 the evacuation of all foreign troops from Lebanese soil was completed in the days of al-Shaykh Bisharah al-Khuri, president of the republic."

Clearly, this is an area that has seen more than its share of strife. The new republic centered there is no exception. Though the Lebanese boast the highest literacy rate in the Arab world, and are quite capable of handling the orderly processes of democratic government, their nation is torn from time to time by political strife. At the heart of Lebanon's dilemma are the divided sympathies of its people. Some (but not all) of those devoted to Arab nationalism are intensely anti-Western. Some, for a variety of unique reasons, are intensely pro-Western. Most of this latter group are Christians, many of them educated at the famous American University of Beirut, which was founded by American missionaries (many Muslims were educated there, too). Finally, thousands of Lebanese maintain close relations with friends and relatives who have emigrated to the West.

Lebanon's devotion to Arab nationalism, therefore, is rather tepid. It has consistently maintained a moderate position in the Arab League. It has mediated between rival power blocs but never

304

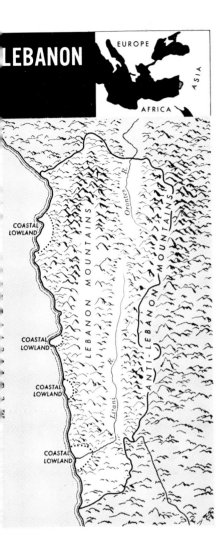

LEBANON

EUROPE
ASIA
AFRICA

COASTAL
LOWLAND

LEBANON MOUNTAINS

ANTI-LEBANON MOUNTAINS

Orontes R.

Litani R.

COASTAL
LOWLAND

COASTAL
LOWLAND

COASTAL
LOWLAND

tionalists (mostly Christians) and the anti-Western Arab nationalists (mostly Muslims) will continue. It depends, however, on the course of relations between the West and the U.A.R. If they are cordial, Lebanon will probably remain relatively quiet. If they are not, stormy days may well return.

Despite its small size, Lebanon plays an important part in Arab life. Lebanon is the main port of entry for Syria. Beirut, the capital, is an intellectual window on the world for the entire Middle East. Here Arab visitors from Iraq, Jordan, Egypt come into close contact with an urban life strongly Western in flavor. Beirut flourishes with schools and colleges. One of them, the American University, has long been a haven for articulate Arabs. It was at this university, under the old Ottoman Empire, that Arab nationalism was first given intellectual impetus. Free speech abounds. Not even the Communists, officially outlawed, are muzzled. On all sides, moreover, material wealth abounds. Buffered by trading revenues, the average income in Beirut is beyond matching by the U.A.R. It is easy to see why the Arab nationalists want to keep Lebanon in friendly hands.

The same vigor that permeates the atmosphere of Beirut stamps Lebanese living abroad. The largest colonies are in New York and Brazil. The New York colony won considerable literary prestige during the 1920's and 1930's by the achievements of Kahlil Gibran (died 1931) and Amin Rihani (died 1940). Gibran's simplicity of style and diction won him many readers in the English-speaking world and altered the course of modern Arabic poetry. In São Paulo, Brazil, the Lebanese circle styled itself the "Andalusian Band" and issued a literary magazine that continued publication until the 1950's.

Both of these colonies did well commercially, too. The arrivals at the turn of the century started by peddling notions, curios and articles from the Holy Land. Soon they were opening lace, kimono, rug and white-goods stores. Today they are establishing import offices with branches

aligned itself with any one of them. Lebanon is the only member of the league that allows ships bound for Israel to pass through its waters. In fact, Lebanon would trade openly with Israel if it did not fear economic reprisals from the United Arab Republic.

Such an attitude hardly endears Lebanon to the more ardent Arab nationalists both within and without its borders. In 1958 the Government, disturbed by pro-Arab uprisings across the country, claimed that U.A.R. agents were responsible. This situation coincided with the revolt in Iraq. Lebanon then asked the United States for troops to maintain the peace. The prospects are that the truce between the pro-Western Lebanese nain half a dozen cities spread over several continents. The success of these émigrés has hardly gone unnoticed back home. In a recent year émigré donations to charities, friends and relatives in Lebanon amounted to $22,000,000, a significant portion of the national income.

Two "Nations"

The Lebanese themselves will tell you that they are divided into two nations: the resident (*al-Muqim*) and the emigrant (*al-Mughtarib*). The existence of this second "nation," along with the other vital ties, gives the West a unique foothold in the Middle East. No other country is so open in its friendship for the United States, the United Kingdom, France and their allies. Lebanon's ability to maintain an independent, prosperous course in the future is thus of great importance.

At the dawn of history a civilization already existed in Lebanon. Archaeologists have established that at Gebal, or Jebeil—today a village of about three thousand people, about twenty miles north of Beirut—there existed a city named Byblos around 3000 B.C. Because of its export of papyrus for making books, the ancient Greeks used the name of Byblos for the word "book," from which came "Bible" and many words containing "biblio." At this early date Byblos ranked above Tyre and Sidon and other flourishing centers of Phoenician culture.

Tripoli and Aradus also existed as coastal ports during this early period. A large maritime trade had been built by the Phoenicians. As shipbuilders they were without peer, and their vessels carried lumber and pine products to Egypt and other parts of the Mediterranean. It is supposed that Phoenician seamen sailed as far as Cornwall, England, where tin was mined.

The timber from the forests of Lebanon was a great source of wealth to the coastal cities, and they were not lacking in other industries. Glassmaking was developed to a high degree. From a small shellfish (murex) they made a purple dye—the Tyrian purple beloved of the Romans centuries later. The name of the dye came from the once flourishing port of Tyre.

Phoenician Trade and Many Rulers

Our alphabet is sometimes said to have been invented by the Phoenicians, but this is only partially true. There is no doubt that these people did evolve one of the earliest alphabets but they were probably helped by their knowledge of the alphabets of other peoples, gained through their activities as traders. However, it was because of the widespread commercial relations of the Phoenicians that languages using an alphabet, such as Aramaic, were transmitted to other peoples throughout the Middle East and as far as Persia.

Because of their riches and their location on the highway from the north to Egypt (they were also the terminal points of the long caravan route from India and China), the Phoenician cities came under the rule of a long line of conquerors. Around 3000 B.C. they were under the protection of Egypt, and then, in turn, they were subdued by the Assyrians, the Persians and Alexander the Great. At times, nevertheless, the cities were able to break away from outside rulers. One instance of this is when Tyre allied herself with Israel during the reign of Solomon, exchanging timber for grain and olive oil. Later the cities became part of the Roman Empire and the Romans built great temples in them. A famous one was to Jupiter, at Baalbek. Its ruins are still magnificent. With the breakup of the Empire, the region became part of the Byzantine realm.

The French Mandate

In the seventh century the Arabs gained power and later the area passed under Ottoman control, which lasted until the end of World War I. Lebanon was then made a French mandate. The country was declared a republic in 1926 under the mandate but was a republic in little more than name. During World War II the Free French forces ousted the Vichy Government in Lebanon and again proclaimed Lebanon a free republic. This became a reality on January 1, 1944. Even then French troops remained stationed in Lebanon and were not withdrawn until 1946.

The tiny Republic of Lebanon is almost squeezed into the eastern end of the Mediterranean Sea by its much larger neighbor, Syria. On the south Lebanon shares a short boundary line with the Republic of Israel.

Much of Lebanon is mountainous. The Lebanon Mountains parallel the coast for more than a hundred miles. In Biblical days they were covered with cedars. The highest peak in this range—Dahr el Qadib—near Tripoli in the north, is more than 10,000 feet high, and one near Beirut —Qurnet es Sauda—is only a little lower. The eastern border is rimmed by the Anti-Lebanon Mountains. Between these chains lies the narrow Bekaa, or Biqa', valley, watered by two rivers, the Orontes and the Litani (called Leontes in ancient days). The Orontes flows north for about 250 miles, entering Turkey and finally emptying into the Mediterranean. The Litani begins close by the Orontes, in the center of the valley, and flows south through deep gorges toward the upper Jordan. Because of the deep ravines, this river is of little use for irrigation.

A SHAWL INSTEAD OF AN OVERCOAT

On a chilly day this man of Beirut wears a camel's-hair shawl over his Western suit.

BLEND OF EAST AND WEST

Lebanese mix Eastern and Western dress with unconcern—old-time trousers and oxfords.

On the watershed of the rivers, at a height of about 3,600 feet above sea level, is the site of the ancient town of Baalbek (which the Greeks called Heliopolis, city of the sun) where Baal, the sun-god, was worshiped. There now remain only the ruins of its once huge temples. Baalbek was destroyed by an earthquake about the middle of the eighteenth century. The Arabs believe that it is the oldest city in the world and that Adam lived there.

Along the narrow coastal plains the climate is subtropical. Winters are mild, summers are moderately hot and there is plenty of rainfall. But in the mountains

A CRUSADERS' CASTLE WEATHERED BY WIND AND WATER

The castle is in the harbor of Sidon, where some Crusaders landed. Deserted and crumbling for long years, the site was later used for a mosque. Its dome is visible in the center.

there is a great change even within as short a distance as five miles from the coastal plains. Here we find snow and cold winters. Snow stays unmelted on the Lebanon range about three months, and the peaks are usually covered with snow from December to June. It is said that the name "Lebanon" comes from a word *Leben* (whiteness) used in the old Aramaic language (spoken by Jesus) and refers to the view of the glistening mountains.

An average of forty-five inches of snow falls in the Lebanon Mountains each year. The Beirut-Damascus railway, which crosses the range, is covered with permanent snowsheds for several miles. The railway rises five thousand feet above sea level so steeply (in some places it was necessary to lay ten miles of winding track to advance two miles) that a cog rail is used for a quarter of the way.

In the Bekaa valley, winters are cool, and summers hot and dry. The rainy season starts in October, and the Bible refers to these autumn rains as the "former rains." The spring rains of April and May are termed the "latter rains." It is from December to March that the downfall is most heavy.

On the western slopes of the Lebanon Mountains, Mediterranean plants are found. Near sea level along the coast there are locust trees and stone pine. Wide areas are covered with brush. Farther up the mountains begin the woodlands, dominated by dwarf hardwood oaks. Still higher on the slopes is a belt of tall pines. At about four thousand feet the famous Lebanon cypress and cedar appear. There are also oaks and other leaf-bearing trees together with coniferous trees, including the rare Cilician silver fir. Extending nearly to the summits, stunted oak, juniper and barberry grow. The Lebanon cedars, you remember, were

308

THE STILL GRACEFUL COLUMNS OF THE TEMPLES AT BAALBEK
Though chipped and eroded, the stones have an impressive dignity. Baalbek is in the Bekaa
Valley and strange gods have been worshiped there: Baal, the sun-god, and later Jupiter.

309

TURKEYS PEER ABOUT CURIOUSLY ON THE WAY TO MARKET

The big birds stroll to market at an amiable pace. They are probably destined for the dinner tables of luxury hotels; for they are hardly the usual diet in a Lebanese home.

used in building Solomon's Temple and palace. Only a few of these cedars are left, in groves considered sacred. Some of the cedars are extremely old and are nearly one hundred feet high and over fourteen feet in diameter.

Beirut, the capital of Lebanon, is the country's only modern seaport. In fact, it is one of the main ports of entry in the Arab world. Close by, in Khalde, is the Middle East's largest airport. Mountains rise almost directly behind the harbor, one of the most beautiful in the world. With its fine beaches, promenades and pine-studded backdrop, Beirut is also a popular resort. In the modern hotel lobbies one finds sheiks on holiday, rich merchants from other lands, cosmopolitan

SIGNS IN ARABIC AND FRENCH IN A BEIRUT ARCADE

There are fine shops in Beirut which sell exquisite imported goods. A French atmosphere lingers in the city and the French language is likely to be heard as often as Arabic.

diplomats, tourists, secret agents, adventurers and promoters. Political intrigue is rife. The atmosphere is French but a great many languages are heard. Many of the city's old streets are steep, winding alleys; but alley or avenue, Lebanese drivers ignore all hazards. Traffic moves at a terrific pace, made possible only by the drivers' lightning alertness. With what seems a natural bent for mechanics, the Lebanese love automobiles, the more powerful the better.

A mountain highway connects Beirut with Damascus, about sixty miles to the east. It is an exciting and sometimes hair-raising experience to motor around the hairpin curves, in the shadow of peaks

or on the very edge of deep gorges. If one dares to look up from the road there are wide views of wild mountain scenery.

The people of Lebanon are about equally divided into Moslems and Christians. For this reason the president is usually a Christian, and the prime minister a Sunni (orthodox) Mohammedan. Chief of the Moslem group is the Sunni sect, although the Shiite sect is almost as large. The Druses may also be considered as a Moslem group.

However, the Druses seem to believe in a mixture of both Christian and Moslem ideas. Unlike Mohammedans, who do not believe in incarnation, the Druses believe that seventy incarnations of God

FISHING BOATS AT A QUAY ON ONE SIDE OF BEIRUT HARBOR

Ships from all over the world anchor in the harbor, and its shores are a semitropical playground. Behind the beaches and shore hotels rears a verdant backdrop of mountains clad with pines.

FREDERIC LEWIS

have occurred, the last one about 1000 A.D.; and Druses say there will be no more until the rest of the world is converted to the beliefs of the Druses, the "true children of God." These people are spread over much of the Lebanon and Anti-Lebanon mountains as well as through Syria. Among the most fierce fighters to be found anywhere, the Druses keep very much apart from their neighbors. They are jealous of their own customs and are especially hostile to Lebanese Christians, particularly the Maronites. In contrast with most other Mohammedans, the Druses are respectful of women. Women are allowed to join the men in religious services. They may also bring suit for divorce, an action unheard-of among orthodox Moslems. Having more than one wife is forbidden. Women must wear a veil but their sober black dress is

A BEDOUIN FAMILY COMES TO TOWN
Almost everywhere in the Middle East one will find Bedouins, the wanderers of the deserts.

relieved by scarlet slippers. Men wear a black robe with a white girdle. As a distinguishing mark from other Mohammedans, a white roll encircles the red fez. Druses are a tall people, with a fairer complexion than is usually found in the Levant.

Like the Druses, the swarthy Maronites are also mountaineers. They make up about a third of the population and form a distinct sect within the Roman Catholic Church. Their religious leader, under the pope, is called the patriarch of Antioch, which is in Turkey. He lives, however, in Lebanon. It is thought that some of the mountain folk were converted to Christianity about the seventh century and became followers of Saint John Maroun, from whom they derive their name. Like many people of a rugged land, the Maronites once engaged in bloody feuds but as a result of their relations with the Western world, their barbarous ways are vanishing. A national festival is held on September 14. The night before, bonfires are lighted and Maronite men and boys

313

A YOUNG GIRL OF THE DRUSES

The clothes she is wearing are light in color and have gay embroidery. When she is grown up, however, among her own people she will wear a black dress, crimson slippers and a veil.

show their bravery by leaping over the flames. At the same time there is an uproar of shouts and gunfire.

In Beirut and the larger towns living conditions are similar to those found in Europe; but village life is quite different. In most parts of the country the huts of the peasants are made of wattle or mudbrick or in part of stone. Interiors are bare of all but the merest necessities. In the far north and south poverty is severe. Villagers cannot afford to buy even rice, but live on lentils, bread and curdled milk.

Most of the villages are owned by a landlord and the people work for him. These landlords are the most important and influential groups in all Middle Eastern countries. There are, however, more

freeholders in Lebanon than elsewhere. Possibly as many as one-half of the rural communities are freeholding peasants with small plots of land. Some of them spend part of the year tending to their crops and the balance working in factories. Methods of tilling the soil are still primitive but better results are obtained than elsewhere in this part of the world. It is not only the heavier rainfall but also a better-informed people that account for this. For instance, in places the western slopes are terraced to keep the soil from being washed away and to hold water. Though the land is cultivated intensively, not enough is grown to supply the country's needs and some grain is imported from Syria. Crops are diversified and include, in addition to various grains, olives, bananas and citrus fruits.

A Gateway for Trade

Despite the fact that two-thirds of the population is engaged in agriculture, trading is the most important economic activity. From the time of the Phoenicians to the present this seems to have been true. It is largely because Lebanon is one of the important gateways to the Far East. Today the country is a major center of foreign exchange and a place where goods are traded that never enter Lebanese territory. Beirut itself is the biggest gold market between Tangiers and Bombay.

The Lebanese factory worker is the best to be found in the Middle East, not excluding Turkey. After the fall of the Ottoman Empire, Lebanon gained rapidly in new factories. Unlike the experience of its neighbors, construction of new plants in Lebanon was due entirely to private enterprise and not to aid from the Government. A large number of small factories now produce various beverages, foodstuffs, cloth, razor blades, cement, soap, matches and other items. The silk industry, which had been a source of considerable wealth, was hurt by the invention of nylon, but is now reviving.

Electric power output is nearly 50 per cent greater than that of Syria, a much larger country. With mountain rivers

314

such as the Litani, the possibilities for greater power generation are enormous. However, the country's known mineral resources are of no consequence. Since the country is already the most densely populated in the Middle East, further expansion appears quite limited. In fact, one of the reasons for the present relatively high living standard is that large amounts of money are sent back to relatives by those who have emigrated, especially to the United States (chiefly Detroit). Since the late 1890's, with little else to export, Lebanon has been exporting its population. It is said that almost every adult Lebanese has lived abroad or intends to; but they come home to retire— and usually bring with them the fastest, shiniest cars they can.

Pipelines from Iraq and Arabia

Two oil pipelines terminate on the Lebanon coast. One line originates in the Kirkuk oil fields of Iraq, with a branch going to Haifa in Israel and another branch ending at Tripoli. There are small refineries at both places. Another pipeline starts on the Persian Gulf, near the Bahrein Islands, crosses Saudi Arabia and ends at Sidon.

Schools and Colleges

Though the Government spends much more on national defense and internal police than it does on such matters as health and education, educational facilities in Lebanon are well above Middle Eastern standards. French Jesuits and American Presbyterians deserve a large part of the credit for this development. The Jesuits staffed numerous schools and founded the University of St. Joseph in Beirut in 1875. Earlier, in 1820, the Americans established several schools and a printing press. The Syrian Protestant College was chartered in 1863, under the laws of the State of New York, from where most of the money for its founding came. Eventually this college became the present internationally known American University of Beirut. For a campus, it has seventy acres of semitropical gardens, all overlooking the blue Mediterranean. No at-

KEYSTONE

A PRIEST OF THE MARONITE SECT

Most Christian Lebanese are Maronites, a distinct sect within the Roman Catholic Church. The priest's vestments include a chasuble, the beautifully embroidered outer garment.

315

DRAWING WATER FROM A WELL DUG BY THE CRUSADERS

Walled in by rough stones, the little well is on the summit of a mountain in a dry region where water is scarce. These women must make a long climb and clamber down heavily laden.

tempt is made to "Americanize" the students, which in a recent year were drawn from forty nations and twenty-one religious groups.

Lebanon has the framework of an educational system from the elementary grades through college. Almost 80 per cent of the Lebanese can read and write, compared with about 10 per cent in the rest of the Arab world.

Health standards are also higher. However, diet is hardly above the subsistence level for many of the people. Bread, milk, olive oil and fruits when in season are the basic foods. Sanitation is poor and disease prevalent. Malaria, typhoid, trachoma and other diseases are chronic. There are few doctors. Some headway in this field is being made, however. An antimalaria campaign has begun, there are a few classes for public-health nurses, and an effort is being made to improve water supplies and other sanitary facilities.

In Lebanon the conflict between the cultures of the East and West is especially sharp. It emerged with the end of the Ottoman Empire and the beginning of French influence. The attempts of the French to bring about a more orderly government, to improve education and health and to correct bad economic conditions met with great opposition from age-long traditions among the illiterate populace led by selfish landlords. Externals were changed but the basic social structure of semifeudalism held. This old order is breaking up and many serious problems arise in the process. To a considerable extent the valuable aspects of the traditional culture are lost while only material things are taken from the West. The forward-looking leaders of Lebanon are keenly aware of this problem. One such leader, Charles Malik—widely admired as Lebanon's delegate to the United Nations —has said that four developments are

PIX

LOOKING OUT OVER TRIPOLI TOWARD THE MEDITERRANEAN
Little of ancient Tripoli survives but the present-day city is thriving as the terminus of an oil pipeline from Iraq. This provides work and income for the city's people.

MULBERRY LEAVES FOR SILKWORMS

To add to the returns from their land, many farmers raise silkworms as a side line.

necessary within Lebanon and the rest of the Middle East: land reform, eliminating the present semifeudal system; replacement of bureaucratic administration with an efficient government; a high order of national leadership; and economic and political freedom for all.

It is interesting to note that one of the elements that has speeded the process of change has been the motion picture.

Another factor, mentioned earlier, is the number of Lebanese who emigrate and then return long years after. Though they remain loyal to their homeland, they cannot help but bring back new ideas.

Today the patriarchal family system—in which the father is all-powerful—is declining. At the same time the country is affected by the deep underlying ferment of Arab nationalism and by the challenge of its modern neighbor, Israel. Thus the peoples of Lebanon are not likely to find an easy solution to their difficulties.

By E. S. FERGUSON

FOOD FOR THE VORACIOUS APPETITES OF YOUNG SILKWORMS

The squirming caterpillars are kept on large, flat baskets in a dark room at a cool temperature. To keep up with their tremendous appetites, they must be fed every six hours.

318

ZAHLE, WHICH CLINGS TO A HILLSIDE IN THE BEKAA VALLEY

The delightfully cool summers of the valley make Zahle a refuge for people from the warmer coast.
They can reach the town easily for it is on the railway between Beirut and Damascus.

HIGH IN THE LEBANON MOUNTAINS A SKIER TRIES THE SNOW

Though Lebanon is usually thought of as a warm country, snow stays unmelted toward the tops of the ranges during the three winter months. Skiing on the firm crust is a popular sport.

LEBANON: FACTS AND FIGURES

THE COUNTRY

A republic in Asia, on the eastern shore of the Mediterranean, which was formed from five Turkish districts in 1920, administered under a French mandate until 1941 and was finally given its full independence in 1944. The country is bounded on the north and east by Syria and on the south by Israel. It has an area of about 3,475 square miles, and a population estimated at 1,400,000.

GOVERNMENT

Lebanon is governed by a president, a prime minister, and a Parliament having 44 seats which are distributed according to religious sects and not parties. The country is a member of the United Nations and of the Arab League.

COMMERCE AND INDUSTRIES

Although less than a quarter of its total area is under cultivation, Lebanon is primarily an agricultural state. Its chief food products, ranked according to the weight of their yield, are grapes, citrus fruits, wheat, onions, barley, potatoes, tomatoes, watermelons, maize, apples, pears and olives. Tobacco and cotton are also important crops. Besides processing crude oil piped in from Iraq, the country manufactures matches, soap, cigarettes, shoes and cotton goods—and weaves silk and woolen materials from imported yarn. There is a little mining of lignite. Tripoli is the terminus of an oil pipeline from Kirkuk, Iraq; and Sidon is the terminus of another pipeline from Abqaiq, Saudi Arabia. Monetary unit, the Lebanese pound.

COMMUNICATIONS

There are 475 miles of railway track and 2,400 miles of highways and secondary roads. Most of the passenger and freight traffic is handled by the hundreds of inexpensive bus and truck companies. Lebanon also has two national airlines and an international airport which is used by a number of foreign lines whose planes offer direct service to and from the Far East. There are 24,368 telephones.

RELIGION AND EDUCATION

Various sects of Christians make up about half of the population, while the rest of the people belong to various Moslem sects. The Government maintains more than 1,000 primary and technical schools; and there are some 850 private and foreign schools. The country has two outstanding universities, the University of St. Joseph and the American University, both located in Beirut.

CHIEF TOWNS

Beirut, the capital, has a population of about 425,000; Tripoli, 80,000; Zahle, 20,000; Saida, 20,000; Tyre, 12,000.

INTERNATIONAL BECHTEL

PLOWING IN THE OLD WAY BESIDE OIL STORAGE TANKS

The crude implement drawn by oxen and the tanks are symbolic of present-day Lebanon. It is at a crossroads in its history where ancient customs and modern ideas are meeting head-on.

Israel

... modern nation with an ancient history

ISRAEL'S achievements since its founding in 1948 are truly magnificent. Homes and jobs have been found for nearly one million immigrants, skilled and unskilled alike. The landscape has been radically altered. Whole villages have been created, new buildings greet the eye on every side, and 52,000,000 trees have been planted. The borders have apparently been secured. Frequent Arab raiding is a thing of the past. To say that all this still does not insure Israel's future safety and progress, however, gives some idea of the massive odds Israel struggles against. Israel has yet to prove that it can absorb into its largely European culture, the hordes of immigrants who flow in from Asia and Africa. The Israelis must yet complete the transformation of the barren Negev desert into productive farmland if they hope to put their economy on a sound, self-sustaining basis. Lastly, the Israelis must somehow pass on from father to son, from the early to the present-day immigrant, the same pioneering spark that has sustained the nation so well in crisis after crisis.

The majority of Israel's immigrants today are from Asia and Africa. Unlike the early settlers, many of the new ones are driven to Israel by sheer desperation rather than Zionist idealism. Worse, they find the job of adapting to Israeli life difficult. When given beds, some of the immigrants from Yemen, for example, crawl *under* them to sleep. Clearly, the Israeli Government is up against no mere language barrier here. It must teach such citizens a whole new way of life—and quickly. Much has already been done, to be sure. In every conceivable way, Israel holds out its hand to the immigrant. Both the Army and the school system provide training in basic conduct and basic Hebrew. The Health Centers provide psychological as well as medical guidance for whole families. Still, the enormity of the job ahead is almost overwhelming. And as one writer observes: "In the twentieth century, miracles are frightfully expensive."

One Israeli miracle is already in the works. The sandy Negev region, occupying the whole southern half of the nation, is being explored, settled, and irrigated. The Israelis plan to tap every available water supply, including the Jordan River, for their parched fields. This project is a potential source of strife with Arab neighbors through whose land the Jordan flows. They have threatened to dam off the waters. The Israelis might be forced to run this risk, however. If the Negev does not soon begin to carry its weight in the economy, Israel's hopes for financial independence from American aid will remain hopes, nothing more. Proof of their determination is the newly finished highway, which runs all the way from Beersheba, through the blazing desert, to Elath, Israel's lifeline to Red Sea shipping.

A third challenge, perhaps the most important of all, remains. Nations, like families, have a tendency to cohere in time of crisis, to relax in time of plenty. Since 1948 this law of human nature has been working in the Israelis' favor. The greater the obstacle placed in their way the stronger has been their response. The hopes of the Israelis for the future depend upon the preservation of their ardent patriotism. No matter how dormant Arab enmity may appear to be, it is still very real. The Arabs, with some justification, resent Israel's eviction of nearly a million of their brothers when the new state was created. They resent, too, the enormous funds sent to Israel from America.

Modern Israel began on May 14, 1948, when thirty-five men and two women signed the Proclamation of Independence, bridging a gap of 1,878 years between the new republic and the ancient Kingdom of Judea. The land had been governed as part of Palestine by British administrators from 1922 to 1948. The United Nations General Assembly, however, voted on November 29, 1947, to divide (partition) Palestine into Jewish and Arab states. The resolution was to become effective upon the withdrawal of the British in 1948.

Real independence came only after a long and bloody battle between Jewish and Arab armies which began the very day the British left, lasting till 1949.

When armistice agreements were finally reached with the governments of Egypt, Lebanon, Jordan and Syria, Israel was left in control of 8,000 square miles out of the total area of Palestine, 10,434 square miles. Thus, the Jewish state now controls 77 per cent of the territory of Palestine as compared with the 56 per cent allotted to it under the United Nations partition plan. This was the plan that the Arab League armies had tried to set aside.

Israel's boundaries include a surprising variety of landscape. In the extreme north are the Galilee hills. In the north-central region (and along most of the coast) the land is flat and fertile. Further inland it rises markedly, then drops suddenly to the hot, dry Jordan Valley. The Negev desert dominates the south.

The holy city of Jerusalem, connected to the coastal area by a broad corridor, is divided. The Old City, walled, sacred to Christians, Jews and Muslims, is within the territory of the Hashemite Kingdom

ISRAEL'S FUTURE depends upon vigorous youths like these, marching on the anniversary of their country's independence.

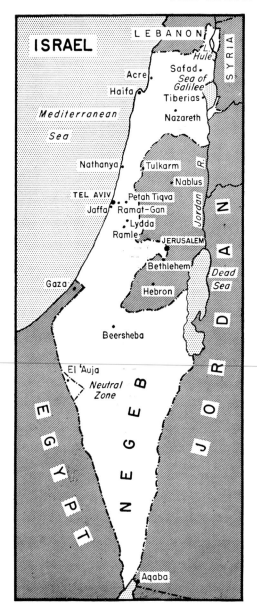

of ministers. In turn, the prime minister and his cabinet are responsible to the Knesset. This body not only makes the laws but also keeps a close watch on all government activities. If the Knesset passes a vote of nonconfidence in the cabinet, which indicates disapproval of the cabinet's actions, the government then automatically falls.

The members of the Knesset represent all the different groups in the Israeli population. They include farmers, rabbis, lawyers and Arabs.

Equality for Israel's Minorities

The minority races of Israel number about 200,000 out of a total population of over 2,000,000. Most of the minority groups are either Muslims or Christian Arabs. In the Proclamation of Independence the Jews guaranteed minorities "complete equality of social and political rights . . . without distinction of creed, race or sex . . . freedom of religion, conscience and . . . culture."

Muslims and Christian Arabs live, for the most part, in Nazareth and the other villages of Galilee. Their children, however, are being educated in the free, compulsory school system of the state of Israel.

Language and Religion

The official language of Israel is Hebrew. The Jewish holy days are national holidays and Saturday is the official day of rest. Minorities, however, choose their own day of rest and celebrate their own holidays.

Trains and buses do not operate from sunset on Friday to sunset on Saturday. Offices, factories and businesses are closed and work on the land is forbidden out of respect for Jewish religious laws. Israel, however, is not a theocracy—that is, a state ruled by religious law. There are no laws to prevent an individual from driving his car or working in his garden on the Sabbath. There has been some friction on this score, however, as Orthodox Jews observe the Mosaic Law with extreme strictness.

The meat imported by the Israeli Gov-

of Jordan. The New City, built outside the walls in the nineteenth and twentieth centuries, is governed by the Jews. The Israeli Parliament, the Knesset, and the officers of the government ministries are housed in the New City of Jerusalem.

The president of Israel has no executive powers. Rather, the real power is held by the prime minister and a cabinet

AN IMMIGRANT FARMER in the Negev of southern Israel prepares the land for crops. The Negev is largely desert country, in the process of reclamation and settlement.

SHEEP-RAISING has been important to the Holy Land's economy since ancient times. The modern Israeli shepherd differs merely in costume from his counterpart of Biblical days.

VIRGINIA TOBACCO, now grown in Israel, is considered superior to the native leaf.

ferred. Instead, in 1950, the Knesset enacted a series of fundamental laws which eventually will be combined into a constitution.

One of these basic laws, passed on July 5, 1950, is the Law of the Return. It states: "Every Jew has the right to immigrate to Israel." This law reaffirmed what had been said earlier in the Proclamation of Independence: "The State of Israel will be open to the immigration of Jews from all countries of the Dispersion."

Accordingly, since the gates of Israel were first opened to immigration, more than 700,000 Jews have poured into the new state. They came from every part of the world, but in particular from regions where Jews were in distress: eastern Europe, North Africa and other countries of the Middle East.

This mass immigration, especially of those peoples from undeveloped countries, had a tremendous impact on the infant state. It strained the country's resources almost to the breaking point as there were already grave shortages in housing, clothing, food, educational and

ernment is kosher—that is, slaughtered in accordance with Jewish ritual. However, nonkosher meat is available for those who desire it. Yom Kippur, the Day of Atonement, is a Jewish fast day and on this most holy of days the Israeli Army does not serve meals. Food, however, is left out for those soldiers who do not wish to observe the fast.

The question of religious observance is one of the most painful and difficult problems facing the leaders of the Jewish state. The Government's attitude is satisfactory neither to the orthodox rabbis, who want stricter observance, nor to those at the other extreme, who complain that the present laws already amount to religious coercion. In order to avoid a showdown on this delicate issue, the writing of a state constitution has been de-

BUILDING a new collective farm, or *kibbutz*, in the Negev region near Beersheba.

KINGSWAY, the main thoroughfare of Haifa, is lined with many modern buildings. The city was founded by German settlers in 1869 and has the only deep-water harbor in Israel.

327

TEL AVIV'S PROMENADE along the sunny Mediterranean coast overlooks a fine bathing beach. Modern, industrial Tel Aviv ranks next to Haifa in importance as a port city.

A NARROW STREET in Nazareth that seems to have changed little since Jesus lived there in his youth. Yet the modern town is far larger than the ancient Galilean village.

MC LEISH

IN ACRE is this mosque, built by a Turk named Jezzar Pasha, who brought columns for its ornamentation from the ruins at Caesarea. Caesarea was the capital of Roman Palestine, but is now only a small village. Acre, a seaport situated on a promontory at the base of Mount Carmel, was regarded as the "Key of Palestine" in the time of the Crusades.

EWING GALLOWAY

ZION SQUARE, in the New City of divided Jerusalem, is the heart of Israel's capital. The historic Old City, containing most of the holy places, is only a short distance away.

ISRAEL OFFICE OF INFORMATION

A MONUMENT to Israel's impressive growth and progress. Hadassah Medical Centre in Jerusalem maintains the most up-to-date equipment and has a staff of excellent doctors.

330

medical facilities, transportation and other basic requirements. In order to insure equal distribution of the meager food and clothing supplies, rationing was put into effect immediately.

Sympathizers throughout the world recognized Israel's plight and contributed hundreds of millions of dollars in the form of grants and loans for her aid.

With this financial assistance the Israelis built scores of new towns and villages to replace the tent cities that newcomers were forced to live in at first.

For some years Jewish settlers have been developing the land, and in many places what was once barren soil has become rich productive earth. Rural villages, as a rule, take one of three forms. The *moshav ovdim* is a co-operative settlement of small privately owned holdings. The *kibbutz* and the *kvutsa* are communal settlements—that is, the land is held in common—usually affiliated with a political party. In the *moshav shitufi,* the land is also held in common but the profits are divided among the members.

In the past few years foreign and local investors have enabled the new state to develop a large number of factories and industries. At the south end of the Dead Sea, for instance, there is a large plant for extracting the mineral wealth from these waters. Potash heads the list of basic chemicals. Education, medicine and transportation are also taking long strides forward.

However, despite Israel's impressive growth, it will take a good many years to restore the standard of living to the level it had attained before the mass immigration began. The task of developing the new state is further complicated by the necessity of maintaining a large standing army to protect its many frontiers. Although the Arab-Israeli war was to have ended with the 1949 armistice, Israel's neighbors, Egypt, Jordan, Syria and Lebanon, are still hostile to the new country.

The armed forces of Israel are composed of all men from the ages of 18 to 45, and women up to the age of 34 who have no children. The older people belong to reserve units and are called up annually for short training periods.

The army of Israel is unique in the world. It trains its men and women not only to be good soldiers but also to be

EWING GALLOWAY

NOT FAR from Jerusalem is Ein Karim, the birthplace of John the Baptist. Today it is one of many villages in which immigrant Jews from all over the world find peaceful homes.

MC LEISH

ACROSS THE SEA OF GALILEE glides this boat with a bright blue sail. Its progress is assisted by the crew bending to their blue-and-white oars. Formerly the sea, which is thirteen miles long and eight miles wide, was crowded with shipping, for on its shore were several important cities, but of these only Tiberias remains today, so that usually only a few fishing boats are now to be seen upon its surface. The Lake of Tiberias is another name for this sheet of water, which, though deep set among steep hills, is often swept by sudden and violent storms.

BY THIS ANCIENT BRIDGE Roman legions crossed the River Jordan in the days of long ago. The bridge spans the river at a point about seven miles south of the Sea of Galilee, and was constructed by Roman engineers. The exact date of its construction is unknown. To the south of this ancient structure is a modern railway bridge, sixty-five yards in length, over which pass trains from Haifa, a port on the Bay of Acre, to E Hamme, a town in southern Syria. In Hebrew times the Jordan valley was regarded as a "wilderness." Only in Roman times was it at all populous

333

FRUIT JUICES are one of the country's chief export items. In the pressing department of a food-processing plant, the juice extracted from oranges flows into enormous basins.

WOOLEN CLOTH from the rollers in this textile plant will reach many world markets.

good citizens. After their basic training, recruits spend several months in agricultural settlements where they are taught farming, geography, Hebrew, history and civics. Many of the recruits are newcomers to Israel and this process speeds up their feeling of identification with their new home. The classes also teach them trades and professions designed to make them useful citizens.

There is an intense interest in music, the theater and other arts in Israel, in villages as well as cities. Such conductors as Toscanini and Leonard Bernstein have led the fine Israel Philharmonic Orchestra. Folk dancing is a favorite recreation in the settlements.

Most of Israel's population is concentrated in the country's three largest cities: Haifa, Tel Aviv-Jaffa and Jerusalem. The Government, however, is making a determined effort to spread the population. New immigrants are urged to settle in outlying farm areas where their skills and labor will be of most benefit to the country.

BY MOSHE BRILLIANT

FREIGHT CARS haul material to a large cement factory. Financial aid, both foreign and domestic, has played a major role in the expansion of Israel's modern industries.

ISRAEL: FACTS AND FIGURES

THE COUNTRY

A republic of the Middle East, bounded on the north by Lebanon, on the east by Syria and the Hashemite Kingdom of Jordan, on the south by Egypt and on the west by the Mediterranean Sea. Area, 8,048 square miles; population, 1,717,800, including 192,000 non-Jews who are mainly Arab Muslims.

GOVERNMENT

The state of Israel came into existence in 1948. It has a president whose functions are largely titular. He is elected by the Knesset (Assembly) for a 5-year term. The Knesset, Israel's unicameral legislature, has 120 members elected for 4 years by proportional representation.

COMMERCE AND INDUSTRIES

Agriculture is the chief occupation in those regions having sufficient rainfall. Barley, wheat, sorghum, olives, grapes and citrus fruits are among the principal crops. Poultry, sheep and goats are raised. Mineral resources include limestone, petroleum, gypsum, sandstone, rock salt, sulfur and potash. Food processing, various manufactures and automobile assembly are among Israel's expanding industries. Chief exports: citrus fruits, fruit juices, textiles, chemicals and cut gem diamonds. Imports: machinery, grain, timber, raw materials, iron and steel, manufactures. Monetary unit, Israeli pound.

COMMUNICATIONS

There are about 325 miles of railway and some 1,500 miles of all-weather roads. Regular airline flights are maintained to many world capitals. There is regular steamer service to and from Haifa and Tel Aviv-Jaffa. Telephone and telegraph lines total about 79,000 miles.

RELIGION AND EDUCATION

A special government ministry supervises the religious affairs of Jews, Christians and Moslems, with the affairs of each community under control of the respective authorities concerned. Education is directed by the Ministry of Education and is free and compulsory through the primary grades. Separate schools exist for Jewish and Arab students. The Hebrew University in Jerusalem, the Israel Institute of Technology at Haifa, the School of Law and Economics at Tel Aviv and Bar Ilan University at Ramat Gan are among the institutions of higher learning.

CHIEF TOWNS

Jerusalem (New City), capital, 144,000; Tel Aviv–Jaffa, 358,500; Haifa, 154,500.

THE BEAUTIFUL traditional costumes of Israeli women are not often seen in the modern land. The headdress of this girl is decorated with overlapping coins. Her head shawl and gown are elaborately embroidered with delicate designs. To complete the picture of former days, the girl follows the Eastern custom of carrying a water jar balanced on her head.

THESE THREE OLD JEWS, who are taking their leisure beneath the ramparts of Jerusalem, have seen the population of that city change considerably since they were young. Among the Jews who are citizens of Israel are some whose families have lived in Palestine for generations; but many more Jews have immigrated to their homeland.

Jordan ... *Hashemite kingdom*

THE country by the River Jordan is beset by many problems. It is desperately poor, has meager natural resources and practically no industries. Indeed it could not exist without outside help. On top of this it has had an influx of more than a half million refugees, mainly Arab Muslims, since the state of Israel was created in 1948. Its situation is further aggravated by the continuing conflict between Israel and the Arab countries; by the United Arab Republic's determined bid for leadership of the Arab world; and by the communist-free world struggle.

From 1921 until 1956 Jordan (Transjordan until 1949) was supported by Great Britain. Then, touched off by

Britain's part in the strife over the Suez Canal in 1956, Jordan broke its bonds with Britain. Jordan thereby gave up a yearly subsidy of about $36,000,000. It has relied chiefly on United States aid since. If Jordan—artificial state that it is—were allowed to collapse a political vacuum would be created. The Communists (outlawed in Jordan) might rush to fill the void.

Jordan belongs to the Arab League and, like the other members, refuses to recognize Israel. Yet this attitude is a material disadvantage to Jordan. Before the division of Palestine in 1948, most of Jordan's trade was with the old mandate. This was halted by the Arab boycott on

EASTER PROCESSION in front of the Church of All Nations in Bethlehem. Many Christian faiths are represented: Roman and Eastern Catholics (Greek, Armenian, Syrian, Coptic, Ethiopian) and Protestants.

Israel. Though the UN Relief and Works Agency provides minimum care (funds are limited) for the refugees, they nevertheless weigh heavily on the poverty-stricken land. There is no adequate work for about a tenth of Jordan's total population. Hostile relations between Israel and Jordan also prevent development of the Jordan River, which could provide irrigation and power for both countries. Quarrels continue over the Gulf of Aqaba, Israel's only outlet to the Red Sea as Egypt bars Israeli shipping from the Suez Canal.

Transjordan was carved out of the Ottoman Empire after World War I. In that conflict the Arabs had played a large part in defeating the Turks. The Arabs served under the leadership of T. E. Lawrence, who organized the guerrilla warfare in the desert. Partly because he had promised an Arab state, Great Britain placed members of the Hashemite family on the thrones of Jordan, Iraq and the Hejaz (Arabia). The Hashemites had been powerful in Arabia for more than a thousand years. They were guardians of Mecca (in the Hejaz). However, Ibn Saud (of another ruling Arab family), in creating Saudi Arabia, drove the Hashemites out of Mecca, in 1924. Until he died, in 1953, ill feeling remained between Saudi Arabia and the Jordan-Iraq kingdoms. Saudi Arabia and Jordan have drawn closer since Saud succeeded his father and Hussein (born in 1935) became king of Jordan in 1952. With the murder of King Faisal, Hussein's cousin, in the July 1958 revolt, Hussein became the last Hashemite king.

Until 1958, Jordan and Iraq had banded together more often than not against Egypt and Syria (today the United Arab Republic). With behind-the-scenes help from Moscow, Egypt and Syria had tried to draw Jordan into a federation extending from the Nile to the Turkish border of Syria. In the same month, January 1958, that the UAR was established, Jordan and Iraq formed the Arab Federal State—which, of course, fell apart after Iraq became a republic, in July.

At the beginning of the 1960's Hussein seemed to be in firm control, at least for the moment. He had shattered the threat, for the time being, of communism at home, made a truce with the UAR, and won the allegiance of the Jordanian Army, the former Arab Legion. Trained by the British it is one of the few effective Arab fighting forces. Nevertheless, Jordan remains dependent on Western help.

Regarding a 1957 report on Jordan by the World Bank the London *Times* stated that, "With the best will in the world the bank cannot find in that arid land . . . any great potential for development." There have been some farm experiments, making grass grow on the desert soil. More roads have been built. Prospectors hopefully search for oil. The Dead Sea, divided between Jordan and Israel, contains vast quantities of valuable mineral salts, especially potassium salts—potash —used as fertilizer. Their development, however, is contingent on co-operation with Israel.

Jordan is mainly an arid, hilly plateau rising about 3,000 feet above sea level. There is a steep drop of several thousand feet from this plateau on the east as it approaches the Dead Sea, which is 1,300 feet below sea level. This sea has no outlet, and the water that pours into it rapidly evaporates in the great heat. Consequently the sea is extremely salty and can support practically no life. In the south are many mountains; close by Aqaba, Jebel Ram pushes to a height of 5,396 feet.

Part of the boundary between Israel and Jordan is formed by the Jordan River, which flows south into the Dead Sea. The valley formed by this river and the Dead Sea is the deepest trench in the earth's land surface.

The few cities in Jordan are located in the western part of the country, mainly in the northwest. To the east are deserts, tremendous seas of sand that extend over

A SHEPHERD leads his flock of sheep and goats through the streets of a town in Jordan. Eighty-five per cent of the people of Jordan make their living by agriculture or from their flocks. The skins, hides and wool of domestic animals give Jordan most of its exports. Because of low rainfall, only about 5 per cent of the land in Jordan can be cultivated without the aid of irrigation. The most fertile land lies in the northwest corner of the country. To secure food for their livestock, the shepherds must wander with their animals in search of grass.

MC LEISH

TWO TURBANED MOSLEMS watch the bustling crowd of traders, pilgrims and travelers that gathers at the Jaffa Gate. Jaffa is one of eight gates in a wall around the Old City of Jerusalem. All of Jerusalem that lies outside this wall is called the New City. Jerusalem has shrines of the Christian, Jewish and Moslem faiths, most of which are in the Old City.

341

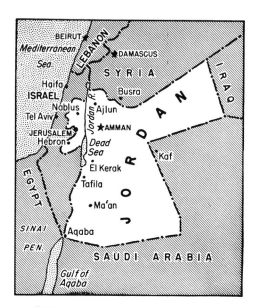

BUTTERFLY-SHAPED KINGDOM

a great part of Saudi Arabia. This desert country is called the "Land of Emptiness."

There is plenty of rainfall in the northwest of Jordan but as you travel eastward it decreases rapidly. Consequently, the land that can be cultivated lies in the small northwest area between the border of Israel and the railroad from Damascus, in Syria, to Amman. This railroad is an extension line from Damascus to the north, and it runs to Ma'an in the south of Jordan. It is called the "Pilgrim Railway" because it carries a large number of Arabs making the pilgrimage to Mecca.

The poorness of the country can be seen from the fact that only about 5 per cent of the land can be cultivated. The peasant farmers, fellahin, farm nearly all of this available land.

Because of little rain over most of the country, irrigation must be used. One means of getting water is by *qanats*, or artificially built subterranean canals. In many places the natural streams disappear underground and run along the rock or hard layer below the ground surface. To get at this water, tunnels are dug, creating artificial underground streams, which carry the water to fields that are to be cultivated. The results are remarkably effective though the method of digging these water tunnels is primitive. Every few hundred yards a well is dug down to the water, and a tunnel is extended toward the land to be irrigated. The earth from the wells is taken up through the wellholes and piled around the edges of the openings at the top. These well openings resemble miniature craters. When seen from an airplane, the land appears to have been peppered with hundreds of meteorites. Then you realize that the wellholes run in too straight a line for this to be possible. The United Nations is endeavoring to help Jordan with irrigation projects in order to gain more land that can be made fertile for the raising of crops.

Some livestock is raised, and wheat, barley and grapes are the main crops grown. Vineyards, to which the hilly country is suited, are extensive. The surplus from the crops is exported to Syria and Iraq. Imports, which are mainly cloth, foodstuffs and livestock, come from the United States, Great Britain and Iraq.

Cities and City Life

There is only one port, Aqaba, located on the Gulf of Aqaba, which opens into the Red Sea. Here by this port, the boundaries of Jordan, Israel, Egypt and Saudi Arabia meet. In ancient times, Aqaba was important as it received valuable goods carried in ships across the Indian Ocean from India and other Far Eastern places. Large caravans were then made up to carry this merchandise on to Mediterranean ports and to Egypt.

Amman, Jordan's capital city, was called Rabbath Ammon during the time of Moses, when it was the capital of the Biblical Ammonites. Later it was rebuilt by a king of Egypt, Ptolemy Philadelphus, and given the name Philadelphia. A theater remains from Roman times. Today it is a typical Arab city. It is treeless but the houses, usually made of stone, are substantial-looking. The streets, through which all the odors of the bazaars are wafted, are crooked and dusty. Several motion-picture houses give the city a modern touch; otherwise, sidewalk cafés with radios are the only entertainment.

Population has leaped with the tide of refugees.

Most of the people are nomadic Bedouins, who tend small herds of sheep or cattle to make a living. Often the tribes move over tremendous distances, even crossing boundaries into other countries. They move wherever there is a supply of water and pasture.

History as Old as the Bible

Even though Jordan is a comparatively new nation the area has a long history dating from Biblical times. It was in Jordanian territory that the Dead Sea Scrolls were found. Between 1947 and 1956 more than five hundred manuscripts, most in fragments, were found in caves clustered about some ruins on the Wadi (River) Qumran, near the Dead Sea. Most of the scrolls are on leather or papyrus, a few on copper. The scrolls belonged originally to a Jewish sect called Essenes, who flourished from about the second century B.C. to the second century A.D. The manuscripts include portions from every book of the Old Testament except the Book of Esther. The Book of Isaiah is almost complete. Other manuscripts seem to foreshadow Christian teachings. It will probably take many years to translate and study thoroughly all of the scrolls. However, the precious fragments are already established as one of the most valuable archaeological finds of all time.

Before World War I, of course, Jordan was a part of Palestine, then in the hands of the Ottoman Empire. The Transjordan created in 1921 was one of the most backward areas in the Middle East. It had no orderly form of government, poverty was widespread and the Bedouins, paying little attention to boundaries, made continual raids upon the few settled villages.

British Support

The first thing Great Britain did was to bring under control the custom of raiding. Gradually the authority and efficiency of the government was built up, largely by means of the Arab Legion.

This army, under the leadership of a Briton, Captain F. G. Peake, was composed of selected Arabs who were given intensive military training.

Since force had been the means of both acquiring land and keeping it, there were no written records of land ownership. With the introduction of law, records were made and a system of establishing boundaries was put into effect. It then became possible and necessary to tax the people to supply the Government with a steady income. Because this income was never enough to fully support the Government, Great Britain added to it by loans.

In 1946, Jordan became a kingdom and made a treaty of alliance with Great Britain. The Arab Legion of Jordan, under the direction of Major John Bagot Glubb, was fast becoming a well-disciplined fighting force. It gave a good account of itself in the Arab-Israeli war of 1948; and as a

BLACK STAR

WHO WILL BUY? Flat loaves of bread, fresh from the oven, in the market place of Amman.

FALLEN is the pomp of the Roman Empire, yet something of its majesty lingers amid the ruins of Jerash, in the hills north of Amman.

ARABS in motley garb pose at Petra. Beginning around the fifth century B.C., the city was carved, not built, out of rose-red sandstone.

A BRISK TRADE goes on inside the Damascus Gate, near the Muslim quarter of the Old City of Jerusalem. There are eight gates in the walls.

CRACK CAVALRY TROOPS of the Jordanian Army. Their handsome mounts are probably descended from the famous Arab horses.

DOME OF THE ROCK. The mosque is built over a huge outcropping of rock, in Old Jerusalem. Solomon's temple was on the same spot, and, by tradition, Abraham prepared to sacrifice Isaac here.

THE HOUSES IN JORDAN are made from blocks of stone, chipped and chiseled to a perfect smoothness by hand. The second worker from the right is checking his stone with a square.

result of the power shown by his army, King Abdullah became an important figure in the Arab world. His dream of a greater Syria seemed possible of realization. This plan and Abdullah's willingness to make a truce with the Israeli caused other Arab nations, especially Egypt and Saudi Arabia, to oppose him. In 1951, he was assassinated.

It is doubtful that Jordan could continue with an orderly government if British support were to be withdrawn, as Jordan does not have the means to support itself. Several plans have been proposed to improve the economic conditions of the country, one by the United Nations Economic Survey Mission in 1949. Progress, which compares favorably with other Arab countries, has already been made under the guidance of Great Britain. Education, though still poor, has been greatly extended. Health standards have been raised, as is shown by the steady decline in the death rate of infants. However, the great influx of refugees from Palestine has increased the country's difficulties. Foreign aid is being given to help care for these refugees, but a more permanent solution must be worked out.

By E. S. Ferguson

THE HASHEMITE KINGDOM OF JORDAN: FACTS AND FIGURES

THE COUNTRY

Bounded on the north by Syria and Israel, on the northeast by Iraq, on the east and south by Saudi Arabia and on the west by Israel. Total area, about 37,500 square miles; population, about 1,403,000.

GOVERNMENT

Independent since 1946, Jordan is a constitutional monarchy, with a king, a cabinet and a legislature consisting of two houses: a lower house elected by male voters, and a senate appointed by the king.

COMMERCE AND INDUSTRIES

Agriculture, including livestock-raising, is chief occupation. Crops include various grains and legumes, olives and grapes. Stock includes goats, sheep, cattle, donkeys and camels. Phosphates and potash are taken from Dead Sea. The unit of currency is the Jordan dinar. There are few industries other than handicrafts.

COMMUNICATIONS

There are about 422 miles of all-weather roads, and 1 railway crosses the country. Airfields are at Amman and Jerusalem; there are 2 small airlines.

RELIGION AND EDUCATION

Practically all the inhabitants are Moslems. There are about 750 government schools.

CHIEF TOWNS, POPULATIONS

Amman, capital, about 202,000; Hebron, 27,000; Nablus, 25,000; Bethlehem, 10,000; Ma'an, 10,000; Mafraq, 2,000.

Bedouins

... the desert rangers

THE wanderers of the deserts of Arabia and North Africa are dwindling. Their numbers have never been counted and probably only a million of them still live as their forefathers did. To find the old Bedouin way of life today one must travel deep into the Empty Quarter—the Rub al Khali desert—of southern Arabia or the interior of the Sahara. There the Bedouins still roam the sands with their herds, setting up their tents of goat or camel hair wherever a little pasture appears around an oasis. In such remote areas, tribal warfare still flares up now and then. The Bedouin and his rifle, usually an old-fashioned make, are practically inseparable.

The only law the Bedouin of the interior knows is that of his tribe. Organized governments have thus far largely ignored him. Besides being half-starved he is also, understandably, illiterate and ignorant. At the same time he is proud and courageous, hospitable and generous. Nature does not interest him; his life is too harsh for him to see any beauty in his environment. Yet he has an ear for poetry and loves stories. Tales and verse and talk while away the tedium of long marches, and they are heard far into the night around campfires.

This kind of life is slowly but surely giving way before the bulldozers and pipelines of modern industrialization. The search for oil penetrates ever farther into the wastes of Arabia. Today, derricks loom in the shimmering heat of the central Sahara.

Before World War II as many as 20,-000 camels would be needed for the *azalai* (salt caravan) that makes a yearly five-hundred-mile journey south from the salt pans of Taoudéni to Timbuktu, in the southwestern Sahara. Today the *azalai* plods the route with only a few hundred camels.

In many parts of the deserts, jeeps and tractors are becoming as common as camels. The Bedouins take to motor vehicles as naturally as a bee to nectar. As drivers they have a reputation for wild recklessness. It is less well known that they have an astonishing gift for mechanics. At an oil-company school in Kuwait, Bedouin youngsters straight from the desert—who can neither read nor write and don't know how old they are—become skilled machinists in record time. Within a year the more intelligent ones are capable of repairing a huge diesel engine or machining a complicated part to a tolerance of 1/1,000 of an inch. However, the Bedouin youths refuse to cut their long hair even though it is dangerous around high-speed machinery.

For many centuries the Bedouin was one of the most picturesque features of the Arabian and North African deserts. His very name means "dweller in the desert"—though the older Bedouins refer to themselves as "people of the tent." From Arabia and Syria, his original home, he spread over Iraq and Egypt and thence farther west into the Sahara. (Some of the western Sahara nomads, however—such as the Tuareg—are not Arabs but Berbers.) The Bedouins remain most closely associated with Arabia and Egypt. Those in the countries of the Middle East may com-

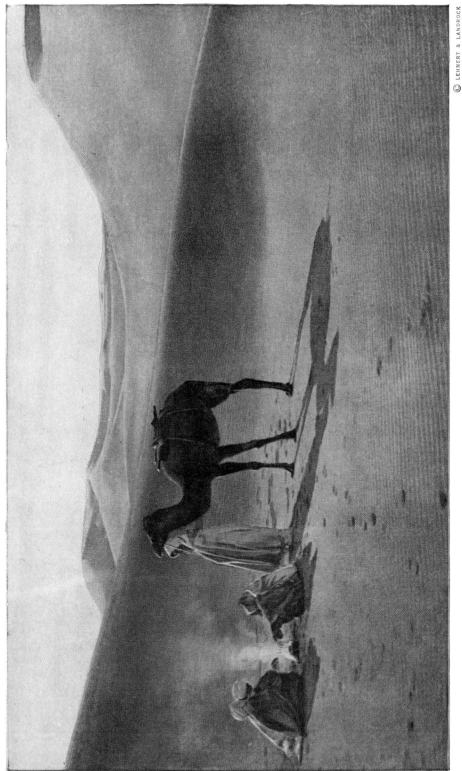

DESERT TWILIGHT shows a glory of color which does not last beyond a few seconds. Soon after, the day's fierce heat is radiated away through the clear dry air and the warmth of a fire is grateful. It is through such country as this that the Beduins wander with their flocks and herds from camp to camp, for the pasturage is scant and often gives out in twelve days. Indeed, the hard life of the desert is today driving many of them coastward to the cities where they often lose their special qualities and soon mingle with the rest of the population.

BEDUIN WOMEN, when they go upon a journey, are usually shut within a litter fixed upon the back of a camel. It is a Moslem practice that women shall be hidden from the public gaze, so they must travel swaying giddily to and fro on their unwieldy covered platform, which is fastened upon the camel's hump, and how uncomfortably hot and stuffy it must be inside.

349

THE LIFE OF A DESERT DWELLER DEPENDS UPON A STURDY MOUNT

Since ancient times the people of Saudi Arabia have been known for their horsemanship and fine steeds. An Arab horse is relatively small, sure-footed, with great physical endurance.

prise about one-fifth of the whole population, including in this estimate the territories of Iraq, Palestine and Syria. How this figure is arrived at one cannot say, for all attempts to get the nomadic tribesmen into a recent census were unsuccessful. The Beduins saw behind the census papers the threatening figure of the tax collector, and as they have never paid tribute to any government they refused to have their heads counted.

Of the higher class Beduins, most live in communities each of which, as has been said, is ruled over by a sheik. It is among such that the more picturesque features of desert life are to be seen. Here are larger and better equipped tents. The sheik himself will be garbed in clothes of fine quality while his tribesmen, in their parti-colored robes, will make a brave show. The national dress consists of the "abba," or camel's-hair cloak—striped gaily with colors or black and white—beneath which is a closely fitting tunic that may be of silk or cotton, according to the owner's means. This is gathered in by a leather girdle or a colored sash, in which a pistol or dagger can be stuck.

How the Desert Men Dress

As headdress is worn a square of cloth —again cotton or silk—brightly hued and striped. This is doubled over the head, the two long ends falling down upon the shoulders. A notable feature of this headgear is the twisted band of camel's hair, which is worn round the top of the head and helps to keep the cloth in position when the front part is pulled forward as a shade for the eyes.

Women's garments among the more settled tribes may also be brightly colored. A blue, red or yellow handkerchief serves for head-covering while the loose robe, fastening with a girdle, is striped or of a striking pattern. But out in the desert the women are drably clothed compared with their husbands. Unlike her Arabian sisters, the Beduin woman does not wear a face veil. Her custom is to cover the lower portion of her face with a corner of her shawl at the approach of a stranger. But she has a feminine weakness for neck-

laces and other trinkets especially for bangles round arm and ankle. Most likely too she will wear a talisman in her headdress, a small transparent stone set in beads, which is supposed to act as a charm against the "evil eye."

With her brown skin, her dark flashing eyes gazing at one from below a well-draped headdress, and with the pleasant jingle of her metal chain necklaces and ornaments, this daughter of the East is quite charming in her youth. But she ages too quickly for her life is one of constant toil with little pleasures.

Workaday Life of the Womenfolk

The Beduin man leaves all the domestic duties to his womenfolk. They grind the wheat in the handmill or pound it in the mortar. It is they who knead and bake the bread, make butter, carry water from the wells, work at the loom and mend the tent covering. To the women also usually falls the task of rolling up the tents when camp is broken and the tribe is moving on to some fresh pasturage.

One of our pictures shows a Beduin mother carrying her baby in the manner usual among this people. The youngster, wrapped in garments of bright colors, is swung over the mother's back in a shawl. At other times it may be set astride her shoulder. As a rule the little ones are strong and healthy for in their babyhood they are left to roll naked in the sun. As they grow up, however, numbers of them suffer from ophthalmia and other eye troubles brought on by dirt and inflammation from the sand or by the sun's glare. In some cases total blindness follows, and then they drift into the towns to join the ranks of the beggars who are so common there.

The Beduin at Close Quarters

If he be less presentable than his more prosperous brothers of the village, the Beduin of the desert, the true nomad who shifts continually from place to place, is even more truly a descendant of Ishmael in the Bible story. Romance and color fall away from this type the closer we get to him. Below middle stature, lean and wiry

BEDUIN GIRLS, like this attractive nomad maid of Tunisia who is shown here with her mother, are as fond of dolls as any young ladies of the same age in our country. It was the Arab conquests of the eighth century which took her forefathers from their original home in the wilder parts of Syria and Arabia along the coast of North Africa as far as Morocco

BABY BEDUINS, carried pickaback in a shawl, soon get tanned a rich clear brown by the desert sun. So too do their mothers, for the Beduins are an independent folk and their womenkind do not always wear the face-veil. They cover the lower part of the features with a corner of their cloak when a man not of their own household is seen approaching.

in physique, he is clad in coarse garments; his tents are of poor quality, and his horses and camels are underfed and shamefully ill-used. With the poorest of these desert gipsies a few wretched goats are often their only livestock.

The Bedouin's treatment of his camel is far from what the "Ship of the Desert" deserves at his hands. It is true that the animal has few good points in his nature; he cannot be described as lovable. He is sulky and refractory and appears to be incapable of affection for his master—though this may only be the result of the treatment he receives. He is made to flop down for loading and unloading pur-

STANDARD OIL CO. (N. J.)

AN ARABIAN BEDOUIN AND HIS FAMILY RELAX BEFORE THEIR TENT

In Abqaiq, Arabia, a Bedouin employed as a watchman in the nearby oil fields builds his tent and clothes his family in the manner of his nomadic tribesmen. The large metal food can the boy to the right holds and the burlap sacking that has been used for the tent are typical of many objects from the modern West that have found a place in Arab life. The women are closely veiled.

THE BEDOUIN IS NO LESS MANLY FOR HIS LONG BRAIDS OF HAIR

A Bedouin of Al Kharj in the Nejd region of Saudi Arabia seems fiercely proud of his distinctive hair style. Al Kharj is one of the best farm regions of the Arabian peninsula. Modern irrigation waters date groves and fields of wheat, alfalfa and millet. Because of the abundance of feed, Bedouins have settled with their herds on the lands about Al Kharj.

poses by blows on the knees; there is no word of command, such as other draught animals learn to obey. When resting with heavy loads on his back, and when taking his food, the ill-fitting framework on which his burden is piled is not removed.

On the other hand he is quite indispensable to his master for he can travel far in a waterless region and can feed on the thorny plants that grow in the sand. His eyes are well protected from the sun by the thick upper eyelids with which he is provided, and when the fierce simoon wind rages across the waste he can close his nostrils to it and the blown sand particles.

A sand storm in the desert is one of the terrors of the nomad's life. When it breaks, the camels crouch down with their backs to it, the travelers seek shelter within

355

ARAB CHILDHOOD does not last very long, and for the girls it ends even earlier than for the boys. At the age of thirteen or fourteen the Beduin girl shown above will be considered to be grown up and a husband will have been found for her. But while she is yet in the playtime of her life she makes the very utmost of it as her cheerful smile suggests

BEDUIN MOTHERS, though they usually have bright wrappings for their babies, often leave them entirely unclothed. It is a common sight in an encampment to see dusky-skinned infants left on their bare backs in the sand to kick in the sun. Notice the chains of metal trinkets that clash at every movement, and the number of different colors and patterns worn.

357

tent or other covering and the women who are fortunate enough to be in litters draw the cloth screens tightly around these for protection. To face the rushing wind, which brings along with it minute grains of sand, is a terrible experience. The Beduin's skin, hardened by exposure and screened by his cloak from the full force of the blast, enables him to bear it; but a foreigner, less accustomed to the elements, will come through the ordeal with his face badly cut and bleeding.

Shepherd and Robber by Turns

From time immemorial the Beduin has been a herdsman and a shepherd. It is the necessity of finding fresh pasturage for his flock that compels him to move from one spot to another. He will pitch his tent in some oasis in the desert with its water wells, until the scanty herbage has been exhausted, then the camp is broken and the journey onward is continued.

But such a peaceable existence as this has never satisfied the restless wanderer. The stern struggle for existence and ever-ready opportunity have made him an outlaw, a highwayman of the desert. To how many travelers and caravans has not the sudden cry of "Beduins" brought terror! The plundering of a caravan is a fierce joy to the Beduin. With rifle, lance and yataghan he descends upon his victims, and woe betide the trader who is not strong enough to beat off the marauders.

Why Caravans Are Looted

The Beduin on a foray is an enemy to be feared. He is merciless in the treatment of his captives and the ransom he extorts is heavy. The Arabs have a proverb which runs: "Entertain a Beduin and he will steal your clothes." So powerful are these marauding bands that they will levy toll even on the safe conduct of pilgrimages to Mecca. They regard the looting of caravans and travelers, indeed, in an original light—namely as the equivalent to the taxes and customs that are exacted in civilized countries. "The land is ours," they argue, "and if you trespass on it you must pay us compensation."

If, however, traveler or trader can show anything in the nature of a permit to enter the territory dominated by a tribe, such a document is generally recognized and respected. A permit of this kind can be purchased from a sheik, who will place some of his followers at the disposal of the travelers and thus pass them on from tribe to tribe across the desert.

Side by side with this lawlessness among Beduins there runs a regard for the laws of hospitality that is almost sacred. They are Mohammedans by religion, and the stranger who has eaten of their salt is safe from molestation. It might be well to amend the statement that they are followers of Mohammed for they are only nominally so. The tribes vary greatly in their religious customs and most of them disregard entirely the Prophet's command to pray five times daily and to make the pilgrimage to Mecca.

Supper in the Tent of a Sheik

Suppose now that we try to picture a sheik who is entertaining some guests. The Beduin camp has been pitched at an oasis. Outside the tent of their chief a little courtyard has been railed off with a hedge of brushwood. A fire blazes in the centre of this enclosure, partly for illumination as the tent is open on this side, and partly for boiling the water. Several of the womenfolk hasten to and fro, busy on the preparation of the coming meal. On the other side of the hedge are to be seen the dark figures of the kneeling camels.

The company gathered in the tent squats upon the mats and begins the meal, a mixture of meat, flour and hot oil, the bowl in which it is served being passed from hand to hand. An earthenware goblet of water makes the circuit of the tent in the same way. Rice is a favorite dish and of course there are dates and some sweetmeats, for the host is a man of position.

As an accompaniment to the feasting, one of the sheik's retinue who enjoys a reputation as a flute-player performs on his instrument. The chief guest—we will assume that he is a newcomer in this country—does his best to converse with his host, and is conscious occasionally of subdued laughter from the screened-off

A BEDOUIN CHILD TAKES A DRINK FROM A GOATSKIN WATER BAG

In a Bedouin camp at an Algerian oasis children take their turns at the goatskin water bag. In the desert water is not easily come by. Everyone must be careful not to waste a drop or to take more than his share, especially when the family is on the move, far from the next well. The Southern Territories of Algeria make up one vast desert broken by few oases.

portion of the tent in which the women have been placed. The more curious of these cannot be restrained from peeping at times over the screen to gaze upon the stranger.

Then, while hookahs and cigarettes are being lighted, coffee is served as a special token of friendship. During the evening, to add to the general comfort, a bowl is handed round in which are some live coals sprinkled with fragrant incense. Each of the company takes a good sniff at this as he passes it on.

With more pleasant converse and entertainment the evening slips away. The various guests make their salutations and depart; blankets are spread upon the tent floors, and soon the whole encampment, except for the watchers posted on the outskirts, is wrapped in sleep.

The Arabian Peninsula

... Saudi Arabia and its neighbors

PETROLEUM lubricates the key to understanding the medley of states into which Arabia is divided. The largest in area, Saudi Arabia, became a political unit as recently as 1932. All are basically tribal organizations. The Sultan, imam or sheik has absolute authority. In such oil-drenched states as Kuwait, however, twentieth-century standards are creeping in as the "black gold" gushes out. On the other hand, Yemen and the other oil-poor (thus far) lands seem hardly to have budged from the tenth century. Slavery still exists to some extent throughout Arabia, and it is still not uncommon for a thief to be punished by having a hand cut off.

Geologists think that the whole area around the Persian Gulf probably holds at least one quarter of the earth's pools of petroleum. The first wells were drilled in Arabia in the 1930's. But only since World War II has production zoomed, largely because the construction of pipelines and refineries has reduced the costs of transportation to the countries of the

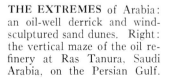

THE EXTREMES of Arabia: an oil-well derrick and wind-sculptured sand dunes. Right: the vertical maze of the oil refinery at Ras Tanura, Saudi Arabia, on the Persian Gulf.

industrialized West, hungry for fuel to provide power.

Lacking trained technicians, the states could not develop the fields themselves. Thus it is foreign companies, mostly American and British, who manage the industry. Concessions (rights for use) are granted by the rulers. The most usual arrangement has been for the profits to be split fifty-fifty between them and the companies. However, Japanese and Italian companies are now beginning to compete for concessions, offering the sultans and sheiks larger shares. The fabulous revenues, naturally, flow into their hands. This makes the Sheik of Kuwait, for example, with a yearly income of $260,000,-000—and it is increasing—one of the wealthiest men in the world. In his case, some two thirds of his royalties are spent on welfare projects—education, hospitals —construction of a sea-water evaporation plant with a capacity of 2,500,000 gallons a day, modernization of the port of Kuwait. Elsewhere the rain of money has seemed to be nourishing mostly fleets of

Cadillacs and enormous air-conditioned palaces.

This wild extravagance went so far in Saudi Arabia that it helped (along with an unsuccessful plot against Egypt's President Nasser) to dislodge King Saud from some of his power in 1958. After a family council, Crown Prince Faisal (Saud's brother) became prime minister in fact as well as name, with control of the country's pursestrings. He has since practiced a policy of stricter economy. Moreover, some of his edicts seem to be making gestures toward constitutional government. Such men as Faisal would seem to be reading the writing on the wall, that the days of absolute monarchy are numbered. Radio itself means that even the most remote village or encampment is beginning to glean some idea of how government is conducted elsewhere.

On the people of Arabia, oil development has had an impact of another kind. Thousands of Western oil men are needed to run the fields and refineries, and many of them bring their families with them. Whole communities have been set down in the midst of the desert, complete with air conditioning, television, Parent-Teacher Associations, garden clubs and the like. Dhahran, Saudi Arabia, for instance, built for oil-company employees, looks like a suburb in the United States. It has its own TV station. Thus the Arabs are seeing for the first time the high standards of living people elsewhere enjoy. Can the Arabs avoid making invidious comparisons?

It must also be said that the oil companies are making a great effort to educate and train the Arabs in oil technology. This effort goes hand in hand with a new passion in the more advanced states— Saudi Arabia and Kuwait in particular— for government-sponsored schools. Most of them thus far are for boys, but girls are beginning to get an education via television. The Dhahran station is popular; its weekly lessons include reading and writing in Arabic. The Saudi Arabian Government recently established its own station, in Riyadh, the capital.

Another sign of the times was the fed-

A YOUNG DATE PICKER gazes longingly at his harvest. Alas, the dates are only half ripe—crunchy and juicy but hard.

eration, in 1959, of six sultanates, emirates and a sheikdom in the Western Aden Protectorate. They became the Federation of the Arab Emirates of the South. By the treaty with the British, the federation has been promised independence in the not too distant future.

The big question for Arabia as a whole seems to be: will the structures of the various states change quickly enough to meet the rising expectations of their people? One Saudi Arabian sheik remarked to a visitor, "Something is happening here. . . . It is something nobody or nothing can stop. This nation is just beginning to go forward. Religion and tradition still may be in the way, but they won't stop it."

The areas dowered with oil are—besides Kuwait and Saudi Arabia—Qatar, the Bahrein Islands and what is called the Neutral Zone (between Kuwait and Saudi Arabia). Yemen, Muscat and Oman, Trucial Oman (or the Trucial States) and the Aden Protectorate may have oil

too but it has been little exploited.

The peninsula of Arabia is perhaps best known as the birthplace of Islam. It is sometimes pictured as a land of sandy wastes. Arabia has indeed many vast stretches of sand but there are arid wastes of stone and gravel with only occasional patches of grass and stunted bush. The whole of Arabia, however, is not desolate. There are oases of palm trees and expanses of green. Here and there are broad valleys dotted with bushes, where wandering tribes of Bedouins graze their herds of cattle, sheep and camels.

The history of Arabia supposedly dates from the Creation. Jidda (Jedda), on the shores of the Red Sea and one of the principal Arabian ports, is said by the Arabs to be the birthplace of Eve. In early times, Arabia was inhabited by many tribes. They did not unite until the time of Mohammed, in the seventh century A.D. Mohammed believed that there is but one God (Allah) and he finally persuaded the people to give up their pagan gods, to accept his belief and to look to him as God's Prophet. At times he fell into trances during which he said he was in communication with God. The messages, eagerly taken down by his listeners, form their Bible, known as the Koran. Among other things it commands a Muslim to be temperate, to pray five times a day—just before sunrise, just before noon, before and

THE OASIS CITY OF QATIF, Saudi Arabia, is almost completely surrounded by a waving green sea of date-palm groves.

after sunset and when the day is closed—to fast from sunrise to sunset during Ramadan, to give alms to the poor, and to make the pilgrimage to Mecca at least once during his lifetime.

At first, Mohammed did not have a large following but the new religion soon swept through the Arab world like wildfire. Moreover, the Arabs, or Saracens as they were then known, gathered under the green flag of Islam and determined to carry it throughout the world. Mohammed died in A.D. 653 but his successors carried out his plans. At its zenith the Arab empire extended through western Asia, across North Africa, into Spain.

However, as time went on, Arabia broke up again. Although the Turks conquered the territory in 1517 and held most of it until World War I, some of the nomadic people were never subdued.

In the middle of the eighteenth century there began the Wahabi movement. It was named for its founder, Wahhab, who sought to reform Islam and to return to the simplicity of the original faith. Later, under Ibn Saud, who organized the kingdom of Saudi Arabia, nationalistic overtones were added to the movement for religious reform.

A SAUDI ARABIAN CHIEFTAIN CLINGS TO HIS ANCIENT FASHIONS

The flowing robes of the desert people are still worn in Jidda, Saudi Arabia's Red Sea port. Light
covering, especially of neck and head, is needed for protection from the desert sun.

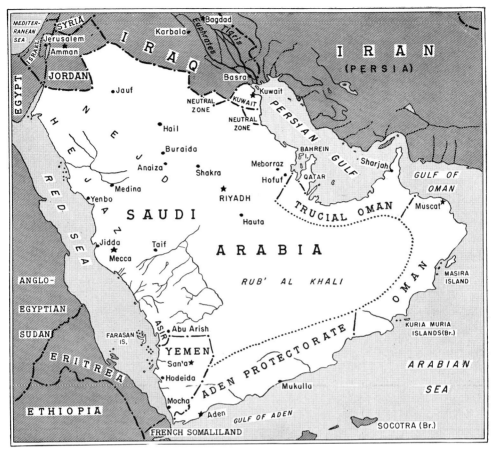

THE STATES OF THE GREAT ARABIAN PENINSULA

Ibn Saud took advantage of the first World War to free his domains from Turkish rule. Later he conquered Hejaz, extended his authority over the larger part of the peninsula, and renamed his kingdom Saudi Arabia. Colonel T. E. Lawrence, a British officer, who sympathized with the cause, did much at that time to develop a spirit of nationality among the Arabs.

Besides Saudi Arabia there are several smaller states, some of them under special treaty arrangements with Britain. In the southwest is the sultanate Yemen and the British colony and Protectorate of Aden. The sultanate of Oman and Muscat is on the Gulf of Oman. On the Persian Gulf are the Trucial Coast sheikdoms and Qatar, the Bahrein Islands and Kuwait.

Mecca and Medina are the two most important towns in Arabia from a religious and political standpoint. Mohammed, the founder of the Moslem faith, was

born in Mecca, and to that city as many as 200,000 devotees make the annual pilgrimage to do honor to the Prophet. Medina, his burial place, is also a place of worship to which unbelievers are denied entrance. It is interesting to note that the religion is divided into two main factions, the Sunnis and the Shiites. The division arose from the fact that Mohammed died without leaving a successor as the temporal and spiritual head of the faith. For twenty-two years after his death Arabia was ruled by three successive Caliphs.

It was then that the two rival factions rose. The Sunnis claimed the right to nominate the Prophet's successor, while the Shiites contended that the divine right of succession lay with Ali, Mohammed's son-in-law, and his descendants. Arising thus, the dispute assumed such proportions that the rival sects still have an undisguised dislike for each other. Cer-

FORBES

THIS WILD RAVINE, the Wadi Musa, on a ledge of which these men are standing, leads to the valley in which are the ruins of the rock-city of Petra. In ancient times this city was extremely prosperous, and controlled the trade route through it, although often captured and sacked by invading armies. To-day little remains except a few temples and tombs cut in the rock.

AN ANCIENT TRADE-ROUTE between Palestine and Arabia runs through this dark narrow gorge of the Wadi Musa near Petra. Although caravans are not so frequent to-day as they were before the Hejaz railway was built, many old-fashioned merchants and pilgrims still prefer to travel by foot or on horse or camel and robbers as in olden times still lie in wait for them.

367

LEVELING SANDY TUFTS TO MAKE WAY FOR IRRIGATED FARMS

A road grader, ungainly master of ruts and tufts, chugs across a bare field near an oasis in the Nejd. Next, plows will turn the soil, and water will pour from irrigation wells, pumps and pipes. Crops will be sown and harvested. Once again science and technology in the hands of an eager people will have pushed farther back the wasted, dry frontiers of the desert.

MORE PLENTIFUL, LESS EXPENSIVE, THE IRREPLACEABLE OXEN

Arabs walk behind yokes of oxen, guiding primitive leveling tools. It is a long, hard day of work, but the effort brings the reward of a smooth field and a fine, porous soil. Though more and more tractors and other farm machines are being brought into Arabia for the development of the irrigated areas, draft animals still must shoulder much of the burden.

MELONS, STOREHOUSES OF WATER FOR DRY DESERT JOURNEYS

An Arab farmer and an American technical expert admire a harvest of watermelons, one of many crops grown on the model farms of Khafs Dhaghra. Nearby are the limestone pits, dug in the 1940's, that irrigate the vast Al Kharj oasis in the Nejd. Because they contain a great amount of water, melons are highly prized by desert travelers of the Middle East.

CARVED BALCONIES, many of them beautifully painted and decorated with Arabic scrolls, overhang the winding streets of Jidda (Jeddah), a Red Sea port. Mohammedan pilgrims on their way to the holy city of Mecca, come here by boat and then, in recent years, make use of the motor bus service to reach their destination. There are several foreign legations in Jidda.

THIS RED STONE TEMPLE of El-Deir at Petra was not built up of separate blocks of stone but was hewn from the solid cliff. To-day it is the most splendid of the remains that tell of the city's vanished glory. It was fashioned by the Romans when they captured Petra in the hope of securing for themselves the wealth and commerce of its inhabitants.

DHOWS AT ANCHOR IN THE HARBOR OF MANAMA, BAHREIN ISLANDS

Bahrein Islands fishermen spend much of their time in the dhow, the heavy craft with the leaning mast and the swinging yard from which is hung a large lateen, or triangular, sail. From Manama, capital of the islands, the fleets go out into the Persian Gulf, where they brave the hottest of suns, and come back laden to the gunwales with pearl oysters and fish.

IN THE MANAMA BAZAAR, MARKETING CENTER OF THE BAHREINS

A ragged canopy of burlap cools a street in the bazaar of Manama. People walk the sun- and shadow-striped way at a summer's pace, haggling at the shops and stalls for a comb, a gem, a watch—perhaps a typewriter or a phonograph. Sometimes the rarest, least expected goods can be produced from shelf or trunk. Then buyer and seller bargain on the price.

Prophet's son-in-law, but that by mistake he handed it on to Mohammed.

The population is more or less divided into the semi-permanent inhabitants of the coast and of the cities and towns, and the wandering tribes of the interior. The latter are constantly migrating for their life is a pastoral one and they must move their encampments in order to find fresh pastures for their flocks and herds.

The dress of the men and women is very much the same. It is designed to give both ease and dignity, and consists of a long linen shirt, baggy trousers of linen that are fastened at the waist with a cord, and a cloak with ample sleeves. In the cold weather the sleeves can be used as gloves by being drawn over the hands. Over this cloak is worn a mantle of bright-colored cloth with, perhaps, a collar of gold or silver work.

A colored handkerchief covers the head and is secured by a woolen band worn in a double circle round the head. For footwear the Arab uses sandals. An Arab when mounted is an imposing sight, with his cartridge belt round his waist, his rifle slung across his shoulder or over the back part of the camel saddle, with his dagger stuck in a belt and his cloak thrown back. Thus arrayed he looks the picture of romance and wild freedom. He has some curious customs regarding the cloak. When entering a town or village it must be worn properly and not thrown back, but when approaching a camp or caravan out in the open plains he waves it as a sign that he has no hostile intentions and that none need fear for life or property.

AVA HAMILTON

WATER VENDOR OF THE MIDDLE EAST

In Saudi Arabia water is so precious a commodity that the thirsty traveler must purchase it by the glass or cup from a merchant who plies his tireless way up and down the hot, dusty streets of the city, heavy urn slung on his back.

tain sects of the Shiites say that they doubt the divine character of the Koran, stating that it was given to the Angel Gabriel for transmission to Ali, the

MECCA'S GREAT MOSQUE is the holiest place on earth to a Mohammedan. He turns towards it when he prays, no matter in what part of the world he may be. The black cube-shaped structure in the centre of the courtyard of the mosque is the Ka'ba, or Holy House, the chief sanctuary of the town of Mecca even long before Mohammed. It is covered with silk. Pilgrims must, as their first duty, walk or run around the Ka'ba seven times murmuring prayers the while. In the courtyard, it can be seen, is a well in which pious Mohammedans dip linen that is later made into shrouds.

HEADLEY

THIS PILGRIM CARAVAN is on its way to the hill of Arafat which Mohammedans hold in the greatest reverence. It lies about thirteen miles east of Mecca. All those who make the pilgrimage to the Holy City go to Arafat. They travel on foot, donkeys, horses and camels. This Caravan has two files of camels; those on the right carry the baggage and provisions, those on the left bear "shugdufs," tents of carpets and curtains which protect the riders from the sun. Every Moslem, financially able, is bound to go to Mecca once in his lifetime, or provide a substitute,

JAGGED PIECES OF GLASS keep prowlers from climbing a wall surrounding a house in Qatif, a Saudi Arabia port on the Persian Gulf. Oil fields were discovered nearby in 1945.

The houses vary according to the district. There are camps of tents and houses of limestone blocks quarried in the vicinity. Let us pay a visit to an ordinary city or town. It is a curious mixture of architecture. There are the dwellings of the rich, with solid walls and exquisite woodwork tracery and carving; houses of mud with flat roofs; reed huts and, upon the outskirts of the towns, the camps of those who have come in from outlying parts to barter and trade. Among the houses are mosques with tall white minarets, from the summits of which the "muezzin," or priest, will call the Faithful to prayer five times during the twenty-four hours.

We may best see the life of Arabia on a bazaar, or market day. Tents of matting are erected and are crowded with all kinds of marketable goods, from wool, cloth, reed mats, palm fibre and dates, to fruit of every description, cattle, sheep, implements and all that goes to make up commercial and pastoral existence in Arabia of to-day.

STANDARD OIL CO. (N. J.)

HAMMERING SILVER INTO USEFUL SHAPES

A silversmith of the Bahrein Islands follows the old ways of his craft in an open shop. With infinite patience he will beat the silver bar, held on the old-fashioned anvil, into a tray or dish or box.

Apart from the booths and tents, there are the permanent shops, which are roofed like arcades in our country. In them we may see tailors, potters, metal-workers, jewelers, dressmakers, carpet-sellers and members of most other trades and professions, with crowds of people always seeking bargains. Every now and then, donkeys heavily laden with merchandise or camels with loads sticking out at dangerous angles force a way through the crowd. They may often unceremoniously hurl passers-by into shop fronts, thereby upsetting the shopkeeper's goods, but no one seems to resent this treatment for it has all been a part of the bazaar for ages past.

In Arabia, religion plays an important part in the daily life of the people, and when the priest gives the call to prayer from the towering minaret all business ceases for the moment and everyone turns to wash their hands and feet before praying. At the conclusion of the prayer business is resumed and the clamor of buying and selling continued.

Marriage in Arabia is a simple affair for it demands no more than the presence of a priest and four witnesses. In the interior of the country it is still further shorn of ceremony, for the legal necessities of the occasion are satisfied by the presence of witnesses from both families, and, a feast having been given, the marriage festivities are over.

From the romantic aspect, the Arabs of the desert are the most interesting to us, for they are the riders of the plains and are forever on the move. The internal

ONE OF THE FORTIFIED GATES TO THE WALLED CITY OF SAN'A, CAPITAL OF YEMEN

San'a lies high in the mountainous interior of Yemen, 7,250 feet above sea level. It is a walled city with eight gates, and within are forty-eight mosques. San'a has been a trading center since ancient times. Tradition has it that San'a was one of the chief cities of the kingdom of the Queen of Sheba (or Saba), whose visit to King Solomon is recorded in the Bible. Today camel caravans, laden with coffee, indigo, safflower, madder, frankincense and myrrh, still plod the road between San'a and its port Hodeida, on the Red Sea, forty miles away.

THE BODYGUARD of the iman (king) of Yemen. Used to going barefoot almost from babyhood, the soldiers do not wear shoes even in uniform. They are nonetheless doughty fighting men.

THE ROYAL PALACE at Sana, Yemen's capital. The present-day city is in the shape of an irregular figure "8," and the extensive palace grounds are where the lines of the "8" cross.

decoration of an Arab tent is often carried out on artistic lines if the owner be moderately wealthy. The floor is covered with carpets, and on one side will be a divan formed of carpets and cushions for the host and his guests. The walls are hung with embroideries worked by the women, who are as clever with the needle as they are at rounding-up cattle and camels. Suspended along the walls will be guns, harness and clothes, and on the floor stand the numerous coffee-pots and cups.

The Arab diet is mainly mutton, rice and bread, with small cakes made from milk and a form of vermicelli. If the camp be near the coast, fish is included. Prawns served dry are very popular. Camels' milk is drunk, and the first thing a thirsty traveler does is to drain a bowl of it.

On the occasion of a big feast, such as the marriage of an important person or some political event, the meat and rice are cooked in a kind of steamer raised a few inches above the ground and are served with bread, cakes, fruit, dates, milk and sundry other dishes. The company disposes of the food without the aid of knives and forks, making use of the fingers as Nature intended. At the end of the repast brass and copper bowls are handed round, in which the guests wash their hands.

An Arab Tribe on the March

When on trek the Arabs have some interesting customs in connection with their camping grounds. They send one of their number ahead, and he reserves the site of the proposed camp by spreading a mantle over a bush in the centre of the chosen ground. Although there may be others moving in the same direction, no one will interfere with the selection, however good the pasturage or attractive its other qualities.

The tribe marches in a long cavalcade, with possibly several thousand head of camels, sheep, goats and cattle. The men are distributed along the convoy directing the line of march. The women and children and all the paraphernalia of the camp are on camels and donkeys, and at the head of the tribe rides the sheik, or chief.

The women are veiled and ride on camels in a sort of huge pannier—a basket-carriage placed on the camel's back —with two large wooden crescents at front and rear, the horns of which stand out on each side of the pannier. From them hang the long tassels and the gaudy embroidery of this queer carriage. These are its most attractive feature, for the pannier is very uncomfortable, and the unfortunate occupants are like hens cooped up in a form of rocking carriage, the motion of which varies in accordance with the ground over which the caravan is passing.

Camp Site Dependent on Water

The camp is always pitched by a well. Water is scarce in Arabia, and the site of a well is usually marked by cairns of stones erected on the surrounding heights, so that the weary traveler may know that water is at hand and he is near his goal. The camels are watered once in every four or five days, but they can exist much longer in cases of dire necessity. The loading and unloading are done by the women, while the men watch the process and drink coffee.

As an Arab caravan leaves its camp in the morning it is a sight that reminds us of the stories of biblical days. Even as the patriarchs and their followers marched across the desert, so in our time do the Arab tribes move across the deserts, their banner leading them on by day and a lamp at night.

Unchanging Ways of the Desert

Thus do the ways of the desert remain the same, for time has not changed the order of things that was in vogue three thousand years ago. Not only in this respect is the life unchanged, for even the drawing of water at the wells is done the same way as in the days of Abraham. A rope is attached to the leather bucket, which is lowered and drawn up by a camel descending and ascending an inclined plane. It is picturesque, but laborious, yet the Arab will not change it for any more modern and rapid system, for it is sanctified by time and a recognized institution of pastoral life.

Among the wild life of Arabia is the ostrich, but it is only met with in certain parts. There are also gazelles and hares and a variety of bustard. The cheetah, or hunting leopard, is found in those parts of the desert frequented by gazelles, its principal prey. Its speed is almost incredible when it gives chase. It covers the ground in a rush that must be seen to be realized. A cheetah that the writer

FRITZ HENLE

CANALS TO COLLECT RAIN WATER FOR THE DESERT TOWN OF ADEN

Aden has little fresh water, and these canals help to conserve the scanty rainfall. Drinking water is also obtained from artesian wells and by distilling sea water. The British-owned fortress town, built partly in the crater of an extinct volcano on a rocky peninsula, guards the southern entrance to the Red Sea. Its climate is normally hot and dry.

A WELL DUG DEEP BELOW THE DESERT SANDS OF SAUDI ARABIA

The well is about 120 feet below the surface, and the refreshing water is hauled up in goatskin bags.
It is then emptied into a trough, also of goatskin, from which the camels drink.

knew brought down an antelope in a run of six hundred yards, the quarry having a start of two hundred yards.

The Beduins, the true children of the desert, have changed least of all in Arabia. They are the wild freemen who harassed the caravans of pilgrims a thousand years ago and they still keep their old wild habits. As they ride along they note every fold in the ground, for it may serve them in case of an attack or a raid by other tribesmen, and they notice every tuft of grass and every bush as possible fodder for their herds or for some sign of foes in the neighborhood.

They guard their flocks and herds like the tribesmen of old. In the heat of the day they recline in the shade of a palm tree, if there be one, or beneath reed matting stuck up on poles. They know the ways of their sheep and goats, and during the noonday siesta we may see a mantle arranged upon sticks so that it resembles a man and serves as a substitute for the shepherd. From time immemorial the goats and sheep have grazed quite placidly round the dummy under the impression that it is their master, and so they do not stray, while the shepherd is enjoying his sleep in peace.

One of the chief occupations of the Arabs is that of camel-breeding and they understand this animal better than any other race. From its hair they make blankets, tents, ropes and even clothing. They drink its milk, eat its flesh and tan its hide for leather; but they have no affection for the beast that gives them so much. Without the camels the Arab would scarcely be able to live in the desert, but all his affection, if he has any, is lavished upon his horse, which is looked upon as a family pet.

The horse is, however, unsuited to life in the desert as is shown in the following story which is current among the Arabs: "The horse complained to Allah that he was not made for desert journeying. His hoofs sank into the sand, the saddle slipped off his back, he could not reach the scanty grass and small shrubs which grew by the roadside. So Allah designed an animal which had a long neck for reaching after food, cushioned feet which did not sink into the sand, a hump on which the load could be balanced. But when the horse saw this animal it started with horror, and knew how foolish it had been to complain. It still may be observed how horses shy at the sight of camels, and sometimes can hardly be induced to pass them."

There is much of interest throughout Arabia. There are tribes whose origin is veiled in the mists of antiquity and there are fertile corners that the Arabs tell us have yet to be explored. There are no rivers, only "wadis," or valleys that are dry during most of the year but are sometimes occupied by streams. There are high mountains, stretches of bleak, arid desert that become fresh green pastures in the months of spring, and wonderful ruins of ancient, deserted cities. It is a fascinating country, for there we seem to be back in early days and among biblical scenes that have altered little in many centuries.

THE ARABIAN PENINSULA: FACTS AND FIGURES

THE COUNTRY

A large eastern peninsula of Asia, bounded on the north by Iraq and Jordan, on the east by the Persian Gulf, on the south by the Arabian Sea, on the west by the Red Sea. Much of the land is desert, and some has never been crossed by Europeans. Includes several more or less independent states with boundaries ill-defined. Total area over 1,000,000 square miles; total population, probably about 12,000,000, but no census has ever been taken.

SAUDI ARABIA

The kingdom of Saudi Arabia is composed of two former kingdoms—Hejaz and Nejd—and their dependencies, and occupies the northwestern and central areas of the peninsula. The area is estimated to be 700,000 square miles, and the population about 7,000,000. All Saudi Arabia is under a single administration with one legislative assembly and a council of ministers. The country is a member of the Arab League and of the United Nations.

In the Nejd, the products are dates, wheat, barley, fruits, hides, clarified butter, wool and livestock. The export trade is of little significance. Imports are cotton piece-goods, tea, coffee, sugar and rice. The towns of Hufuf and Riyadh have populations of about 50,000.

Hejaz produces dates, honey and fruit. The Beduin products are hides, wool and butter. Foreign oil concessions are of great value to the country. The annual pilgrimage to Mecca is another source of revenue. There are few roads. Routes are made suitable for motor traffic especially for carrying the pilgrims. The populations of chief towns are: Mecca, 100,000; Jidda, 250,000; Riyadh, 120,000; Medina, 50,000.

YEMEN

An independent imamate in southwest corner of peninsula; on March 8, 1958, federated with the United Arab Republic under name of United Arab States. Area: 75,000 sq. mi.; population, about 5,000,000. Products include barley, wheat, millet and especially coffee. Hides and coffee are exported. San'a, the capital, has a population of 50,000.

MUSCAT AND OMAN

An independent state located in the easterly corner of the peninsula with an area of about 82,000 sq. mi. and a population estimated at 750,000 chiefly Arabs though there are also negroes. It is governed by a sultan. Date cultivation and the breeding of camels are the chief occupations. Dates, pomegranates, limes, and dried fish are exported. Imports are rice and coffee. The capital, Muscat, has a population of 5,500.

KOWEIT (KUWEIT OR KUWAIT)

A state located on the northwestern coast of the Persian Gulf, governed by a sheik. Area, 6,000 sq. mi.; population, 250,000.

ADEN

A British colony (since 1937) on the southwest coast of the peninsula which is important as a bunkering station on the highway to the east. Its area is 75 sq. mi. and that of Perim Island, 5 sq. mi. The total population is 140,000. A British governor and commander-in-chief have charge of the government which includes the Aden Protectorate and Hadhramaut (combined area, 112,000 sq. mi.); pop., 650,000. Attached for the purpose of government is Sokotra Island. The five Kuria Muria Islands, south of Oman, are also part of the colony.

BAHREIN

The Bahrein Islands, in the Persian Gulf, are an independent state; area, 213 sq. mi.; pop., about 125,000. Oil and pearl fishing are the chief industries.

TRUCIAL OMAN

A territory composed of 7 sheikdoms on the southern end of the Persian Gulf. Area, 6,000 sq. mi.; pop., 115,000. Pearl fishing and raising of dates and sorghum are the chief occupations.

A R C T I C

O C E A N

GREENLAN

Baffin
Bay

Bank I.

Victoria
I.

Baffin I.

Davis
Strait

Great Bear
Lake

ASIA

Yukon

Mackenzie River

Great Slave
Lake

Hudson
Bay

R. Nelson

L. Winnipeg

Bering Strait

Bering Sea

Aleutian Islands

Vancouver
Island

N O R T H

Great Lakes

St. Lawrence R.

Newfoundlo

Columbia R.

Missouri R.

R O C K Y

A M E R I C A

APPALACHIAN MTS.

ATLANTIC

Azo

Bermuda I.

MTS.

Colo. R.

Rio Grande

Miss.

Gulf of
Mexico

Bahama Is.

West

Cuba

Indies

Hawaii
Islands

CENTRAL
AMERICA

Caribbean
Sea

OCEAN

P A C I F I C

Gilbert Is.

Panama
Canal

Orinoco R.

EQUATOR

Amazon River

Phoenix Is.

Solomon Is.

Marquesas Is.

ANDES

S O U T H

Madeira R.

R. Sáo

New
Hebrides

Society Is.

O C E A N

A M E R I C A

R.

Francisco

New
Caledonia

Fiji Is.

Tuamotu
Archipelago

MTS.

Parana R.

NEW
ZEALAND

Strait of Magellan

Falkland
Islands

Cape Horn

Drake Strait.

ANTARCTIC

CIRCLE

Weddell Sea